The absurdity of bureaucracy

MANCHESTER
1824

Manchester University Press

POLITICAL AND ADMINISTRATIVE ETHNOGRAPHY

The Political Ethnography series is an outlet for ethnographic research into politics and administration and builds an interdisciplinary platform for a readership interested in qualitative research in this area. Such work cuts across traditional scholarly boundaries of political science, public administration, anthropology, social policy studies and development studies and facilitates a conversation across disciplines. It will provoke a re-thinking of how researchers can understand politics and administration.

The absurdity of bureaucracy

How implementation works

Nina Holm Vohnsen

Manchester University Press

Published by Manchester University Press
Altrincham Street, Manchester M1 7JA, UK
www.manchesteruniversitypress.co.uk

British Library Cataloguing-in-Publication Data is available

ISBN 978 1 5261 0134 1   hardback
ISBN 978 1 5261 5006 6   paperback

First published by Manchester University Press in hardback 2017

This edition published 2020

Typeset by Servis Filmsetting Ltd, Stockport, Cheshire

To the public sector with love and affection

We cannot live human lives without energy and attention, nor without making choices which show that we take some things more seriously than others. Yet we have always available a point of view outside the particular form of our lives, from which the seriousness appears gratuitous. These two inescapable viewpoints collide in us, and that is what makes life absurd. (Thomas Nagel 1971: 719)

Contents

Series editor's preface

Ethnography reaches the parts of politics that other methods cannot reach. It captures the lived experience of politics; the everyday life of political elites and street-level bureaucrats. It identifies what we fail to learn, and what we fail to understand, from other approaches. Specifically:

1. It is a source of data not available elsewhere.
2. It is often the only way to identify key individuals and core processes.
3. It identifies 'voices' all too often ignored.
4. By disaggregating organisations, it leads to an understanding of 'the black box', or the internal processes of groups and organisations.
5. It recovers the beliefs and practices of actors.
6. It gets below and behind the surface of official accounts by providing texture, depth and nuance, so our stories have richness as well as context.
7. It lets interviewees explain the meaning of their actions, providing an authenticity that can only come from the main characters involved in the story.
8. It allows us to frame (and reframe, and reframe) research questions in a way that recognises our understandings about how things work around here evolve during the fieldwork.
9. It admits of surprises – of moments of epiphany, serendipity and happenstance – that can open new research agendas.
10. It helps us to see and analyse the symbolic, performative aspects of political action.

Despite this distinct and distinctive contribution, ethnography's potential is rarely realised in political science and related disciplines. It is considered an endangered species or at best a minority sport. This series seeks to promote the use of ethnography in political science, public administration and public policy.

The series has two key aims:

1. To establish an outlet for ethnographic research into politics, public administration and public policy.
2. To build an interdisciplinary platform for a readership interested in quali-

tative research into politics and administration. We expect such work to cut across the traditional scholarly boundaries of political science, public administration, anthropology, organisation studies, social policy, and development studies.

The first book in the series is *The absurdity of bureaucracy: How implementation works,* by Nina Holm Vohnsen of the Department of Anthropology, Aarhus University, Denmark. She offers a humorous and sobering account of policy implementation set in contemporary Danish bureaucracy. Taking the reader deep into the hallways of governmental administration and municipal caseworkers' offices, the book explores labour market policy. The randomised controlled trial known as *Active – Back Sooner* was a central component of the Danish Government's *Action Plan on Sickness Benefit.* It sought to reduce the cost of sickness benefit and to secure an 'active labour force'. Using the notions of *absurdity* and *sense-making* as lenses through which to explore the dynamic relationship between a policy and its effects, the book reclaims 'implementation studies' for the qualitative sciences. It emphasises the existential dilemma confronting any policymaker and public official; namely, whatever you do, you will regret you did not do the opposite as well. Following step-by-step the planning and implementation of the policy, the book sets out to show that 'going wrong' is not a question of implementation failure but is the only way in which implementation can happen.

The book develops a novel theory of policy implementation that incorporates the absurd and the incoherent in implementation. Its findings will intrigue all students of public administration and public policy. However, much as I admire the fieldwork, I was first drawn to this book by its innovative writing. As a political science professor, I was trained in a 'professional' way of writing that discourages experimentation and encourages many clumsy neologisms. This book opens with a montage of 'ethnographic snapshots'. Each is 10–15 lines long and might be a conversation, a dilemma, a scene from a bureaucratic setting, a decision taken or a situation confronted. They serve to introduce the reader to the book's analytical heart; the dilemma between sensible decisions and the resulting experience of absurdity. The montage makes use of two writing techniques: American novelist Kurt Vonnegut's abandonment of the 'beginning, middle and end' in narratives, and Russian film-maker Sergei Eisenstein's 'intellectual' montage. I had never read such a bold – at first I thought rash – way of starting a book. But it works. Such self-aware experimentation with the craft of writing is an example not only to my political science colleagues but to everyone who seeks to contribute to the series.

Professor R. A. W. Rhodes
University of Southampton
Series editor

Acknowledgements

First and foremost I would like to express my gratitude to those caseworkers and managers, civil servants, privately employed social workers, psychologists, and job consultants who have trusted me with a degree of openness that leaves them potentially vulnerable to criticisms. I will not, for reasons of confidentiality, mention any names here. I also wish to acknowledge the men and women who by virtue of having received sickness benefit for a shorter or longer period of time during 2009 have crossed my path and wound up in my study. They do not figure as prominently in this book as I initially thought they would, but my conversations with them have shaped this book in other ways. I hope with this book to do justice to their confidence.

I wish to express my deepest gratitude to Anne Line Dalsgård, my supervisor during my years as a PhD student, who lovingly and carefully guided me forward, sideways, and out on important detours. My thanks to Christian Bason, former Director of MindLab, for never failing to inspire me: your confidence in me and support has been unparalleled and a humbling experience. I feel spoiled by having been subjected to what is possibly the best management in the world. My thanks to Professor Nigel Rapport, the second supervisor during my years as a PhD student, who broadens the scope of what anthropology can be. I am grateful for your friendship, for coffees, for TLS, literature, and even Greggs. And I am grateful too for your intellectual generosity and your refusal to lead me in any direction except down the beach and up the hills. My thanks to Professor Rod Rhodes for appointing himself my academic mentor when I most needed one and for insisting that I never conform but merely find the proper wrapping: just when I thought academia was no longer for me, you pulled me back in. Special thanks to Lars Frølund from AU Outreach; to former Permanent Secretary to the Minister of Employment Bo Smith; to an unnamed and unshakable Head of Office in the National Labor Market Authority; and finally to a Municipal Director without whom this research could never have happened.

I would like to thank my former colleagues at MindLab: my former research assistant, the incredibly bright and kind Rasmus Kolding; fellow PhD students Karen Boll and Jesper Christiansen who have continued to be good companions throughout the years. Jesper has been the closest colleague one can have in academia and I thank you for sharing office space, students, thoughts, and articles.

My thanks to colleagues at the Department for Anthropology at Aarhus University: to Anders Emil Rasmussen and Martin Demant Frederiksen for support, advice, and fellowship during PhD years – I wish we never again in our lives have to go through anything like writing our theses; to Maj Nygaard-Christensen for ideas, valuable thinking, and too many other things to mention here; to Morten Nielsen for critical readings of and input to my analyses – in attempting to follow your arguments I think things I would not have thought otherwise; to Mads Daugbjerg for valuable critique in the process of writing this book.

Thanks to the Department of Social Anthropology at the University of St Andrews for hosting me as a PhD student and later for granting me a research fellowship and allowing me to develop my thinking. Thanks especially to Victor Cova for thoughts, ideas, literature, readings, suggestions, and an unparalleled intellectual scope to benefit from.

Thanks too, to the anonymous readers who have provided suggestions and critique of the book in its various stages of being a manuscript.

Especially thank you to my mother, Susanne Holm, for teaching me how to think critically and systematically about the conditions of life. "If people behave strange and counter to their own interests, always ask about their alternatives" has been a guiding principle in my intellectual life.

Reading guide

To the policy-maker at every level and in every kind of organization:

This book is really for you. I know you are busy, so you can skip ahead to the portrait section beginning in Chapter 1. Chapters 1 through 4 have brief analyses of three to four pages summarizing the main analytical themes brought up in the portraits. Chapter 5 departs from the premise that implementation invariably fails but that it does so in predictable and systematic ways. The chapter presents this argument structured around five theses detailing how implementation works.

To the political scientist:

When I last submitted an article to a journal run by political scientists it came back with the judgement: "Insightful and well-written, sometimes even amusing, but it fails to live up to any academic standards known to us." Perhaps this speaks of sloppy work on my behalf (in my attempt to straddle academic boundaries, the article had become a mongrel and certainly no longer lived up to my own academic standards), perhaps it speaks of the conservative nature of Danish political science. My fear is that is speaks of the fact that in our attempt to safeguard academic standards we cast aside valuable insights because they come in a shape and genre unfamiliar to us. I hope you will recognize this book as an honest attempt to reach across disciplinary boarders.

To the anthropology student:

When I was a student of anthropology, I didn't read all the stuff on the history of Western bureaucracy – like Weber and Foucault. I was interested in Latin America with the regional tradition for personal accounts and drama and emotions going everywhere. Bureaucracy and public administration were as far from that as I could imagine. I finished my MA in anthropology after prolonged field-work among middle-class women in Guatemala who tried to break with classic gender roles which would have them stay at home, obey their husbands, and do all the house work. Alongside my studies, I was involved in rural development work in Guatemala. So I also read a lot of literature on third-world development or development in 'the south' as it was later called. After graduating, I got a job in a Danish municipality. And it was here that it struck me, that the basic problems faced by the municipal administrations and civil servants were the same ones faced by the indigenous grass roots organizations in Guatemala and those faced by the urban middle-class women who struggled to realize their plans for an educated and independent life, namely that the road to the desired future is riddled with resistance. Then I understood that bureaucracy is just another mode of human agency: a mode of dreaming, hoping, making plans, and trying to make them come true. In Western societies we have constructed powerful and elaborate institutions that nurse this mode of human behavior. But really, it's the same problems encountered by every human in every aspect of their lives. Our plans never go quite the way we intend them to and life takes us in surprising directions. Regardless of your interest in implementation and bureaucracy I therefore hope you will enjoy the book.

To the middle manager and the leader:

I know you are busy too. You might find it insightful to read Chapter 4 which deals with employees' disobedience of the rules and regulations that it is your job to make them to follow. After that, skip ahead to the Epilogue (written as a game book) to gain some hands-on experience of the reality your employees and co-workers face. This might make you more empathetic to their complaints and see that tiresome as complaints may be, there resides an enormous organizational potential in listening to the structures they portray.

To the reader who won't accept my premise that implementation invariably "goes wrong" because they have themselves been involved in implementation of policy resulting in "success":

My point is not that implementation cannot lead to results deemed successful by those involved. My point is that this judgement tells us very little about how implementation works in practice. Also it tells us nothing about the self-generating aspects of bureaucracy and the "development machinery." What are called unintended outcome and side effects are not something "extra" that "just happen." Rather such effects are central to understanding the processes through which we generate the structural aspects of our democracies. If you are particularly interested in the ways in which "success" and "failure" are often constructed with little or no relationship to the actual outcome of implementation, British anthropologist David Mosse has written a wonderful article based on his extensive experience as a consultant in the British aid industry. I recommend this article to anyone who works with implementation. It is called "Is good policy unimplementable? Reflections on the ethnography of aid policy and practice" (Mosse 2007).

To the scholar of development work, social work or other policy areas:

The book is about policy-driven interventions in the broadest sense and I hope it will speak to you regardless of the area of intervention you examine.

To the consultant:

Stop wasting our taxes by charging huge fees for consultancy work for public sector institutions. The public sector is under pressure these days and you are among those bleeding it. Have the decency not to pretend that you can make implementation work. If you are going to tap into public funds and channel money away from service delivery at least have the guts to tell us like it is; there is no easy solution, no policy will pan out the way it was intended; and often the most important (good or detrimental) effects of policy are not those you are asked to evaluate or focus on. "But you are hopelessly naïve," you might object, "if I say this I won't get another assignment." Fair enough, but count yourself among those sponging on the system.

To the reader who is looking for a good story and has no theoretical interest:

You might enjoy the prologue. Then proceed to read the eight portraits you can find in chapters 1 through 4. Then try the game book in the epilogue.

To the easily bored reader:

I am myself an easily bored reader so your concerns are most close to my heart. I have tried my best to write this book so that I would not myself be bored reading it and so that I would feel excited picking it up. Give it a try. If the prologue does not do it for you, skip ahead to the portrait section in chapters 1 through 4. The epilogue (written as a game book) might interest you too.

To the reader looking for something to quote:

Chapter 5 is the place to look. I've packed this chapter with one-liners (even put some in the headlines) and it contains a summary of my main points as they relate to the empirical material. It is built up around five theses and repeatedly refers back to the empirical material in the portrait section so that you can easily identify the portrait you might want to read for background information.

To the critical reader:

I'd love to have your feedback. Please contact me etnnhv@cas.au.dk.

To the reader concerned already about the format:

I refer you to the section in the Introduction entitled "writing complexity." Further information about methodology, my position in the field, and the character of my data can be found in the appendix.

Central people, documents, and organizations

Documents and organizations

Action Plan on Sickness Benefit: A conclusion paper containing 39 proposals aimed at preventing and shortening the Danes' long-tern sickness absence. It was first approved in September 2008 during tripartite negotiations between the Danish Government, the Danish employers' organizations, and the Danish employees' organizations. Subsequently it was adopted politically in November 2008 during the annual negotiations for the National Budget.

Active—Back Sooner: An elaboration of the action plan's proposal 32. Officially, a randomized controlled trial. Many thought its purpose was to test key elements in a planned revision of the sickness benefit legislation. It was implemented in 16 Danish municipalities during the spring and summer of 2009. However, the revised legislation was adopted in Parliament months before the trial's conclusion.

Danish National Labor Market Authority: Formerly a policy-producing subsection of the Danish Ministry of Employment. In 2009 it was charged with implementing the proposals in the *Action Plan on Sickness Benefit*.

Danish Ministry of Employment: The Ministry comprises "the Department" headed by the Permanent Secretary to the Minister and an ever-changing configuration of subsections headed by Directors. Among these subsections were—in the years this book details—the Danish National Labor Market Authority and the National Research Center for the Working Environment [NFA].

ENGA: A private agency which had answered and won the municipal public tender in the sickness benefit and unemployment area. They provided the municipalities with such things as "work ability assessments" for applications for early retirement benefit, and with other assessments of people on social benefits. In relation to the implementation of *Active—Back Sooner* they were asked to provide an offer of "at least ten hours of activity" to which participants who could not go back to work were referred.

job center: A municipal unit responsible for administering—among other things—the sickness benefit legislation and the legislation pertaining to unemployment and maternity leave.

Ministry

Minister of Employment: "The intervention in this trial is planned according to the individual's preconditions, the individual's need, the individual's health, and the individual's resources."

Permanent Secretary: "you have to bear in mind that one minister who might be involved in several negotiations cannot possibly have a deep knowledge of all the matters that have to be decided on."

Vice Director: "It is expensive for society to have this many people walking about sick and we would rather spend the money on something else."

Lea (senior civil servant): "there are limits to the extent to which you can change things and still expect them to happen in practice."

Jytte (lawyer): "I would get sick if I were to calculate how much time we have spent correcting these errors."

Job center

Ulla (manager of job center): "being a manager primarily consists in passing numbers upwards."

Peter (team leader): "It all comes down to a question of showing consideration for the person versus showing consideration for the caseworker and the project design."

Marie (caseworker): "Initially, when we wrote our local project description, I guess we thought it would be more "project-like." But we have moved towards what is compatible with our day-to-day business."

Ida (caseworker): "You don't question every single thing you are asked to do."

Kirsten (caseworker): "The worst thing about it is that in terms of the project this will look like a success."

Ann (caseworker): "I cannot help feeling that whenever I need help with a case the advice I am given is random."

Frank (caseworker): "we already told you that your numbers do not reflect our reality."

Sara (caseworker): "mostly I maintain the system for the sake of the system."

Ian (caseworker): "there is nothing I can do. I will have to shut her case."

Ena (caseworker): "all I think of is how fast I can get rid of the cases by referring them somewhere else where I can pretend things are taken care of."

Merete (caseworker): "So what are we NOT to do then?"

Jane (caseworker): "suddenly I am filled up and then come the sleepless nights where I lie and think about all the things I ought to have done."

ENGA

Jane (local director): "We know very well that you bend and stretch and work beyond the things we are paid to do but you must stop this. And I know this is tough."

Marianne (team leader): "From an economic point of view I should just take this contract here but I think a little decency is warranted. I kind of have to do their work."

Sofie (social worker): "What you will observe in just a few minutes is that none of the people who are about to arrive have more than an inkling of why they have been sent here."

Joan (social worker): "If we don't put in the extra hours, the ones we are not paid for … the rest is utterly pointless."

Louise (recipient of sickness benefit): "It is nice being here but I can't help thinking what is it that is supposed to come out of it?"

Other people

Reporter: "The political arena has been substituted—as I see it—by evidence battles.

Psychiatrist: "Where the general practitioners go wrong is when they make the mistake of believing what their patients tell them."

Prologue: Labor days[1]—an empirical montage from Denmark

Hard work

On the first day of May, when the sun beats down on a central street in the city and burns my hand that, as it reaches for my lukewarm iced coffee, is still semi-sedated by sleep (it could, for instance, easily have knocked something over had the table not been empty except for the sticky substance—perhaps dried-up beer—that reflects the sun back from the rough wooden table), the air is stagnant and the street has a distinctive smell. I notice it as soon as I step out of my front door in the middle of the afternoon, the sun having long worked on the multiple dried puddles of juices, whose creation and death this street witnesses every night. Resuscitated, they now appear sticky, sparkling, glittering, and release odors that mix with lotions and perfumes, car exhaust and evaporating asphalt: the sweet and spicy concentrate of human, sun, and city.

Your own words

In the municipal office where citizens' rights to sickness benefit are evaluated, citizens who are called in for the initial meeting often have only the vaguest idea about the meeting's purpose. What they *do* understand is that they are going to be checked out. This is why you frequently see citizens arriving with special hand-bags or briefcases where they have collected all the different pieces of information they envisage might be needed to *prove* their illness to the caseworker. For the same reason, when they rummage around in their bags for some specific piece of paper, it often happens that medical journals, prescriptions, official letters, and little cards with scribbled appointments with physical therapists or psychologists spill onto the floor or out onto the caseworker's desk. The caseworker will try to stop this presentation of evidence: "Just tell me in your own words why you are not at work." If this is requested of a person of non-Danish nationality, the following almost invariably occurs: the citizen says (for instance in Polish, Russian, or in broken Danish), "Why, because I am sick!" upon which he or she resumes the rummaging for evidence to confirm this circumstance. Perhaps a sick note or alternatively a direct phone number to the doctor is brought to light and offered to the caseworker. Then the caseworker might say something along the lines of

"Yes, I know you are sick, that's why you are here today, but explain to me what it is about your illness that makes you unable to go to work." If, on the other hand, the citizen guesses what the caseworker is driving at, the conversation might move forward more smoothly.

Much obliged

On the Danish National Labor Market Authority's (*Arbejdsmarkedsstyrelsen*) webpage, you could, in the early months of 2010, read the following under the heading "sickness absence" (*sygefravær*):

> If you are absent from work due to illness for a longer period of time, you can get support from your municipality to help regain your ability to work and return to the labor market as soon as possible. You are also eligible for economic compensation in case of absence due to illness in the form of sickness benefit [*sygedagpenge*]. ... If you are absent due to illness for more than eight weeks, the municipality will send you an information form that you must return within eight days. Subsequently, the municipality will summon you to a follow-up conversation or call you up [...]. The purpose of the conversation with the municipality is to assist you in keeping your job and your connection to the labor market. ... It is your obligation to participate in the municipal follow-up. (Arbejdsmarkedsstyrelsen 2010, my translation)

After the summer of 2009, municipal caseworkers in Denmark had the option of referring citizens who received sickness benefit to other organizations who specialized in programs aimed at shortening the period of sickness absence by keeping the citizens "active" while they were unable to work. In the spring of 2009, before these new rules were included in the law on sickness benefit, a controlled trial (*Active—Back Sooner*) was carried out in order to test central elements of the amendments to the law. During the trial period, citizens who received sickness benefit and who had certain birth dates were randomly drafted for an obligatory offer of a program of activity for ten or more hours a week. These offers of activity could be, and were in several cases, outsourced to private employment agencies. The activities could consist of physical exercise, applying for jobs or writing CVs, or classroom sessions guided by psychologists or medical doctors with the aim of reorienting the sick citizens' understanding of their current situation and getting them back to work more quickly than they would otherwise have done.

The privilege

If you are ill and you get referred to a private employment agency that specializes in "sickness benefit package solutions" [*sygedagpengepakker*] the goal of your referral might be "to train for stable attendance." If you have been away from "the ordinary labor market" for a long period, the mere task of showing up every day at 9am can prove challenging. It certainly poses a challenge for the researcher, and few are the days on which she makes it on time. While this has no immediate consequences for the researcher, this is not so in the case of Irene. Irene is not there voluntarily and might lose her right to sickness benefit if she does not show up. These are the main differences between the researcher and Irene: in the fall of 2009, the researcher is twenty-eight years old and fit as a fiddle; Irene is fifty-nine and suffers from diffuse pain, a metabolic disorder, and diabetes that has recently taken a turn for the worse. With the exception of three years, the researcher has been enrolled in different sorts of education since she was five; Irene has been working full-time in restaurants and shops since she left school aged 15. The researcher is paid a salary; Irene receives sickness benefit. That is why it is the privilege of the researcher to stroll down to her local coffee bar, Nosewise, on a given Wednesday at 10:15am to have a coffee and a late breakfast while Irene, for the nth week in a row, must sit in the private employment agency's computer room and work at her curriculum vitae or play Minesweeper until her pain gets so severe she might be allowed to go home.

Piss and coffee

In a different street in the city, a man is sitting in a particular spot on the ground. He is embracing his knees while his entire slovenly being trembles. He is sitting in the exact spot where a public urinal stood until recently. The penetrating and nauseating smell of decades of pissing has impregnated the surroundings to the extent that I have to hold my breath when I pass on my bicycle, even half a year after its removal. Sitting in this specific spot is this young man—junky, thief, or whatever else might explain the presence of the equally young but, in contrast, sparkling clean police officers who stand in a circle around him. A sorry excuse for a citizen sitting in the middle of a puddle of piss that spreads around him between the cobblestones and forms channels that run toward the doorway of the local pub, forced by the slight tilt of the street. Not far away, if you turn right just after the National Bank, on the other side of the bridge separating the former military bastion at Christian's Harbour from the Royal Dockyard and Copenhagen's commercial center, sits a big square building. Above the building's entrance is a large stone section into which the word *Overformynderiet* was chiseled decades ago, the popular meaning of which is akin to "super-patronizing." The fact that the National Labor Market Authority resides here seems especially appealing to the Danish sense of self-irony, and causes many knowing looks to be exchanged by visitors and employees alike. To the extent that this building can be said to possess a smell, it must be the vague scent of a civil servant's perfume, or maybe the bitter odor of filtered coffee, or the particular smell of large quantities of paper gathered in one place. The sound of a pair of well-dressed and determined medium heels and a discreet but rhetorical knock on a door. This is where the most recent version of the law on sickness benefit was drafted.

Calling in sick: I

Afterwards, she kept thinking it should have been pretty straight forward. She received unemployment benefit and when one week she was down with a case of flu she called in sick to her local job center as she had been instructed to do by her unemployment fund. Yet, when the next payment of her unemployment benefit was due she received no money. Encouraged by the staff in her unemployment fund she notified the job center about the mistake and a few days later she received a letter stating that matters would be corrected. They were not. A significant period of time therefore passed where the young woman had no money to pay her rent and other living expenses while she tried to sort out the mistake with the job center. She called in with a few days' interval to call attention to the missing payment and each time she was asked the same questions: How long had she been sick? Two days. What was the cause? She had been down with the flu. Why had she not notified the job center that she was no longer ill? Well, she had actually. Could she prove her case? Yes, she could and she referred to the letter she had sent them and the one she had received in return. "Don't you have all this information already?" she asked, referring to her previous phone calls. They did not. The days passed and no payment landed in her bank account.

Gap

Intellectual montage is, according to Russian film-maker Sergei Eisenstein (1994), the juxtaposition of (in the case of film-making) shots that elicit a specific intellectual meaning. A classic example of intellectual montage is Eisenstein's *Strike*, in which he cross-clips between shots of a crowd of people being beaten down by the military and shots of a cow being slaughtered. Here the interpretation of the violent event is explicitly locked down as "system treats people like cattle." Had the cross-clip been from the birth of a child or from a ballet, the suggested interpretations would have been different: the bloodshed involved in transitions and new beginnings, or the careful and aesthetic orchestration of a State intervention. In this form of narration, one line of shots constitutes the main storyline while other shots are placed at key moments to suggest parallelisms intended to lead the spectator to consider specific interpretations of the events portrayed. However, in the attempt to write about the complexities of labor market politics it would be misleading to present the field as having, to quote American novelist Kurt Vonnegut, "leading characters, minor characters, significant details, that it has lessons to be learned, tests to be passed, and a beginning, a middle, and an end" (1973: 209). By dispensing with a narrative based on a leading argument and an explicit storyline, the resulting intellectual montage has as its aim the multiplication of meaning rather than its reduction; it aims for interpretations that are more open than they are closed.

Not your average citizen

In the summer of 2009, a taller-than-average woman sits in her garden and offers the researcher a cup of coffee. The taller-than-average woman would be forced to bend down further than average was she to console, say, a one-year-old in a day care institution, as she used to do. And she has been doing a lot of bending, so now she sits in her garden five months after her back pain stopped feeling like your average back pain, and she is still waiting for the scanning that will indicate if the physical rehabilitation she has been on the waiting list for since she got ill will be sufficient, or whether an operation is warranted. She does not know whether she has been waiting longer than average.

Fitting

It is best if none of the randomly chosen recipients of sickness benefit get exempted from the controlled trial (even if what the caseworker can offer is not likely to get them back to work sooner) because that would compromise the project design. This consideration can be voiced in several ways. Listen:

> *A municipal caseworker*: We would really like it if you would participate in the project. If we only include the people it is sure to help then we will not be able to show when it does not help, OK? It is in order to ensure the best results possible that we want you to participate. So if you can, you must.

> *An employee from the National Labor Market Authority*: What a controlled trial like this can do is to debunk some myths. Make us wiser. If we think this approach makes sense then we must also dare test it and see if it perhaps does not.

> *Another municipal caseworker*: We cannot give you any treatment that will shorten your period of absence from work, but we have to find a way to plan your illness period so that it fits with the project's demand for activity.

> *A citizen*: It is fine that you make such a project, you know, I just do not think I fit into your box, OK? I mean, what do you want to talk about? If you do not know that, I cannot be bothered with it. Or 'bothered'—it sounds a bit harsh perhaps— but I am not doing it just for the fun of it, OK? It is a waste of your time and mine.

36

My adult working life began on 15 October 2007. A recent graduate with a degree in social anthropology, I got a job as an internal consultant in a municipality in Northern Zealand. My first task was to report numbers to Statistics Denmark and to the National Board of Social Services. I remember coming to work the first day and being left alone in a small and naked office. On the table before me some manager had placed eight sheets of paper filled with little boxes and paragraphs from the Law on Social Services (*serviceloven*). On each sheet I was required to report the frequency, amount, and/or size of the municipality's offers in the service areas they inquired into. The simplest of the questions addressed the use of so-called day centers. I was to report the "daily average number of visits" in a given week six months ago. I stared at the sheet. "What is a day center?" I thought to myself. I got up and began to ask around, getting a different answer from each person I asked. Three weeks and many phone calls later, I knew there were three such "day centers"; that primarily elderly people came there during the day to be kept active; and that nobody knew how many people used them. I nevertheless had to fill in the form, since returning it incomplete to Statistics Denmark was not an option. I do not remember what I wrote, perhaps "36." In any case, the number was the sum of the added guesses of the day center staff I happened to get hold of. "Well," one staff member cautioned me, "it's just a guess because we don't jot it down every time someone comes in, OK?"

Clash

According to Charles Sanders Peirce's theory of consciousness (1955 [1940]: 28), we are inclined toward the establishment of thought habits in our intellectual life. A thought habit consists of our adaptation of a specific interpretation of causation or our settling on a fixed belief about the true state of things that we subsequently will be likely to subscribe to without further reflection or critical examination. Eisenstein's classic application of the intellectual montage, as in *Strike*, is associated with this type of conditioning, so that having watched this sequence in *Strike*, it becomes more likely that, the next time we watch a State intervention, we will accept the proposal that "the people" are being treated like mere cattle. With Peirce we see that these interpretations might be random, even false. He proposes that the potential for specific interpretations already resides as qualities in the individual phenomena we relate to (ibid.: 98ff.). Since qualities are multiple, any interpretation will omit a number of qualities that in any moment might be actualized in alternative interpretations. In the intellectual montage, we might use this insight to work against conclusion and fixed interpretation by continuing to juxtapose our "shots" in numerous ways.

Overdose

Today in the municipal job center, caseworker Ida has just decided that she wants to get a motorcycle driver's license. In her office, a woman pulls down her blouse and points with her right index finger toward the place on her left chest where, instead of a breast, we now see a topography of scarred skin. In another office, caseworker Marie, who at this moment in time still does not know whether she is finally pregnant, just manages to prevent a man from pulling down his trousers. Instead he now inches the tight jeans up over his knee in order to prove the existence of a scar caused by the knife he intended for something completely different and work-related, but which cut a 10cm line from his knee up along his inner thigh when large sacks fell on him as he unloaded a lorry. At the fifth office down to your left, a woman cries furious and humiliated tears in Ian's office as she understands there is no way around it: she will have to tell this young, unfamiliar man why she, who has been able to take care of herself for sixty years, now suddenly cannot. Ian himself just buried a friend. Overdose.

Calling in sick: II

One day she was particularly insistent, hoping to get the matter concerning her unemployment benefit settled. As a result her call was forwarded a number of times and each time she had to explain her case from the beginning. At one point, she told me, she had started tearing up with frustration and found herself begging (her by now quite warm mobile phone made her cheek glow and itch) to be allowed to talk to the caseworker she had spoken to on the previous day. As a matter of fact, the caseworker in question happened to be sitting next to the person she spoke to. However, since that caseworker had just begun her break she could not be reached. "Apart from that" the caseworker said in what the young woman thought was a confrontational tone of voice "I can see in my papers that you're an early retirement pensioner. Why have you withheld this information?" The young woman, astounded, said she most certainly was not an early retirement pensioner. She had just finished her university education and by virtue of having made monthly payments to her unemployment fund was now entitled to receiving unemployment benefit while looking for a job. The caseworker would not be convinced. "It clearly says so in your papers," she argued. At this point in the conversation the young woman ended the call.

What Kate did not do

Kate, an employee at the private employment agency ENGA, says, "I might as well say right away that those feedback charts on the participants in the controlled trial—I have not completed them. And I feel bad about it but I do not know where to begin. I just did not do it." The researcher now watches Marie—who by now knows she is pregnant—tell Kate how she herself would have approached the job had it been hers, while Kate's team manager says, "of course we will solve that task. That is part of the agreement." Kate is responsible for one of the citizens Marie has referred to the private employment agency as part of the controlled trial, but she has no idea what the woman in question has been doing during the four weeks she has been involuntarily participating in the controlled trial. Except that she has seen her psychologist but—by the way—that had nothing to do with the project, and then she has been on the internet searching for something Kate does not know about. "We only know them from the group sessions, so we will have to pass on the specific questions," says the team manager. Apparently nobody knows anything about the people who are participating in the controlled trial, to Marie's irritation and the researcher's amazement. In the end, Marie asks if they can be certain that they have been informed about cases in which the citizens have not showed up for the controlled trial? Kate says she is pretty sure the Municipality has not been informed about that, no.

Barriers

When the municipal caseworkers refer a citizen to a private employment agency, they need to fill out an electronic form that serves as the contract with the private employment agency. On this form, the municipal caseworkers must indicate what the purpose of the referral is. This is what a "purpose of referral" might look like when the private employment agency receives such a contract from the municipal caseworker:

> "The barriers need to be broken down."

This is how a conversation between the researcher and the privately employed social worker might then sound:

> *Researcher*: Is that all you know when the citizen is referred here?
>
> *Social worker*: Yes, that is a typical contract. And then you might wonder why they want to pay for a thirteen-week program without specifying which barriers they intend us to "break down."

Shrubberies

At the private employment agency called ENGA, the team leader, Marianne, found herself overwhelmed by the grotesqueness of the fact that she and her colleagues had for a moment seriously discussed whether to lay out shrubberies in their yard in the hope that the homeless people and vagabonds whose work ability they were sometimes commissioned to assess would remain at their property. The discussion had been a response to the fact that that the employees had noted that these people repeatedly got their applications for early retirement pension rejected on the grounds that the applicant had participated "too little" in the work ability testing for the caseworkers to have sufficient grounds for assessing their ability to work. The employees at ENGA felt compelled to react to the circumstance that those worst off and who were not even able to attend the work ability testing, those who in their professional opinion lived up to the criteria for early retirement pension the most, were by the same token cut off from receiving it. It seemed that whatever they did, it would lead to an absurd condition—a continuation of the present practice if they did nothing, an equally absurd condition if they build flowerbeds for the vagabonds to sleep in while they documented it.

A helping hand

During those first months of my employment in the Municipality, I struggled continuously with the numbers I had to report to Statistics Denmark. The report on the delivery of "personal care and practical assistance" proved to be a particularly tough one. The data system could not extract the numbers we needed and nobody had mastered spreadsheets beyond the simplest commands and sorting. Apart from that, dead citizens still had to be removed from the files and we knew that people who no longer received any kind of help continued to figure in the system as well. What lent an additional touch of fiction to the exercise was that Statistics Denmark required that we indicate the total amount of time for which each citizen received such services. Unlike most other municipalities where services were granted in minutes (for example, forty-five minutes of cleaning a week), in this Municipality people were granted specific services (cleaning the floor, watering the plants) regardless of the time it might take to complete them. I called up Statistics Denmark and explained the situation on more than one occasion but it was not an option to hand in an incomplete form. Furthermore, some boss further up the municipal system had been to a meeting at which our Municipality had been singled out as one of only three that had still not reported our numbers, and the pressure to make sure our numbers were in before his next meeting had traveled down the system from manager to manager until, finally, I was the one presented with the task of getting it done. I also received emails from employees in Statistics Denmark who were themselves under pressure to get the statistics out before the end of the year. Finally, one of my managers took me aside and told me to make up some numbers that were not too far off those we had reported the previous year.

What Kate does not *get*

Kate has just had a discussion with one of the municipal caseworkers about the case of a woman who has been referred to the private employment agency for twenty-five hours of activity each week. The woman has repeatedly left early or has not shown up at all because she is in pain. Since Kate is contractually obliged to inform the Municipality of the total number of hours the woman has been present, this situation has resulted in a stream of formal letters from the Municipality to the woman inquiring into the existence of "valid reasons" for her non-attendance.

> So I phoned the caseworker to ask what the purpose of this referral was. I asked her if these twenty-five hours a week is the key issue or if we can accommodate the attendance to the woman's pain. But without answering me the caseworker starts talking about booking another three months of the program for the woman. Then I asked her, in a straightforward manner, what the purpose of that would be. And if she had said "to work on a stable attendance" or "to handle the health-related issues" which this woman finds so disturbing then the situation would have been different. But no! The caseworker was only interested in whether or not she could be here twenty-five hours. This is where this turns into a discussion about whether it is my job to place myself in the doorway and say "No, you cannot leave." Where would that take us? This is where I begin to think that this whole system is extremely odd.

19 percent

Wednesday, 10 June 2009: on the front page of *Politiken*, one of the largest Danish national newspapers, you can read that Danish social workers break the law on a daily basis. The subheading clarifies that one out of two social workers is unable to live up to the legal requirements on a regular basis. The question posed by the Danish Social Workers' Union to its members on behalf of *Politiken* was as follows: "Have you been able to live up to the guidelines for your social work as defined by the law within the past three years?" A pie chart shows that 49 percent responded that they did, 32 percent responded that they did not, and 19 percent did not know. In the text you are given the additional information that most of the social workers indicate that these breaches of the law happen on a daily or weekly basis. The journalistic angle on the story is the increasing workload in the public sector and the unfortunate incidents that happen due to a general lack of time for processing cases.

A guiding principle

The montage principle is not new to ethnographic attempts to address and unfold perspectives on themes or objects of research. Examples include Michael Taussig's attempt to capture some of the characteristics of the State in *The Nervous System* (1992); Marilyn Strathern's *Partial Connections* (2004 [1991]), in which she revives comparison as an anthropological core project after the relativistic turn of the 1980s; and Nigel Rapport's insistence on the heterogeneous nature of individual social lives as discussed in *Transcendent Individual* (1997; also Rapport 1992, 1994). Despite differing agendas, the basic principle shared by these accounts is that the portrayal of any situation might lend us a perspective through which to look at and wonder about other situations. Approached this way, analysis is not merely a question of presenting a convincing argument or juxtaposing different perspectives on the same reality—of different viewpoints adding up to *the* reality—but of addressing separate realities that might intersect and overlap, while remaining distinct. In contrast to the intellectual montage as applied by Eisenstein in *Strike*, this approach requires that we accept and cultivate ambiguity: from one perspective, Kate is a nuisance who has not understood the first thing about the task she has been given by the municipal caseworker, but she could also be seen as the only sensible person in the system. Both perspectives might be considered situated truths about Kate and her work, but they will not add up to a truth or a coherent picture.

Something extra

Do not hold it against a civil servant that the following thought occurs to her at 4pm after she has been observed by an anthropologist for an entire day:

> We are 200 people who are just sitting here, writing ... making paper. We just sit here and write about what ought to be done ... without doing. I sit here and

when I look out of my window over at the Ministry of Social Affairs, I think ... "I wonder what they are writing over there."

Such a thought might occur on an afternoon in the fall of 2009. But, she adds, she knows that even if she is not directly involved in the implementation of programs and plans themselves, her work sets the framework for how political agendas might be put into practice elsewhere. One of her colleagues, for instance, has written the framework for the controlled trial in which citizens on sickness benefit were subjected to obligatory offers of "activity" intended to help them return to work as soon as possible. In such a case, policy stops being merely paper and can acquire life, as in the following interaction between a citizen, John, and our municipal caseworker, Marie:

> *John*: You had me confused there for a moment because I thought you said it was an offer. So it is something I am forced to do?
>
> *Marie*: Well, you *are* actually ... perhaps I should have mentioned that. But you have to look at it as if we are giving you something extra.
>
> *John*: But then maybe I should not join the fitness center anyway… or start swimming as I had planned. ... If I *have* to participate in your activity. I mean, I would not want to overburden myself either, right?
>
> *Marie*: No, that would not be smart.

Calling in sick: III

The following day she braced herself. She called up again and having been through the now familiar movements where her numerous calls and stated information were nowhere to be found in the system and she had been referred a few times from caseworker to caseworker she finally came across a caseworker who claimed to know what had happened. If the young woman's information was nowhere to be found in the system, it was simply because she had never in the first place contacted the job center concerning her period of sickness. "But," the young woman argued, "if I had not contacted you in the first place, then how could you have sent me a letter in response in which you state that things will be corrected?" The young woman told me afterwards that she thought this argument of hers was pretty clever. However, the caseworker could find no information in her files that such a letter had ever been sent and she stuck to her explanation: The young woman had never reported her sickness to the job center as she was obliged to. That was the core of the problem and this would affect her entitlement to unemployment benefit. The young woman, now highly frustrated, asked if she could come by the caseworker's office and personally present the letter and all her papers so that they could once and for all set matters straight. But had she for a moment eyed a final way out of the situation she was about to be disappointed. The caseworker told her that such a place where she could come by did not exist. "But," the young woman tried "you must be sitting somewhere?" At least, she argued, there had to be a reception desk or perhaps just an entrance where she could present the letter? "No," the caseworker persisted, to the young woman's disbelief and amusement— there were no doors and no entrance to where she worked.

Upsetting

One evening in the spring of 2009, a group of top government officials from a range of different ministries gather to discuss the current conditions for policy-making. They are concerned about their respective ministers' tendency toward "response politics"—politics that directly answer criticism raised in the media. The following exchange about an important piece of legislation that has just been adopted in Parliament takes place:

> A [in a polite, careful tone of voice]: You *can* get the impression that parts of the act were not wholly thought through.

> B [who has written large parts of the legislation in question]: Not thought through!!! Jesus, no! It is a shoddy job! But what would you expect? We had two weeks to come up with it.

In another office in another building a group of project workers are being told by an official from a Ministry that in their investigation of the current state of their front-desk services they are being too critical. They would not want to upset the staff too much.

Beside the point

19 percent of the social workers did not know whether they had broken the law or not.

Rule of law

After a meeting between a group of developers from across the different sections of the Municipality a tired senior public servant addresses the researcher:

> You know what? ... I've been on the municipal committee for social benefits for quite a while and I have said time and again that we need to have some rules that the citizens understand ... or at least some that the caseworkers understand. ... As a minimum we will have to demand that those who adopted them understand them. ...
>
> Apart from that, you know what? ... I have really been wondering about this tender we are discussing now. As you know, we are sitting here at the municipal level trying to draft some sensible tender documents and to describe the content of some courses for sick people. And this is before the law has even been passed by Parliament—before we know any of the results from the controlled trial. But if

we do not do it now we will not make it in time. And if we do not make it in time we will not be able to collect the reimbursement from the State. As a municipality we cannot afford that.

Writing complexity

How does one write about the complexity of an empirical field; about the multitude of connections and intersecting realities without reducing the overall impressions of messiness and absurdity to coherence and clarity? The dilemma Glenn Goodwin (1971) raised in his article "On transcending the absurd" stands at the heart of this challenge: being "expert at constructing explanations," he asks, how does one write a readable text that has not, by the same token, lost its "sensitivity to the absurdity of things" (ibid.: 842)? I am convinced that Kurt Vonnegut's (1973) break with the skewed attention paid to main and minor characters in fiction is relevant in the context of writing about the drafting of politics and the development of the Danish labor market system. By placing side by side in writing what in the physical world is separate, I want to contrast and link a number of situations where people do their best, and generate not only a labor market system, but a society.

Puzzling

In March 2009 a journalist from the Danish Broadcasting Corporation's Program 1 casts his inquiring eyes on the legal foundation of the controlled trial, and he is on to something. Actually he is not a journalist, but who would have guessed? With a self-image as the constitutional watchdog and his thoroughness and fierce mannerisms, the only thing lacking to complete the stereotypical picture of the classic journalist is a cigarette wedged behind his ear. He prefers black coffee from the machine to the freshly ground French press, also available, as he makes himself comfortable in an editing room deep inside the colossus that constitutes the Danish Broadcasting Corporation. While the researcher marvels at the technology, the reporter brings in the sound directly from Parliament, where an interpellation caused by his in-depth journalism has just begun. At the National Labor Market Authority, where his reports have caused significant overtime work, he is suspected of "politicizing." Is it political scheming that drives him? Or is it his sense of the logical flaw that in his childhood drove him to solve every mathematical puzzle on the back page of the journal, *The Engineer*?

Front line

On the radio, they argue that the controlled trial targeting recipients of sickness benefits is illegal. A professor of social law says there is no doubt about its illegality. The National Labor Market Authority says there is no doubt about its legality. Ida from the municipal job center thinks it is uncomfortable: "It makes me feel rather like a foot soldier, the orders come down from above and you just toe the line."

Questions for Carl

How did you feel when you were sitting at home on your couch, alone, your health deteriorated, job gone? Did you want to give up? Did you suspect that getting back on your feet would be an uphill struggle? Did you feel dizzy?

Failure

Carl felt as if his life had ended. As if, at age 51, life had nothing left in store for him. Carl just sat there on the couch every day. We might imagine him staring into space or at the television screen. An outdoorsman now sitting in his apartment; a strong man reduced to passivity. He grew grumpy; his friend told him he was not "himself" anymore:

> *Carl:* The first two or three days, I really did not want to be here at the private employment agency. I had already accepted that it was all over. But now I know that there is more in life for me. And my friends tell me that I am a much happier person again. This group of people I have met here ... it is like having good colleagues, it makes me want to get up in the morning and go "to work."

In the statistics Carl's case will appear as a failure; the Municipality has invested in a "sickness benefit package" to get him back on track; in other words, back to full-time employment. The private employment agency had four weeks available. They were paid around 1000 Danish kroner (or £100) a week for 25 hours in which he—the citizen—was to be brought closer to the labor market through an approach centered on his needs. Carl was not, however, ready for full-time employment after four weeks.

Success

Eventually, when I handed in the last sheet to Statistics Denmark, it felt like a victory. It mattered less that the calculations should have been based on a specific week in March and that it had been necessary for me to base my calculations on a random week in December. It mattered less that it was fictional, as we did not grant people a "time slot" but a service—meaning that I eventually had to make up numbers based on my own assumptions such as: "It probably takes ten minutes a week to water plants twice a week." It mattered less that I had spent two months, on-and-off, plus my colleague's time, to create this fiction. It mattered less that both my colleague and I *knew* that our files were incomplete. What did matter was that I was finally able to conclude the task that had been haunting our unit and that had caused problems for our management and Statistics Denmark. I received much praise for my handling of the task and from then on all kinds of statistical charts landed on my desk.

Irene

"And by 'system' I guess I mean all the people who unknown to me and without having ever met me or spoken to me make decisions that affect my life in tangible ways."

Motivating

One Monday afternoon a man is summoned to a meeting at the private employment agency. He does not know why. He has been through two programs of work ability testing at the employment agency before and extensive files have been written on his case. A testament to this is the 5cm-tall pile of documents placed on the table in the meeting room by Sophie. Sophie is the social worker who has been commissioned by the Municipality to "motivate" the man to participate in a third program at the employment agency. The man holds a letter in his hand as he walks behind Sophie down the hallway. It tells him to report this Monday at this hour to this agency but the letter does not tell him why he has to do so. Therefore, he tells Sophie as they sit down by the table, he called his caseworker before the meeting to ask her why he had been referred to the employment agency again. He was left none the wiser since his caseworker could only inform him that she no longer worked his case and did not know who did. "Do *you* know who my caseworker is?" he asks Sophie. Sophie looks through her documents. She cannot find the information. The man presses on: "But I have been through the work ability testing twice already. How can they just keep referring me here? This is meaningless!" He tells Sophie he has lodged an appeal against the Municipality's decision to reject his application for early retirement pension. Sophie in her turn informs the man that he *must* participate in the program in order to maintain his right to social security until the appeal has been processed. She does *not* explain to him that the Municipality's processing of appeal cases takes so long that she expects the man will long have gone through the program when they make their decision. And she does not tell him that the Municipality will most likely use his very participation in the program as a means to reject the appeal case. In her experience they might very likely argue that if he can participate in that program, he can work. Sophie tells him that it cannot be any other way, that this is the law.

Writing absurdity

Absurdity is a perspective that appreciates the total sum of a series of events, decisions, links, or implications. Absurdity provides a lens through which to appreciate the multitude of organizational links, and of competing goals, purposes, and ways of framing decisions as being sensible. In relation to understanding how policy-driven development takes place, and why it rarely happens according to the plan, it draws our attention to the simple and banal but repeatedly ignored fact: that implementation of a given course of action does not happen in a vacuum. A policy provides but one set of goals or values which will have to struggle for the implementers' attentions with a string of other and often contradictory goals and purposes. It is this abundance which will cause the individual plan to be bent out of shape or reinterpreted beyond recognition. This is not an exception to how implementation happens, and while it might be called "unintended outcome" it is the very mode in which any implementation process in a complex setting happens. Implementation happens non-linearly and it is characterized by mutation caused by individual decisions which—seen in isolation—are very sensible.

Beginning, middle, and end

Kate does a shoddy job. A focal point for a municipal caseworker is to comply with the law. Kate struggles to fill in the gaps. According to the news, 19 percent of the social workers do not know if they break the law. A focal point for a municipal caseworker is to comply with the project design. A focal point for the citizen is to get well. The letter in the young woman's hand does not exist. A reporter has noted a logical flaw. A policy-maker has two weeks to draft an important piece of legislation. A "sickness benefit package" has given Carl back his hope for the future. There was no door to where the caseworker worked. An authority says there is no logical flaw. It is a focal point for the National Labor Market Authority to ensure that the citizens get the help they need to get back to work as soon as possible. Carl's case was a failure. One citizen refuses to do it "just for the fun of it." Statistics are essential for estimating the success or failure of the employment effort. A citizen sits in a puddle of piss surrounded by police officers. A citizen sits in a garden waiting for treatment. All kinds of statistics land on my desk. A policy-maker drinks her coffee surrounded by reports, laws, and drafts. A caseworker handles her pile of cardboard case-files that grows higher by the hour. On a street in Denmark citizens have sex, sell drugs, get pissed, fall in love, and drink iced coffee. Sophie tells him that it cannot be any other way, that this is the law.

Note

1 This prologue is an adaptation of a chapter published as Vohnsen, N. (2013a), "Labor days: a non-linear narrative of development," in Suhr, C. and Willerslev, R. (Eds), Transcultural Montage, Berghahn Books, New York, Oxford, pp. 131–144.

Introduction: the absurdity of bureaucracy

The story I want to tell in this book is not the story of a dysfunctional employment system, although I realize it might be read this way. Had that been my agenda, I would not have made the slightest contribution to what has long been a popular conception in Denmark. Since I concluded my ethnographic fieldwork in December 2009 the Danish employment effort has seen its share of evaluations and newspaper articles that report the dysfunctionalities of the system; for some time a popular blog brought witty live reports written by people subjected to the employment effort (www.dagpengeland.dk); in 2012 the Danish Broadcasting Corporation took a job center as the topic for its annual TV satire; the National Audit Department (*rigsrevisionen*) has repeatedly cast its dissatisfied eyes on the topic. The legislation governing the subject has been reformed various times in the years following my study. It seems that somehow things never really work out the way they are supposed to in the employment system.

The story I *do* mean to tell is a more general one about an area of political intervention where the documented complexity of laws and of conflicting goals has reached such a pitch that it seems that the slightest administrative movement or organizational adjustment immediately distorts the totality. The people you will meet in the course of this book are people who do their best to make sound and sustainable administrative decisions; who are as loyal as practically possible to a politically adopted project and law; who put in extra time to respond to the citizens who pass through their offices; who toss and turn in bed at night in despair; and who energetically restructure and readjust organizations and work routines. It is a story of human beings who, in their attempt to produce a meaningful "system" and make sensible decisions, by that very same token reproduce a bureaucratic system that at any moment has the potential of appearing utterly absurd to its spectators, to its planners, and to the subjects of its interventions.

In the course of telling this story I address the following questions: How is it that bureaucracy continues to beget bureaucracy despite repeated attempts to downsize and deregulate? How does implementation actually happen, and what are the principles by which carefully planned policies come to have such unpredictable results? The main protagonist of my story will be a randomized controlled trial first conceived in the Danish Ministry of Employment in the fall of 2008.

The failure of *Active—Back Sooner*

On 8 October 2010, the quantitative evaluation (Rambøll 2010) of the controlled trial *Active—Back Sooner*[1] targeting the Danish recipients of sickness benefits was published. The evaluation concluded that the intervention had failed to abbreviate the period over which the intervention group received public benefits (as had been the purpose), and furthermore that the intervention had cost significantly more than the equally effective "normal procedure" (ibid.: 1f). However, the "normal procedure" (received by a control group which had been established for the purpose of comparison) had at the time of the evaluation's publication long ceased to exist: immediately following the trial period and nine months before the publication of the evaluation, central elements in the project had been integrated into a revised law on sickness benefit. This included the possibility to refer people against their will (if they did not want to lose their income) to "activities" (which could include physical exercise or sessions on stress management) and the duty to assess whether people could return part-time to work while sick.

The revised law had been adopted by the Danish Parliament some months before the controlled trial was completed; the first draft for the law had been placed for public hearing in December 2008, some weeks before the controlled trial started. This was only gradually realized by those municipal caseworkers, who labored under the impression that the results from the controlled trial would be used to assess whether or not such an intervention would be recommended to Parliament. In other words, these employees had thought of their effort as an attempt (and it had indeed been promoted as such by the Ministry of Employment) to make "evidence-based policy" and some continued to think of it as such even after the new legislation had gone through the first of three readings in Parliament only a few months into the trial's implementation phase. The controlled trial itself had come about partly as a result of many Danish caseworkers' wishes to "make a difference" and to be able to offer something "that made sense" to the sick citizens who moved through their offices and electronic case management systems. However, for the caseworkers included in my study the intervention ultimately came to be experienced as even more senseless than the "normal procedure" it was meant to replace. Statements such as "this is absurd," "this is meaningless," "this makes no sense," and "this serves no purpose" remained common when the caseworkers talked about their work both before, during, and after the implementation of *Active—Back Sooner*.

How might we best understand these paradoxes and contradictions between what was intended and what took place? One analytical strategy could be to dissolve the contradictions by claiming that the project was just a tool in larger political negotiations; that the politicians never meant to use the results of the project for anything, and that the intention had been something else all along; or perhaps even that this was just an example of plain sloppy work. However, that solving contradictions discursively does not make them go away is a daily experience of the civil servants and caseworkers the reader will meet in this book. Contradictions will return to resist the interpretations and decisions made. How then might we understand the policy's apparent failure and the contradictions that characterized it?

Implementation "gone wrong"

That policy does not easily translate into the prescribed practice is one of the fundamental problems addressed by scholars of policy implementation and public administration (e.g. Brehm & Gates 1999; deLeon & deLeon 2002; Durose 2009, 2011; Hjern & Porter 1981; Lin 2002; Lipsky 1980, Maynard-Moody & Musheno 2000; Mulgan 2009; Osborne & Gaebler 1992; O'Toole 2000; Pressman & Wildavsky 1984 [1973]; Scott 1998; Winter et al. 2008; however, see Kettl 1993: 60–1 for a critique). Taking a top-down or bottom-up approach, these studies point to the implementing administrations as one of the main sources of distortion: policy implementation "goes wrong" because those whose job it is to implement a policy (e.g. doctors, caseworkers, police officers, teachers) decide to disregard, bend, or wrongly apply rules and directives (for an overview, see deLeon & deLeon 2002; O'Toole 2000). While these different analyses may explain certain actions which may shape implementation, they nevertheless rest on one or more of the following problematic assumptions: a) that the crafting of a policy precedes its implementation; b) that the crafting of a policy and its implementation are carried out by two distinct groups of people; and finally c) that these two groups of people are concerned with different things (statistics versus achieving results in individual cases; politics versus practicalities; money versus people) and approach the world differently (e.g. abstractly versus concretely; indifferently versus personally).

That these dichotomies are difficult to uphold when looking at concrete cases has been demonstrated thoroughly by the vast body of ethnographic literature which examines the everyday life of corporate policy implementation (e.g. Krause-Jensen 2011; Ong 1988), national policy implementation (Boll 2011; Das 2004; Gupta 2012; Hyatt 1997; Latour 1996; Lea 2008; Shore & Wright 1997; Shore et al. 2011; Vohnsen 2015; Wright 2008), and international development (Ferguson 1994; Li 2007; Mosse 2005, 2007; Nygaard-Christensen 2011). However, with the exception of David Mosse (2005), these findings have not been turned into concrete implementation theories. This book follows in the tradition of David Mosse in aiming to provide an empirically founded understanding of how implementation works, which may substitute or radically nuance the above mentioned assumptions.

The complexity of inter-organizational implementation which this book exemplifies is recognized as particularly challenging within the field of public policy implementation (e.g. Hjern & Porter 1981; Lin 2002; Lipsky 1980; O'Toole 2000). Thus in 2000 O'Toole criticized his own generation of implementation scholars for endlessly introducing new variables, and mused over Ken Meier's definition of contemporary implementation theory as "forty-seven variables that completely explain five case studies" (Meier in O'Toole 2000: 268). Yet, what their generation was actually documenting, this book claims, was the endlessly intertwined nature of human social life, of which implementation is but one instance. Rather than seeking to either fully document or reduce this complexity to make an operational model, this book argues that it is more enlightening to regard implementation as exactly this—as but an instance of human social life. With this approach it is the book's ambition to reclaim implementation studies for the qualitative sciences. Thus, if Goggins et al. (1990) in their call for a third generation of implementation research wanted to "be more scientific" (ibid.: 18) and "shed new light on implementation behavior by explaining why the behavior varies across time, policies, and units of government" (ibid.: 17), then this book wants to do the same but "be more philosophical" and argue that the fundamental mechanisms and dilemmas confronted in the process of implementing policy are not confined to administration and management. The central dilemma faced by the civil servants—that whatever you do there is always something else you could have done and probably should have done—is universally shared by humans and has been conceptualized and theorized within Western societies by the literary figure of "the absurd."

Theoretical framework: the absurd

Despite the fact that institutional absurdity has been treated expertly by authors such as Kafka in his novel *The Process* or by Herman Melville in his short story *Bartleby The Scribe*, and might be said to constitute a genre of its own within TV series—e.g. *The Office, Yes Minister, In the Loop, The Wire*—scholars of State organizations and bureaucracy have left this topic all but unexplored (for a recent exploration, see Graeber 2015). Even ethnographic analyses which pride themselves in departing from vernacular accounts are curiously silent when it comes to people's experience of the absurdity and meaninglessness of bureaucracy. But perhaps this is not strange at all. The trademark of anthropology—the mother discipline of ethnography—has been, throughout its disciplinary history, to make the exotic familiar, the irrational rational, the incoherent coherent. Perhaps we have come to see it as our duty to do so and regard the failure to make sense of things—as Matt Tomlinson (2007) suggests in *The limits of meaning*—as our personal failure as analysts? There does seem to exist, as Joel Robbins comments in the same volume, a particular, strong, anthropological will to make sense out of everything (Robbins 2007: 221). Whether this is something proper to anthropology as a discipline or to science in general I will not pursue here, but I will take to heart the warning from the sociologist Glenn Goodwin (1971) that social scientists risk losing their sensitivity to the absurdity of things as they become more and more expert at constructing explanations (ibid.: 842).

Absurdity in the social sciences

Meaninglessness and absurdity arose as explicitly pursued topics in the sociology of the 1970s and 1980s (Boorstein 1969; Broadhead 1974; Goodwin 1971; Lyman & Scott 1989 [1970]; Seidman 1983; also Casey 2002). A key work from this period is Stanford Lyman and Marvin Scott's *A sociology of the absurd* (Lyman & Scott 1970). In this book they identified the philosophical roots and analytical potentials in a "new wave of thought" (ibid.: 2) in sociology. "The world is essentially without meaning" they proclaimed, and there is no "real meaning of action" to discover (ibid.). Theirs was an attempt to break with the Parsonian functionalism which was dominating at the time. Instead of searching for "the functional meaning of things"—i.e. meaning given already—the task of the new sociology should be to examine how people "carve out meaning in a world that is meaningless" (ibid.). The key examples of this new sociology which Lyman and Scott saw themselves as heir to was "labelling theory," represented in Erving Goffman's *Presentation of self* (1959), Howard Becker's *Outsiders* (1997 [1963]), David Matza's *Becoming deviant* (1969), and the "ethnomethodology" of Harold Garfinkel (1967). Meaninglessness was, from this perspective, a condition that underlies and orders social interaction and conflict to become a key focus (Lyman & Scott 1970; also Goodwin 1971).

This fundamental assumption—that meaning is not given but socially constructed—became highly influential in anthropology through the popularity of the work of Goffman, Becker, Matza, and Garfinkel. However, this did not lead to empirical explorations of said "absurdity" and "meaninglessness." There are but few exceptions to this rule: "The meaninglessness of ritual" by Fritz Staal (1979), "What's in a word: the meaning of meaninglessness in Telefolmin"[2] by Dan Jorgensen (1980), and the aforementioned edited volume on Christianity, *The limits of meaning* edited by Matthew Engelke and Matt Tomlinson (2007). These three pieces of work differ from their sociological counterparts in that they treat meaninglessness as empirical categories to be explored ethnographically rather than as a fundamental condition of human existence. However, they do so in distinct ways: Dan Jorgensen's aim was to make analysts of religious belief systems pay attention to the role of ambiguity and incoherence by looking at classic theories of belief systems through a Telefolmin theory of meaninglessness (captured by the trickster figure Magalim). Fritz Staal conversely departed from a Western theorization of meaninglessness in order to elaborate a new theorization of Ayurvedic ritual praxis which was more loyal to his empirical observations. Joel Robbins' analytical move was to make a synthesis of the empirical material presented in the volume, Engelske and Tomlinson's *The limits of meaning*, in order to explore how meaninglessness is socially constructed as the backdrop of a meaningful (more specifically, Christian) existence, a condition necessarily external to what is perceived to be "the system" (Robbins 2007). Most recently, Nils Bubandt (2014) has treated the absurd characteristics of witchcraft (which he terms "the aporia") in Buli, Indonesia. Drawing, among others, on the work of Jorgensen, Bubandt argues that witchcraft should not be understood as a belief system but rather as a condition of doubt. In this book, I will follow in the footsteps of these anthropologists in looking empirically at the kind of work routines and the sort of outcome labelled by my informants as meaningless and absurd. I take from Robbins his point that meaninglessness seems always to be treated like a system fault rather than a constitutive characteristic of a system, and I follow Jorgensen in paying attention to the role of ambiguity and incoherence in producing the experience of meaninglessness.

Absurdity in this book

The dynamic nature of absurdity and sense-making will be the concurrent analytical figures throughout the analytical chapters on implementation and decision-making that comprise this book: here I will unravel the multitude of decisions, purposes, goals, and criteria for success that constitute one small but significant corner of Danish labor market politics. I use absurdity as an analytical umbrella for emic statements such as "this is purposeless" (formålsløst), "this makes no sense" (giver ingen mening), "this is futile" (nytteløst), "this is ridiculous" (latterligt), "this is absurd" (absurd), and "this is meaningless" (meningsløst), which were used by my informants to judge the content of their work and the labor market effort in general. These various usages fall close to philosopher Steven Luper-Foy's (1992) definition of absurdity as covering "the ridiculous," "the incongruous," and "the meaningless," with the latter in the three senses of "the senseless" (that which is unintelligible or the activity that does not fit a purposeful pattern), "the futile" (that which has a purpose but fails to achieve it) and "the pointless" (that which has no purpose at all) (ibid.: 97).

While I talk of sense-making, I wish from the beginning to make it clear that I depart from the before mentioned sociological theorizations of absurdity and sense-making in important respects: I cannot empirically regard sense-making as happening in a vacuum and cannot agree that "the world is essentially without meaning" (Lyman & Scott 1989 [1970]: 2). Contrary to Zygmunt Bauman's stipulation that "purposes and meanings are not 'given'" (Bauman 1992: 6) in my material they are given, and in abundance. So while I agree that "purpose can be chosen" (ibid.), I do not agree that "meaning can be created ab nihilo" (ibid.: italics in original). This too was what Robert Broadhead (1974) pointed out in his review of A sociology of the absurd (Lyman & Scott 1970) when he cautioned against what he regarded as Lyman and Scott's confusion of the "the meaninglessness of 'metaphysical reality'" with the "social construction of reality" (Broadhead 1974: 43). The experience of meaninglessness is far from being an exhaustive description of social reality.

In this book I shall therefore argue that the Danish labor market effort is experientially absurd. Absurdity (in the sense of senselessness, purposelessness, futility, meaninglessness) arises in my empirical material as the emic judgement that there is no logic to what takes place, that something has ceased to make sense, and serves no purpose. In support of philosopher Thomas Nagel's (1971) argument that the sentiment of absurdity is the result of the human capacity to step back and look at one's own practice in a disengaged way, absurdity and meaninglessness appear in my empirical material as a perspective belonging to the momentarily disengaged person, and not to the practitioner of policy crafting or delivery of public services in the moments of being engaged in responding to the tasks at hand. In summary, I take absurdity to be a perspective the human can move in and out of and not an objective condition that underlies and orders social reality.

The theoretical purpose of this book is to unravel this experience of absurdity in order to show the multiplicity of logics at work in implementation of law and policy. It is not so, I shall argue, that the situations that provoke the various sentiments of absurdity are characterized by an absence of meaning or logic, but rather a presence of competing goals and conflicting purposes, and a multiplicity of parameters by which to judge the sensibility of one's actions. Therefore to call the Danish labor market effort absurd is not only to do justice to a sentiment shared by many Danish citizens (whether its practitioners or those subjected to it); it also offers a perspective from which to appreciate the totality of the different goals and criteria for success that compete for civil servants' and caseworkers' attention.

Empirical interest: repercussions of policy

Since the mid-1990s, anthropology has produced a rich literature on the effects of international development schemes. Common to these ethnographies is the refusal to take the "failures" or "successes" of policy implementation at face value (Das 2004; Ferguson 1994; Lewis & Mosse 2006; Li 2005, 2007; Mosse 2005, 2007; Shore & Wright 1997, Shore et al. 2011; Tsing 2005;). While other social sciences have taken an analytical interest in identifying reasons for failed implementation, anthropological studies have turned their attention to the practices and effects of implementation and of the development schemes regardless of the relation of these effects to pre-defined criteria for success. I carry this tradition forward and provide ethnographic accounts of how the controlled trial *Active—Back Sooner*, designed and adopted politically to be applied locally, quickly resulted in the creation of several parallel projects that evolved or mutated in anything but linear ways, often with only little relationship to the original policy. In the following I will position my approach as it relates to anthropological key debates on "effects" of interventions and the "intentionality" behind them.

A reassessment of "effect"

The anti-politics machine (1994) by James Ferguson is an empirical description of a failed development project in Lesotho. Ferguson turns his analytical attention to what the project accomplished rather than what it failed to do, asserting that "'failure' ... does not mean doing nothing; it means doing something else' (Ferguson 2005: 284). Ferguson argues that while the project failed to bring about the expected agricultural development, it was instrumental in establishing a vast social infrastructure consisting of roads, post offices, health care clinics, and numerous local bureaucratic institutions (ibid.: 271f.). Rather than seeing these outcomes as side-effects of a failed project, he wants us to see them as "instrument-effects" (ibid.: 272), as both concrete effects of the project and outcomes that were instrumental in "expanding the exercise of bureaucratic State power" (ibid.: 273). The tendency of development projects to work this way is what he calls the "anti-politics machine": first a political question (in his case poverty) is reduced to technical problems (nutrition and distribution of resources), and then, in the process of solving them (through technical agricultural advice), they become instrumental in carrying out what is essentially a deeply political operation (the expansion of the State system and the advocacy for economic redistribution). Ferguson sees no conspiracy here; this is not the way the planners intend it, he emphasizes; "it really does just happen to be the way things work out" (ibid.).

There is an interesting parallel between Ferguson's observation from the development work in Lesotho and an article that raised a public debate in Denmark when it was published in 2007 in one of the largest daily newspapers. The article, called "Forgive us—we did not know what we did" (Gjørup et al. 2007, my translation), was written by eight former senior civil servants from the Danish Ministry of Finance as a warning and as a response to the Prime Minister's heralding of a public sector "quality reform." In the 1990s these eight civil servants had promoted the introduction of contract management as a model for managing relationships in the public sector. In the article, they described how the model, with which they had intended to introduce an unusually high level of freedom and autonomy in the relationship between public sector institutions and their auditing authorities (they had initially been successful in doing so) had, in time, evolved into an all-pervading contract system, which was not only highly resource consuming but which removed focus from the quality of the services provided and instead gave rise to an ever increasing elaboration of target figures. "Instead of collaboration and dialogue we got [...] more paper and more bureaucracy" they wrote (Gjørup et al. 2007, my translation). The way contract management had been used by practitioners was clearly a failure in the eyes of the planners (that is, Gjørup et al.). But it is equally clear that the implementation of contract management has had enormous effects on the way the Danish public sector is run and there seems to be universal agreement between politicians, civil servants, and front-staff employees (such as doctors, teachers, caseworkers, and police officers) in the public sector that the ever increasing demand for paperwork has reached an intolerable level (i.e. Finansministeriet 2011; Bræmer 2008). In Ferguson's and Gjørup et al.'s accounts the failures of the interventions (the agricultural development scheme and the introduction of contract management, respectively) are presented as straightforward. The Lesotho development project failed because it did not bring about the rural development it promised; the introduction of contract management failed because it turned out to function contrary to the intention of introducing greater freedom and trust in the relationship between public sector units.

Anthropologist and former consultant for the UK Department for International Development, David Mosse, would advise us to begin our inquiry differently by examining how the judgements "success" and "failure" relate to the practices they are meant to evaluate (Mosse 2005; 2007). Drawing on ten years of experience with a project that was promoted as the blueprint for the "participatory approach" in international development work he demonstrates that the evaluation and promotion of the project as successful and later failing had little, if anything, to do with its practical effects. In his monograph, *Cultivating development* (Mosse 2005) he offers a detailed account of the crafting and implementation of the above mentioned British aid project set in rural India. He shows how in the period when the project was being promoted most successfully as an example of the "participatory approach," most of its core "outputs" were results of the exercise of "vertical control over program delivery" (Mosse 2005: 161). The project's "success," argues Mosse, was the result of the theoretical linkage in the project design (the policy) which allowed the target groups' participation in activities to be read as signs of a good and sustainable development (ibid.). When the project eventually "failed" it had nothing to do with a change in the project's practice, nor had it anything to do with the review team's ability to "penetrate the reality of project practice" (Mosse 2007: 470). Rather, he argues, the project's failure was occasioned ("socially produced") by the review team's refusal to accept the project's underlying theoretical assumption that participation in project activities necessarily leads to better livelihoods. As a result the "review team did not ask the project to change what it did, but to modify its *theory*" (ibid.: 471, italics in original). Thus evaluations, according to Mosse, serve primarily to sustain or undermine a policy's theoretical basis but will not inform us of what took place in practice.

Mosse's analysis is similar to Ferguson's in seeking effects and impacts away from official evaluations but they are looking for different things. Ferguson wants us to explore the effects of failure, Mosse wants us to explore how judgements such as "failure" relate to the actual project practice. With Ferguson we see an anti-politics machine where power is free-floating and things just happen to turn out the way they do; Mosse, on the other hand, theorizes a hyper-political network in which power is unequally distributed between people whose energy is bound up in sustaining the policy through translation back and forth between theory, plan, and practice. What I take from these two approaches in my own exploration of the implementation of *Active—Back Sooner*, and later the revised law on sickness benefit, are their sensitivities to the wider project context and to the actual project practice: if Ferguson, observing the Lesotho development project from afar, begins by asking if the effects of failure are not relevant for understanding implementation, and Mosse steps into the whirlwind of consultancy, brokerage, and translation and asks what failure and success are, I direct my attention to the details of policy-makers' and implementers' everyday work life and ask *what* it is that fails, succeeds, or has effects? *What* is implemented—a piece of national policy, a locally adapted project, or a myriad time-bound solutions?

In moving between the administrative levels on which *Active—Back Sooner* lived—sometimes as paper, sometimes as political ideal, sometimes as decision or subject of debates—my analysis will zoom in and out on the project, sometimes coinciding with a view that allows for the ideas of Ferguson or Mosse to be explored. Where my approach differs from Ferguson's and Mosse's, it is as a result of scale. The closer we look at the moments in which decisions pertaining to the project are made, the more the project dissolves into a multiplicity of logics and strivings for conflicting goals and it seems that in those moments the project relates to the politically adopted project in nothing but name. How does all this happen? What brings about the dissolution of the project? How are the effects of political interventions produced concretely? To answer this we need people and with the introduction of people into the equation the question of intentionality surfaces.

The question of intentionality

When Ferguson encourages us to look at the tangible outcome of development projects regardless of the relation of these outcomes to pre-defined criteria of success he wants us to accept that the impact of development schemes leads to an extension of the bureaucratic sphere and that this happens despite the planner's best intentions. Planners are up against a powerful machine—the anti-politics machine. Seen through this lens, intentionality loses its import; the effects of development happen "behind the backs or against the will" of those who planned them (Ferguson 1994: 20). While the development of contract management in Denmark could certainly be argued to have happened behind the backs or against the will of the former Danish civil servants (i.e. Gjørup et al. 2007) who introduced it, their analysis draws attention to a set of people who, in Ferguson's analysis, receive little attention; namely the individual man or woman whose job it became to craft the contracts. What happened once Gjørup et al. had let contract management loose in Denmark and what caused their intention to fail in practice, they write, was "the incessant human drive towards perfecting the instrument" (ibid., my translation[3]).

Note that this "human drive towards perfecting the instrument" is very different from what Tania Murray Li (2007) calls "the will to improve," a mentality proper to development work, which she places in the theoretical framework of a Foucauldian governmentality analysis. In Li's framework "government" is seen as "the attempt to shape human conduct by calculated means" (ibid.: 5). She identifies two key practices as central for understanding the "will to improve": one is the identification of deficiencies that need to be rectified, the other the practice of "rendering technical" (ibid.: 7), involving the process that Nikolas Rose has described as "defining boundaries, rendering that within them visible, assembling information about that which is included and devising techniques to mobilize the forces and entities thus revealed" (Rose in Li 2007: 7). Li describes these two practices (of identifying a problem and of collecting information about an area of intervention which will allow for the identified problem to be rectified) as parallel to Ferguson's anti-politics machine which reduces political problems to technical ones (Ferguson 2005: 273). She too is interested in the practical outcome of such interventions. In her analysis she therefore brings together the genealogy of governmental interventions and an "analysis of what happens when those interventions become entangled with the processes they would regulate and improve" (Li 2007: 27). However, in this separation of the world into "the plan" and "the practice" she bypasses the steps that Gjørup et al. draw attention to, namely the practices of planning and the hopes and attempts to do good and make sensible decisions involved therein.

Unlike Li's discursively constituted "will to improve" then, Gjørup et al.'s "human drive towards perfecting the instrument" introduces *an intentional person*, yet one who is *driven by something general*: —a drive to respond to the tasks at hand and possessed by a will to perfect the instruments given; in other words, "the planner." In their poetic sentence they simultaneously place individual intentionality at the core of development processes while inserting the question of "implementation-gone-wrong" in the wider context of human creativity—here understood in the pragmatic sense of continuously producing and solving problems (Joas in Joas & Sennett 2006: 11). It is the perspective of Gjørup et al., rather than Li, that I will adopt in this book: I wish to address the messiness and contradictions that characterize human experience and practice and the human planning as a response to this mess. Adopting this view will allow me to show how the planning of an intervention not only precedes its implementation but that planning and implementation of interventions might happen simultaneously and continuously on all organizational levels. The "planners" in this book are therefore not only the politicians or the centrally placed civil servants in the Ministry of Employment and its sub-sections that drafted the initial policy document which set the framework for the controlled trial, but also the municipal bosses, middle-managers and caseworkers, as well as the bosses and employees in the private employment agencies who became involved in the execution of central parts of *Active—Back Sooner.*

Writing complexity

Analytical strategy

My ethnographic exploration of the crafting, planning, and implementation of *Active—Back Sooner* took place primarily during the year 2009. My research can best be summed up as an example of what Susan Wright and Sue Reinhold (2011) have called "studying through"—a research approach to studying policy that "avoids presuming a hierarchical relation between policy-makers determining policy and implementing it on the governed" (Wright & Reinhold 2011: 19). In the research strategy Wright and Reinhold lay out, the researcher follows "a discussion or a conflict as it ranges back and forth and back again between protagonists, and up and down and up again between a range of local and national sites" in order to study a "process of political transformation" (ibid.). In my case, the "thing" I studied "through" was the project *Active—Back Sooner.* I conducted ethnographic fieldwork[4] in three organizational units where I knew "it"[5] would have effects (an office in the National Labor Market Authority, a unit in a municipal job center, and a team in a private employment agency) but as the discussions surrounding *Active—Back Sooner* took hold in the public debate, I expanded my research to include the comments and discussions in the media and Parliament.

Central to Wright and Reinhold's approach is that while researchers physically move themselves between different organizational contexts, they exercise a special awareness to the ways in which events have "multiple potential effects with unpredictable significances for the future" (ibid.). This will reveal, they predict, how keywords "involved in one incident reappeared or changed in the next" (ibid.). While Wright and Reinhold are attentive to "events" or "incidents," my focus has been on decision-making as moments in which *Active—Back Sooner* was either produced as plans or public documents or used as a warrant for decisions. Their prediction, however, holds water when tested against my material; *Active—Back Sooner* as it was invoked in one situation of decision-making was not necessarily the same *Active—Back Sooner* invoked in the next. Still, *Active—Back Sooner* in all "its" versions had effects and it is these effects that I trace in the chapters 1 through 4.

Context

"Context," Roy Dilley writes, "involves making connections and, by implication, disconnections" (Dilley 1999: x). Following this, context and text are produced simultaneously by the analytical focus. When Peter Miller & Nikolas Rose (2008) proposed an analytical approach in which we examine how parts of a population come to be singled out as being in want of political intervention, they place at the center of analytical attention the discursive aspect of human practice. Though Miller and Rose's approach might help us see—as we will—how the conditions were established for regarding sickness benefit as an area of intervention in Denmark in 2007–09, and how certain ideas about sickness and health sneaked into the public and political debate, it will, however, not help us understand the practical effects of *Active—Back Sooner*, nor will it be informative of the messy details and contradictions inherent to either the implementation of development projects or the inexhaustive nature of decision-making. Seen from the close-up perspective on the practicalities of decision-making, what Miller and Rose's analytical framework offers seems purely contextual in that it facilitates an exploration of the larger picture and the bigger structure that allow situated decisions or suggestions to be made. With "The making of law" (2010) Bruno Latour, on the other hand, claims to have written a context-free, zoom-free monograph invoking only those contextual details needed to allow us to move to the next analytical step in his analysis so as not to lose his reader totally in the foreign terrain of French administrative law. As in the case of the analyses of Miller and Rose (2008), the result is beautiful and convincing—well-rounded. My interest, as I wrote earlier, is different. If by context we mean that which surrounds what is at the center of immediate attention then it follows that what is at the center of attention for someone is, potentially, somebody else's context.

My approach will therefore encompass both viewpoints. If Latour wants us to see how translation takes place by tracing the transition of knowledge from one place to another, as he does most beautifully in his essay "Circulating reference" (1999), I want us also to see the disruptions, the surplus, the rejected. I will zoom in and out, move between scales, institutional levels, situations and people (also Wright & Reinhold 2011). My aim is not to thereby approximate my analysis to any more "complete" or "truer" understanding of the labor market area but to provide context by means of comparison (Rapport 1992; Strathern 2004 [1991]) in displaying a multitude of different situations and incidents that will both serve as the ground for mutual comparison and contextualize each other. Therefore I will not, in this book, provide a detailed account of subjective life-worlds contextualized by the larger political, economic, and cultural schemes of things. Rather, I will provide an account in which we will see how a policy is created multiple times and mutates continuously in different places and times. This means that the central subject of this book is not so much a specific group of individuals as it is a policy and those people who by virtue of having a particular job end up being its "planners." But then how does one write complexity without either imitating it or reducing it to simplicity? How does one render complexity intelligible without making things appear straightforward? In this book I apply three different writing principles: montage; the environmental portrait; and the branching-plot principle found in game books.

Montage

I opened this book with a montage of empirical situations from the Danish public sector. For the sake of overview and for the benefit of those who might have skipped past it, I will repeat the explanatory sections here: intellectual montage is, according to Russian film-maker Sergei Eisenstein (1994), the juxtaposition of (in the case of film-making) shots that elicit a specific intellectual meaning. A classic example of intellectual montage is Eisenstein's *Strike* in which he cross-clips between shots of a crowd of people being beaten by the military and shots of a cow being slaughtered. Here the interpretation of the violent event is explicitly locked down as "system treats people like cattle." Had the cross-clip been from the birth of a child or from a ballet the suggested interpretations would have been different: the bloodshed involved in transitions and new beginnings, or the careful and aesthetic orchestration of a State intervention. In this form of narration, one line of shots constitutes the main storyline while other shots are placed at key moments to suggest parallelisms intended to lead the spectator to consider specific interpretations of the events portrayed. However, in the attempt to write about the complexities of labor market politics it would be misleading to present the field as having, to quote American novelist Kurt Vonnegut, "leading characters, minor characters, significant details, that it has lessons to be learned, tests to be passed, and a beginning, a middle, and an end" (1973: 209). By dispensing with a narrative based on a leading argument and explicit storyline, the resulting intellectual montage has as its aim the multiplication of meaning rather than its reduction; it aims on interpretations that are more open than they are closed.

According to Charles Sanders Peirce's theory of consciousness (1955 [1940]) we are inclined towards the establishment of thought habits (ibid.: 28) in our intellectual life; we tend to fix our beliefs about the true state of things. Eisenstein's classic application of the intellectual montage, as in *Strike*, is associated with this type of conditioning, so that having watched this sequence in *Strike* it becomes more likely that, the next time we watch a State intervention, we will think of people being treated like mere cattle. In Eisenstein's thinking it is the juxtaposition of shots that initiates this process towards the fixation of interpretation. As Peirce puts it, we see that the potential for specific interpretations already resides as qualities (ibid.: 98ff.) in the individual shots and that interpretations are actualized in the clash between shots in numerous ways. The montage principle is not new to anthropological attempts to address and unfold perspectives on themes or objects of research. Examples include Michael Taussig's attempt to capture some of the characteristics of the State in *The nervous system* (Taussig 1992); Marilyn Strathern's book, *Partial connections* (Strathern 2004 [1991]), in which she revives comparison as an anthropological core project after the relativistic turn of the 1980s; and Nigel Rapport's insistence on the heterogeneous nature of individual social lives as discussed in *Transcendent Individual* (Rapport 1997; also 1992, 1994). What I aim for it to do is to destabilize fundamentally the idea that policy implementation may be bracketed off from the wider political, organizational, and social context in which it takes place. It destabilizes dichotomies such as center and periphery, beginnings and ends, relevance and irrelevance, focus and context, and undermines any linier understanding of policy implementation.

Environmental portraiture

It has been a challenge to write about the complexity of my empirical field, and about the multitude of connections and intersecting realities, without reducing the overall impressions of messiness and absurdity to coherence and clarity. The dilemma Goodwin (1971) raised in his article, which I quoted above, stands at the heart of this challenge: Being an "expert at constructing explanations" (ibid.: 842) how do I write a readable text that has not, by the same token, lost its "sensitivity to the absurdity of things" (ibid.)? As a means of writing about the implementation processes and about the bureaucratic decisions I am interested in, I have therefore chosen the "environmental portrait" as a guiding form of the writing style I am aiming for in this book, most explicitly in chapters 1–4. Photographer Kenneth Kobré (2008) distinguishes the environmental portrait from other kinds of portraiture by the role attributed to the background in the photograph (Kobré 2008: 92): the background details are a means to help "report the story" (ibid.: 92). Rather than pulling the subject out of its environment and isolating it by placing it in front of "a plain seamless paper background" (ibid.: 93), in environmental portraiture "the subject is photographed at home, at the office, or on location" (ibid.: 92); in other words, we are allowed to see the subject of an environmental portrait "amid the everyday objects of his or her life" (ibid.: 93).

This approach speaks convincingly to the research strategy George Marcus (1995) labelled as "multi-sited" and described as the mode of ethnographic research in which we "examine the circulation of cultural meanings, objects, and identities in diffuse time-space" (ibid.: 96). Rather than concentrating ethnographic research on a singular site (in my case this could be an office in the Ministry, Parliament, or a unit in the municipal job center), the research centers on tracking "a thing" (ibid.: 106) in the various "diffuse time-spaces" through which it passes (also Wright & Reinhold 2011). While my methodological approach to data gathering might be called "multi-sited" in so far as I tracked a policy through different "sites," I hesitate to call my ethnography (i.e. the written material presented in this book) multi-sited. The primary realization won by "following the thing" (ibid.) was that it immediately became clear that the "thing" I followed had no stability—the project, in singular, did not exist. In addition, the "sites" through which the project(s) *Active—Back Sooner* moved were not the physical "sites" I moved through but rather diffuse intellectual "sites," as varied as a legal debate and a local attempt to reach statistical goals. Since I wish to draw out the multiple nature of the project(s), what best helps me describe the implementation process is not physical "sites" but rather the different "backgrounds" on which *Active— Back Sooner* was cast; in other words, different environments in which it can be inserted analytically to highlight its several properties and lives.

Branching-plot novel

A final writing principle I use is the "game book." This principle is used in the types of book mainly popular in the "choose-your-own-adventure" literature of the 1980s (Katz 2011), in which the reader makes choices at key moments that define the course of the narrative. The simplest form of this literature is the branching-plot novel, which is like a normal linear narrative except for the choices the reader makes. Since my argument is about decision-making I thought it interesting to explore how such a writing technique could be used in an academic context. The branching-plot principle will be applied in the epilogue "Bureaucracy—choose your own adventure," in which the reader gets to make a series of decisions pertaining to sickness benefit cases in the municipal job center. With this piece I want to move understanding from a merely academic appropriation of arguments to an approximated experiential level. It is a trivial point that civil servants and bureaucrats are busy and that their work life is full of contradictions. It has been reiterated to death. Yet what the cognitive and agentive effects of being busy are is not something that is necessarily appreciated best theoretically. By exposing the reader to the totality of decisions and interruptions faced by street-level workers the branching-plot novel aims to force the reader to give up the intellectual distance and step into the whirl-wind of casework.

The validity of "Bureaucracy—choose your own adventure" as a piece of academic rather than fictional writing rests on a close commitment to the empirical data. Each situation described in this story did take place in November 2009. Each decision has been made by one of the municipal caseworkers. The internal, reflective voices narrated in the text echo explicitly voiced considerations and concerns. What is fictional is, therefore, the linking of decisions made by several different caseworkers to one deciding agent—the reader. I maintain the editorial authority in the structuring and juxtaposition of the different dilemmas and choices the reader will be asked to make. Whether the reader chooses to follow my instructions I, like any other planner, cannot control; ultimately, it is your decision.

Notes

1 Translated from the Danish title *Aktive—Hurtigere Tilbage*.
2 The Telefol are a people in Papua New Guinea.
3 In Danish "den bestandige menneskelige drift imod perfektionering af instrumentet" (Gjørup et al. 2007).
4 For specifics, see appendix.
5 I write "it" in quotation marks, as a central point of the book will be to demonstrate the lack of unity and coherency in *Active—Back Sooner*. I will elaborate on this later in this introduction.

1

Anticipations

The first two portraits will introduce the reader to the municipal and ministerial reality respectively. While introducing some of the central people in the book they will tell some stories of the genesis of *Active—Back Sooner*. Their central question is "Where does a policy come from?" The conclusion they will reach is that "it" comes from no one place, that "it" has from the outset no unity but rather is a container of discrete agendas, held momentarily together by means of the dissimilar materials of statistics and hopes. It is the hopes and statistics, then, which these portraits will explore while we follow the stitching together of the *Action Plan on Sickness Benefit* by the civil servants in the Ministry of Employment.

Portrait 1: "making a difference"

I begin my account a couple of minutes before 9:30am, the last Friday before Christmas in 2008, as I run through the drizzle down a street in Denmark towards the town's job center. I was late. It was still dark and I sweated in my winter clothes as I passed the graffiti-adorned apartment houses in the street for the first time. The job center was situated in an old hospital building in a shabby part of the town. While the sliding glass doors leading into the reception were new, the tiny wooden elevator creaked and bounced on its way up to the fourth floor where I had a meeting with the manager of the section, Ulla, and the team leader, Peter, who was in charge of the team that would be responsible for implementing the controlled trial *Active—Back Sooner*. When I reached the fourth floor I easily found Ulla's office. Her door was wide open but I knocked as I entered. Ulla looked up from her computer screen and launched straight into a complaint about her inbox:

> Ulla: Phew! Work just keeps pouring in today. Everything needs to be dealt with before the holidays start. I received an email last night at 8pm in which I am asked to respond and have some papers ready within two hours. The Central Administration seem to assume that I work 24 hours a day. You will have to excuse me briefly. I just need to make a phone call.

The Municipality was of a considerable size and the employment area was divided into several sections that each answered to the Central Administration placed in the heart of the town some distance away from the job center. I had been introduced to some of the people from the Central Administration at a conference we had all attended a few days earlier but as yet I had no impression of the relationship between the administrative levels. However, I remembered that Ulla had remarked laconically during the lunch we had shared, that "being a manager primarily consists in passing numbers upwards," a remark I was yet to understand the full implication of.

I was still sweating after the running, and so while Ulla was on the phone, I went looking for the toilet to get a sip of water and wash my hands. While there was no water in the warm tap, there were both water and what looked like small stones in the cold. The contrast between the Capital's ministerial buildings where I had so far spent my time and the town's municipal buildings was tangible. Confident I would be offered coffee at the meeting (no Danish meeting is complete without it) I decided against the water and left the toilet. In the corridor leading past Ulla's office, Peter had appeared, leaning against the wall. Ulla was still on the phone so I asked Peter about his role in the project. He told me that for the past year he had been managing the team of caseworkers who worked with recipients of sickness benefit until their 26th week of sickness absence. After the 26th week, the cases would be transferred to another team. The 26-week limit had been recommended, he added, by a consultancy company that had analysed their case flow but he no longer remembered the reason why they had arrived at this particular limit.

I asked Peter why the job center had decided to join the project. While I had negotiated my access to the job center I had repeatedly been told that they were extremely busy in Peter's team and yet they had taken on this time-consuming task. Peter explained they anticipated the elements in the project would become obligatory by law sometime during the summer of 2009 and being a municipality of considerable size they needed to be conversant with the development. At the same time, the elements in the project answered some of the wishes that the caseworkers had been voicing—the possibility of referring people to psychologists or physiotherapy. He explained that they had already done a lot to create such offers oriented towards treatment rather than returning to the labor market since the recipients of sickness benefit were generally very happy with such offers and found that they benefitted from them. "I think that ought to count," Peter said as Ulla called for us to enter her office.

While Ulla passed around cups of coffee I explained to her and Peter that I was interested in the implementation of *Active—Back Sooner* and the context it would be implemented in. I explained to them that the caseworkers—or street-level workers as they were sometimes referred to in the social sciences—were generally singled out in the literature on implementation as the ones who did, in the long run, decide whether or not a certain policy would be followed. Furthermore, as Ulla and Peter were well aware, the caseworkers in the municipal job centers were often blamed, both in the Danish press and by the Minister of Employment, for being conservative or unwilling to follow new national policy, for professional reasons or for reasons of ideology. What I would like to do, I said, was to undertake an empirical study that looked into these caseworkers' everyday work life and the conditions under which central policy was translated into practice. My dream scenario, I pressed on, would be to simply "hang out" in the job center for an uncertain period of time and follow the caseworkers in whatever they did, especially those affiliated with *Active—Back Sooner*.

After the meeting I was very excited. Ulla had promised to get back to me before the New Year and I had the feeling that my wish would be granted. It felt like something of an accomplishment. It had not been easy to get this far. Ulla was a busy woman and the person from the Central Administration who had promised to forward my request to her some weeks earlier had cautioned me: "Do not expect anything. The caseworkers are extremely busy and our first priority is to make sure they do not feel we impose all sorts of things on them," a remark several of the caseworkers would later laugh at, reluctant to believe that any such considerations were ever taken. Before the meeting, Ulla too had told me not to expect anything, again with reference to the workload in the section. However, from the moment the decision arrived a week or so later to let me do my research in the section they welcomed me with open arms.

In order to provide a background for understanding the subsequent analysis of the implementation of the controlled trial and the planned revision of the sickness benefit legislation, I will ask the reader to follow me through a series of "introductory conversations," which were not part of the controlled trial. The casework described in the following sections was therefore regulated by the legislation which the proposed legislative revision projected in the *Action Plan on Sickness Benefit* would substitute. This was—in other words— the "normal intervention" which the trial's control group would receive.

The "normal intervention"

There were three successive "intake" hours on Monday mornings in early January: 32 citizens[1] per hour had received letters telling them to present themselves at 9am, 10am or 11am respectively for an "introductory conversation." The meetings were called thus because it was the first time during their sickness absence that they had any interaction with their municipality in this regard. The recipients of sickness benefit were obliged by law to attend this municipal "follow-up" of their cases in order to maintain their right to the public benefit. On this specific Monday morning only 19 of the 32 citizens had shown up for the 9am intake. The remaining 13 would later receive a letter enquiring into the reasons for their absence. This collection of personal statements was part of a procedure that took place before the municipality could either shut their cases or set a new date for a meeting. It was not unusual, I was told, that only half of those summoned showed up.

Entering through the sliding doors to the job center one walked directly up to the reception desk where the recipients of sickness benefit were supposed make their arrival known. After the receptionist had located the yellow-brown card-board file with their name on, and moved it from the pile of folders belonging to those who were supposed to show up to the pile of those who actually showed up, they were asked to take a seat in the waiting area surrounding the reception on three sides. On this morning nine people were sitting by nine small coffee tables in one section of the waiting area while the rest had scattered along the walls. At 9am the caseworkers began to arrive from the hallway running perpendicular to the reception desk. Their offices were either distributed along a corridor running at an angle to the main hallway or on different levels of a tower rising above the point where the corridor met the hallway. The caseworkers lined up behind a tall coffee table inside the reception and turned towards the waiting area every few seconds to call out the name of one or other of the waiting people.

At 9:10am those whose name did not get called in the first round began to move about. There was a shelf by one of the walls on which a few brochures were placed. A few people walked up and fidgeted with them for a few seconds then walked away. There was a rack supposed to contain magazines on the wall but it was empty. Instead, people passed the time by staring into space. It was very quiet and bits and pieces of the conversations between the receptionists were audible: "he just *has* to show up or we will shut down his money." They lowered their voices. One of them giggled. At 9:30am a young woman got up to ask whether she had been registered. "It said in my letter that the appointment was for 9am?" She was told not to worry and just await her turn. A man stood up, walked to the shelf and looked at the brochures, then returned to his seat and continued to stare into the distance. Every now and again a caseworker returned and called somebody's name. At 9:40am a man walked through the door and started an argument with the receptionist. He wanted a meeting immediately. He was loud and insistent but the receptionist kept repeating that she could do nothing to help him besides noting in his file that it was urgent. At 9:45am the young woman went up to the reception again and asked them to check if they were sure she had been registered. She had seen four caseworkers walk up to the coffee table and leave again without calling anyone's name. I left the waiting room to join one of the caseworkers, Ian.

"Pulling a case"

At 10am, Ian and I left his office and walked out into the corridor towards the waiting room. A few doors down he stopped by Ida's open door and tapped her door post gently. "At it again Ida," he said cheerfully. A few meters further down the corridor we turned right and continued down the hallway leading from the office area to the reception area. To our left we passed the waiting room, now again full of people. Ian headed towards the coffee table where a new stack of card-board case-files had been placed. With his back towards the waiting area, Ian took the top folder and scanned the flap for a name. He then found the corresponding name, Maria Hansen, on a sheet of A4 paper placed next to the cardboard folders, ticked the box by her name to indicate she had shown up and then signed his name on the line next to her name. With this gesture he had become and would continue to be Maria's caseworker either until her case was shut or until it reached 26 weeks of administrative age, when it would be referred to another unit in the Municipality.

The folder contained an information chart (*oplysningsskema*) which Maria had filled in and returned to a separate part of the Municipality called Benefit Service (*ydelsesservice*). They handled the actual payment of benefits. Because Maria's contract with her employer entitled her to be paid a full salary during periods of sickness absence her employer could, after the first three weeks of sickness absence, get a sum equivalent to the sickness benefit rate reimbursed by the Municipality (Retsinformation 2008).[2] Had she not been entitled to a full salary or had she been self-employed the sickness benefit would have gone directly to her. When her employer filed for reimbursement, Benefit Service sent the information chart to Maria Hansen and the payout then depended on her submission of the chart. If filled in correctly the chart ought to contain information about the cause for the sickness absence and ongoing treatment, details about her current employment situation and the date of expected return to work. Apart from the information chart, the folder contained a copy of the notice letter (*indkaldelsesbrev*) Maria had received. This letter informed her that she had to present herself at the job center today at this hour. Still with his back to the waiting area Ian quickly read on Maria's information chart that she suffered from "pain in the arms and inflammation in the shoulders." Apart from this Ian knew nothing about the woman whose name he was about to call: "Maria Hansen?"

An "introductory conversation"

Maria got up and after some introductions she followed Ian and me through the hallway and down the corridor towards his office. Ian's office lay in a corridor with five bright offices of around 8 square meters on either side. The doors had large windows in them but were relatively soundproof. Most offices had a tall narrow wardrobe on the right side of the door where the caseworkers kept their coats, bags, and often bicycle helmets, since most lived in the town and cycled to work. A spacious desk with a computer and writing materials occupied the left wall, while bookshelves stood along the right wall. The walls at the far end of the offices were all dominated by one large window looking out into green yards. Before them one or two chairs were placed. This was where Ian asked Maria to take a seat. I had placed a chair just left of the door with the result that Maria could see me while Ian had his back turned towards me to indicate that I was not part of the conversation, a routine I had soon slipped into with all the caseworkers. As with all the caseworkers I had followed, Ian had a particular order in which he liked to do things. He began the meeting by telling Maria why she had been summoned to the meeting and what they were going to talk about:

> *Ian*: First we will talk about the background for your sickness absence and what will happen from here on. Then I will tell you some things about the law that you need to know as a recipient of sickness benefit. Finally, I would like you to fill out

a declaration of informed consent so I can get access to your medical papers and other information I might need to work on your case. You do not have to sign this declaration but if you do not, I might not be able to access the information I need to work on your case. Whatever information I do obtain will only pertain to this specific case of sickness and you can withdraw the consent at any time.

People generally expected the caseworker to be well informed about their situation when they showed up. Quite a few people said they thought the caseworkers already had access to their medical papers and seemed unaware of the fact that information given to one party (for example, their union or their GP) was not automatically transferred to other parties (such as the Municipality or the private employment agency). To many, all of these diverse actors constituted "the system." Since Ian's section of the Municipality dealt primarily with people who either had a job or who had only just been fired, most had not had sufficient dealings with or interest in this "system" to realize that "it" consisted of many separate entities that were by law not allowed to communicate unless people had given their explicit and written consent. Seemingly not listening to Ian's explanations about the workings of "informed consent," Maria interrupted him:

> Maria: I think it is ridiculous that I have to come here to attend a meeting and go to meetings with my employer when I am sick.

Maria's reaction was not unusual. From the dozens of conversations I sat through that year it was clear that most people considered "sickness" a strictly personal matter between them and their doctors, and their "sickness absence" a matter between them and their employer, if they had one. It surprised many that the Municipality had any say in these matters, and many had no idea that their employers were being reimbursed by the Municipality. Yet, while the origin of the Municipality's involvement in the set-up was obscure to most, there was no uncertainty when it came to guessing the purpose of the meeting. They were convinced they would have to prove they were "really" sick. The caseworkers knew this was the general conception among people who had never been to such meetings before and they did their best to kill this idea swiftly.

> Ian: Well, we do not ask you to come in order to check up on you. We are obliged by law to have these meetings because we need to inform you of your duties and rights as a recipient of sickness benefit. We must ensure you get the treatment you need and see if we can help you get back to work sooner in any way.

> Maria: [Appearing not to listen] But then at my work they ask me *why* I have been feeling better recently. What shall I reply? I do not know *why* I feel better, or *why* I feel worse, do I?

Not knowing how to reply, Ian returned to his normal procedure and asked Maria about her health problems and whether she was currently receiving any treatment. She told him she was seeing a rheumatologist. Since the rheumatologist could not find anything to explain the pain she felt in her arms and shoulders, she had insisted on getting an MR scan. However, the rheumatologist had been unwilling to refer her to one. Ian wrote this information down on a blank sheet of A4 paper which he then placed in the cardboard file. He then asked her to fill out the declaration of informed consent which, he explained, he would use to obtain a statement from her rheumatologist. He then moved on to inform her about her legal rights and duties as a recipient of sickness benefit: she was not allowed to do anything that would prolong her sickness absence or worsen her condition; she was obliged to follow the treatment prescribed by the doctors and therapists she saw; she was not allowed to apply for a job while she was receiving sickness benefit;[3] and finally, she was obliged to participate in the municipal follow-up in her case, which meant coming to meetings and answering letters and phone calls.[4] Since Maria had not applied for professional rehabilitation, a "flex job"[5] (a reduced ability job) or early retirement pension—and Ian did not think it relevant to bring it up—her case would stay with him. Ian therefore told her that she could expect either a phone call or to be called in for another meeting in eight weeks' time if she were still sick. As in most cases Maria was startled by the prospect of still being sick in eight weeks and replied that she certainly did not think she would be.

'Making a difference'

After Maria had left, Ian turned to me and said that her case had been standard in the sense that she was obviously in a lot of pain but the health care system was unable to help her. As was Ian: "Unless the rheumatologist finds something and can begin a treatment," he said, "there is nothing I can do. I will have to shut her case." Maria's case was typical in that Ian's involvement as a caseworker was limited to giving information about the law and potentially shutting the case. In Maria's case Ian guessed that this would mean she would get fired if she did not return to work, despite her pain, because her employer would stop receiving the reimbursement from the Municipality. The conversation was also typical in that Maria had entered Ian's office with the clear understanding that Ian was checking to see if she was really sick. Sara, one of Ian's colleagues who would later become involved in the local implementation of *Active—Back Sooner*, disliked this aspect of her job:

> Sara: I hate my job the most when it seems that all we can do is drag people in here and tell them about a law they do not understand; then demand that they tell us the most personal details from their lives and then say, "OK, I'll see you again in eight weeks' time." And for what purpose exactly?

The cases in which the caseworkers felt unable to "do something" were typically the cases they liked the least. Sara summed it up in an interview:

> Sara: I often have the feeling that we are here just for the sake of being here. In a few cases I might make a difference in another person's life, but mostly I

maintain the system for the sake of the system. I register things. I call up and ask if they are still sick. I note they are still sick. And it has made no difference whether I did it or not. Except sometimes you get to shut some cases.

The types of cases preferred by the individual caseworkers I spoke to could be as different as "a straightforward broken-leg case" and a "heavy and complicated, diffuse case" but what was characteristic of the cases they each preferred was that they felt able to "make a difference." This "difference" could be offering something concrete (such as a referral to physical rehabilitation or assisting the practical planning of the return to work by participating in meetings with employers) or it could simply be demonstrating that "the system" to which they as caseworkers were seen to belong had a human face and a shoulder to cry on.

For Sara's colleague Ida, who sat a few doors down the corridor from Ian, wanting to "make a difference" was the reason she had decided to join the group who would work with the controlled trial when Peter sent an email around the unit asking for volunteers. For Ida, "making a difference" meant assisting people in getting back to work as soon as possible. She hoped that the trial would be similar to another controlled trial they were part of called *Back to Work*. This was the project Peter had mentioned that day outside Ulla's office as an example of the kind of "offers" he hoped the Municipality would be able to present to their citizens in the future. The *Back to Work* project was meant for people who suffered from musculoskeletal conditions, who were still employed. It was run from a clinic for occupational medicine in a nearby hospital and was staffed by psychologists, physiotherapists, and doctors specializing in occupational medicine. Ida liked it for its thoroughness. People were examined by the physiotherapist and the doctors and had to fill in a questionnaire, based on which the psychologist would assess their need for psychological consultations and courses in pain management. If the doctors agreed that they qualified for the project, the physiotherapist would furthermore visit the work place to see if any changes could be made in terms of work routines or providing equipment.

> *Ida*: What I like about these cases is the closeness with which they are followed by all parties involved.

The close contact and concrete future-oriented offers were two elements in the *Back to Work* project that Ida found highly important and which she knew would play a central role in *Active—Back Sooner*. She contrasted this anticipated way of working with the "normal intervention," which she found unsatisfying:

> *Ida*: Although in the beginning I tried to speak to all my citizens at least every four weeks, it soon proved impossible and now I am back to contact only every eight weeks as required by the law.[6] And since I am only obliged to speak to them in person every second time and it is so much quicker to "follow-up" over the phone it often happens that people have been sick close to half a year before I see them in person again.

Marie, Ida, Sara, and Ann, the four caseworkers who would in time come to constitute the core project-group, all entered the project because they reckoned they would, for once, get an opportunity to do all the things they normally had no time for. To Marie, who had been involved in the drafting of the internal project description, the project was precisely an opportunity to "try out some of the things we as caseworkers had dreamt of being able to offer."

A week into my fieldwork in the job center, I had a late lunch in the municipal canteen. I joined some of the caseworkers—three middle-aged women and a young man who I recognized as Marie's and Ida's colleagues. They were talking about the difficulties they had keeping up with the intake of new citizens. I had only been following the work in the unit for a few days but I had already picked up on the general feeling of being too busy, which most conversations between colleagues revolved around. Jane, a middle-aged woman, said:

> *Jane*: I have my strategies and I keep telling myself it is not my fault. I distance myself and try not to let people's troubles sink in. But suddenly I am filled up and then come the sleepless nights where I lie and think about all the things I ought to have done.
>
> *Nina*: What is it you do not have time for?
>
> *Jane*: The close follow-up that some people require to ever move on from here.

They continued their discussion about whether or not "the management," embodied most immediately by Peter and Ulla, were aware of the paradoxical situation in which they found themselves:

> *Marianne*: We are actually too busy to report them "fit for duty" [raskmelde dem].

The paradox she identified in her own work was that there was a mismatch between the management's efforts to get the caseworkers to "shut more cases," that is, to remove people from the publically financed sickness benefit by terminating their cases (preferably because they were now ready to go back to work), and the fact that as a result of that strategy they now had so little time to follow up in the individual cases as to prevent them from doing what they felt *would* lead to more cases being shut. The feeling that "quantity" took priority over "quality" was expressed continuously in a multitude of different ways. As Ena, a young employee, said during lunch later in the week:

> *Ena*: When we are this busy all I think of is how fast I can get rid of the cases by referring them somewhere else where I can pretend things are taken care of.

She had referred seven of the morning's nine people who had come in for "introductory conversations" to either the *Back to Work* project or to the MPD project.[7] Ena's tone of voice was ironical and her tough pragmatic strategy which was used by several of her colleagues expressed a genuine hope that somewhere else in "the system" people would have the time to take proper care of things. At the same time, she acknowledged that she was probably fooling herself. These were the circumstances under which the implementation of *Active—Back Sooner* would soon begin: on the one hand the busyness gave rise to a strong hope that things could be different (and would be in this new project) but on the other, the same busyness would, as we shall soon see, undermine the fulfilment of these hopes.

Portrait 2: the perfect plan[8]

A few months earlier, around the end of November 2008, I had been on the look-out for a piece of labor market policy that could serve as the focus of my empirical research. Employed by the Ministry of Employment and seconded to the cross ministerial R&D unit MindLab I had been given the broadest possible brief: produce some useful research. Useful to whom and in which way were questions I would grapple with throughout my employment, not least when the object of my research quickly turned out to be highly politically controversial and my clear impression was that many of my informants in the Ministry would have preferred that I abandon it altogether. I refer the reader to the appendix for a more detailed account of my position vis-a-vis the Ministry. For now it suffices to write that in a primary attempt to be "useful" I had read through the Ministry's internal strategic papers and was content to find that gaining a better understanding of how their policies were implemented in practice was an organizational priority. So on this morning in late November 2008 I was reading through the recently approved *Action Plan on Sickness Benefit* (Beskæftigelsesministeriet 2008a) in search of a suitable object for an ethnographic implementation study.

The *Action Plan*'s proposition 32, "experiment with preventive and clarifying offers," which targeted recipients of sickness benefit, immediately caught my interest: Before assuming the position as researcher in MindLab, I had been employed as an internal consultant in a municipality where, among other things, I worked with the development of preventive health care offers. At that time, in 2007–2008, the National Board of Health, in alliance with major patient organizations and the renowned Nordic Cochrane Center (Sundhedsstyrelsen 2007), pushed for the public health sector in Denmark to work in a manner that was "evidence-based" and made use of "best practices." I recognized the planned experiment as a part of this broader trend and was curious to see how this could be done in the employment area. I asked around in MindLab and learned from my colleagues, who unlike me were involved in actual policy work, that some of the people who had been closely involved in designing the planned experiment had been on a field trip to the United States arranged by the Danish consultancy company Rambøll Management, during which "randomized control trials" were being advocated as the golden standard for determining the effectiveness of public interventions. According to a colleague who had participated in one of these trips, about 200 top managers from the public sector in Denmark had so far been on such a trip and randomized control trials were generally taken to be *the* new paradigm of public sector development.

I took a closer look at "proposal 32." The heading expressed an instruction ("Active during sickness absence") and the sub-heading a hypothesis ("The sick who are active can more easily return to work"). Below the heading followed the title of the proposition ("Experiment with preventive and clarifying offers") and eight bullet points that summarized its purpose, target group, content, time frame, and overall budget. The time frame meant I would be able to follow the experiment from beginning to end (bullet point six stated that it would be implemented during 2009), and there was enough "meat" on it to interest me academically: It outlined the basic principles behind one of the first large scale attempts to run a controlled trial out of a Ministry in Denmark; the context in which it would be implemented was extremely complex and relied on the cooperation of many different actors. The project would be, it said in the first bullet point, a controlled trial in which the participating municipalities were, according to bullets four and five, relatively free to choose the content of the intervention. The paradoxical adaptation of a strict methodology from the medical world, coupled with autonomy regarding choice of method, was now being introduced into an uncontrollable setting where the target group, if they objected to participate, would no longer be entitled to sickness benefit. In other words, from its very conception the trial violated the most basic principles such a trial would normally rest on:[9] a) it was not clear which intervention would be given and whichever it was would not be comparable across the intervention group; b) participation was, in all but theory, compulsory. With these characteristics, the trial was, for me, an impossibly irresistible research object.

The *Action Plan on Sickness Benefit*

The proposal itself was less than a page long. Apart from the above mentioned information there was not much more to go on and when, out of academic habit, I flicked through the pages searching for a list of references I found none. I was about to learn that reading bureaucratic documents was a different business altogether than reading the academic publications I was used to. First of all, bureaucratic documents are not attributed to individual authors but to organizations, for instance "the Government," "the Ministry of Employment," or "the National Labor Market Authority." Secondly, the closer a document comes to having the status as official government policy the fewer arguments and references it contains and the more matter-of-fact the text becomes. Hence the *Action Plan on Sickness Benefit* was completely void of references and arguments to underpin its suggestions and conclusions.

I began, therefore, with the help of my research assistant, Rasmus Kolding, a sort of excavation job where we tried to back-track the evidence and research on which the different proposals in the *Action Plan* supposedly rested. Despite being attributed to organizations, it is not particularly difficult to find out who the actual writers of a particular bureaucratic document are (nor that these authors do not receive acknowledgement, in fact, writing a "good note" is a way to make yourself known in the organization and improve your chances of promotion): I picked up the phone, called the main number of the National Labor Market Authority and asked to speak to someone who had been involved in the drafting of the *Action Plan*. I was put through to one of the lawyers who had been involved in designing the controlled trial I was currently interested in and, referring to my position as a researcher employed by the Ministry of Employment, I got an appointment to come by and see her immediately.

So I picked up my notebook and left the office on foot. My walk amounted to a total distance of a few hundred meters through the power center of Danish politics. Leaving MindLab's office on the ground floor of the Ministry of Economy I stepped onto a street that led me past the former Danish stock market, now owned by the Confederation of Danish Industry, on my right hand, while the Ministry of Justice, the Ministry of Finance, and the Parliament followed in rapid succession on my left. I then crossed the main road and walked on between the Ministry of Social Affairs and the National Bank before entering the National Labor Market Authority. I had been to a meeting in the building previously. The lawyer I now had an appointment with was employed in the same office, so I bypassed the reception, took the stairs a few floors up, and found her easily enough. Despite being forthcoming she was able to give me but the most sketchy summary of the evolution of the *Action Plan*. It turned out she had not herself become involved until recently and despite being in charge of the implementation of the controlled trial she did not know how it had originated, nor had she any specific knowledge of the "evidence base." She did, however, equip me with a stack of analytical reports and encouraged me to look up a senior civil servant, Lea, who had been in charge of the process leading up to the political adoption of the *Action Plan*.

Deviating numbers

The origin of the *Action Plan on Sickness Benefit* was unusual. So Lea told me when months later I finally got the chance to interview her about the preparatory stages of the *Action Plan* and the included trial. Usually, she explained, policy work would be initiated in one of three ways. One third would be what she called "strategic policy work." These policies would be elaborated on the basis of the Government program's stated objectives (for instance that, upon being elected, the Government declares its intention to reduce sickness absence by 20 percent before 2015) and would result from comparatively long development processes. Another third of the policies, referred to as "response policy," would be crafted in response to criticisms raised in the media or in Parliament (for example, unintended consequences of current legislation needing adjustments) or in response to unforeseen events (such as a global financial crisis). The last type of policy she described as a kind of proactive policy work, designed to preempt criticism rumored to be in the pipeline from major interest groups or professional organizations (such as the Confederation of Danish Industry or Local Government Denmark). The work processes leading to the two latter types of policy were characterized, she said, by being unpredictable and by the need for immediate response. What was unusual about the origin of the *Action Plan*, then, was that the policy work was initiated by the civil service rather than any of these three triggers.

It all began in the National Directorate of Labor in the autumn of 2007, Lea remembered. Here the analysts noticed an atypical development in the expenses for sickness benefit. That the expenses had "exploded," Lea explained, was something the civil servants had to take seriously. Not so much the expenses *per se* as the fact that this indicated an increase in the number of people who, as a result of sickness, were outside the "active" labor force. This development was first brought to Lea's attention when her colleagues in the National Directorate of Labor sent an analysis report one step up the organizational hierarchy to the Department of Employment working directly under the Minister, specifically to Lea's Office.[10]

> *Lea*: Just before this there had been a lot of media attention because—among others—the Municipality of Copenhagen[11] did not comply with the legal demands for when to speak to people on sickness benefit and they did not give people the service they were obliged to provide. Whether it was due to the recent municipal reform[12] or if it was an internal organizational issue I do not know, but as a result we already had this feeling that things weren't going particularly well in this area. So my colleagues in the Directorate of Labor looked into the existing research and analyses of the area and drafted an analysis report which they sent to the Ministry.

This first analysis report was based primarily on available statistical material and pointed out what seemed to have changed; what had caught the civil servants attention was the "long-term sickness absence" designating sickness absence of more than eight weeks. Eight weeks was an important analytical unit built into the statistical module because it was the administrative limit after which the municipalities' obligation to "follow-up" (*opfølgning*) in sickness benefit cases became effective. It seemed that a relatively small group of people—the long-term sick—was responsible for the larger part of the collective sickness absence in Denmark. Presented with this analysis, the Permanent Secretary (*Departementschefen*) decided to host a series of meetings where employees from the Ministry's different sub-sections were invited to discuss the challenges pertaining to "long-term sickness absence."

The unconditional duty to be loyal

The Permanent Secretary had been the administrative head of the Ministry of Employment (formerly the Ministry of Labor) since May 1998. He was appointed Permanent Secretary by the former coalition government formed by the Danish Social Democrats and the Danish Social-Liberal Party. He had continued to hold this position when the coalition consisting of the Liberal Party of Denmark and the Conservative People's Party won the general election in 2001 (and changed the Ministry's name to the Ministry of Employment) and when they were re-elected in 2005 and 2007. This meant the Permanent Secretary had held this position for more than 11 years when I interviewed him in December 2009 about the crafting of the *Action Plan*. At this point I was relatively ignorant when it came to the concrete workings of the Danish political system but the Permanent Secretary was kind enough to explain to me the basics of the civil service's relationship to the political level as this was a topic close to his heart.

> P.S.: We must be able to switch agenda and color[13] overnight when the government changes. I tried it in 2001 when the government changed from a social democratic government to a liberal one, and I have tried it on a more person-based scale with the three different Ministers of Employment we have had since 2001.

In 2009 in Denmark there were only one or two people in each Ministry, he explained to me, who were appointed politically; the Minister and—as of recent times—possibly a "spin doctor" or "special advisor" appointed directly by the Minister. The remaining employees were all civil servants who remained in the ministries through the changing governments. Since he knew I was not trained in the political sciences, unlike a considerable part of the civil service, the Permanent Secretary elaborated on his role as a civil servant:

> P.S.: As civil servants we have the unconditional duty to be loyal to our Minister. This means that you give advice in which you respect what the current Minister wants to do and you help the Minister reach his or her goals. The other duty you have is to ensure that the advice you give rests on as good a professional and unbiased foundation as possible. We need to be guarantors to the Minister and to the rest of the politicians in the political negotiations that things have been properly examined; that the analyses they use and the facts they base their decisions on when they decide something are sound [*i orden*], and that what we plan is practically implementable. Because you have to bear in mind that a Minister might be involved in several negotiations at any one time and cannot possibly have a deep knowledge of all the matters that have to be decided on. So, as Permanent Secretary to the Minister, I have to guarantee this.

While he had held the position as Permanent Secretary a main focus of his had been to develop the practice of "knowledge-based" working and to build up the analytical capacity in the Ministry. The aim of this was two-fold: firstly to be able to foresee which issues might become politically important and secondly, being prepared to provide solid advice on these issues. As an example of this kind of work, he turned to the area of sickness benefit. In 2003, he explained, civil servants in the Ministry had observed that absence due to sickness was escalating. This was a problem they shared with a series of other countries, among these the other Scandinavian countries, Sweden, Norway, and Finland, with which Denmark would often be compared. It had been a moment in time where there was a general concern regarding the scarce labor supply (*arbejdsudbuddet*). The loss of labor power due to sickness absence was alarming, he remembered—especially because it seemed to be steadily increasing. Back then they had looked for international experiences on the basis of which some initiatives had been elaborated.

This latest initiative (he now referred to the *Action Plan on Sickness Benefit* I was interviewing him about) had come about as the result of a similar situation—shortage of labor supply and an increase in the expenses of sickness benefit. But contrary to earlier, this present *Action Plan* was an example in which the civil service had been prepared. They had recommended, on a solid foundation of analyses and knowledge, that the politicians should adopt a new policy and begin working towards a "paradigm shift"[14] in their effort to reduce sickness absence. When I asked him, curious that in both his and Lea's description this *Action Plan* seemed to have been developed autonomously by the civil service, whether this new policy was in fact civil service policy and not Government policy, he replied:

> P.S.: "What originates from where" is really a futile discussion. We would never have gone ahead with something like this—or at least only rarely and on a preliminary scale—without having consulted our Minister first. I cannot remember the history of this most recent *Action Plan on Sickness Absence* but normally the working procedure would be—and I think it was too in this case—that we undertake a discussion with our Minister. We express our concern for the drastic rise in sickness absence and ask him if we should concern ourselves with the matter. He would of course agree and then we would begin our analytical work.

In this narrative, as in Lea's, it seemed impossible that things could have gone any differently. The numbers were alarming and it was the duty of the civil service to be concerned about it. Not responding would be unthinkable. Should the analysis remain loyal to the narrative provided by Lea and the Permanent Secretary the real driver of the *Action Plan* was neither they nor the politicians, but numbers. Not that we should grant numbers intentionality or even agency—these I will reserve for the human actors in this book, but the statistical deviation prompted people around it to respond, and to respond in a particular way. The way Lea and the Permanent Secretary described it, neither they nor the Minister seemed to have any other option than to create a plan to *reduce* the numbers.

After the initial meetings, remembered Lea, the Permanent Secretary decided it was time to look at what might be done to address the increase in sickness absence. Curious about the sources from which they had drawn these suggestions, I asked her about it. She told me that at this early stage they were limited to what was already known in the civil service. Some civil servants had good and frequent contact with Local Government Denmark, the organization of the Danish municipalities, and felt they had a good idea about the municipalities' more general wants. Others had regular contact with both recipients of sickness benefit and the individual caseworkers in the municipalities who phoned in to complain about or ask questions concerning particular rules in the current law they found difficult to apply or counterproductive. Also, the employment area was continually being evaluated, and the different sections in the Ministry disposed of quite a few reports. It was part of Lea's job to translate all this information into a set of challenges and corresponding proposals for solutions intended for the Minister.

Inclusion into the Government program

Until this point in time, Lea continued, they had not really involved the Minister. What they had been doing was, she said, just providing "proper service to the Minister" (*almindelig god ministerbetjening*): they had kept an eye on how things evolved and helped the Minister by pointing out irregularities he might want to do something about. But then in October 2007 the Prime Minister called a general election.

> *Lea:* Then we stopped working. Once an election has been called, in effect we have no Minister. This was when they [the politicians] formulated the Government program and here the reduction of sickness absence by 20 percent before 201515 was included as a political target. I do not know where this number—20 percent—came from because the Government program is something the politicians make themselves without our involvement. If there was a professional[16] [*faglig*] reason for deciding this, I do not know it. There might be. 20 percent is a rather high number but I think it most likely that they just wanted to signal they were ambitious.

When the Government was re-elected in November 2007 the civil servants took up where they had left off. Something entirely new could have come into the Government program but the politicians had decided to adopt as a political strategy what the civil servants had already begun. So immediately after the election, strategic meetings with the Minister began and the work was speeded up to complete "a package," including a draft for the soon to be published analysis report and a "gross catalogue" (*bruttokatalog*) with challenges and possible solutions, for the Minister to take home for Christmas.

The civil servants in the Ministry's sub-sections were asked to contribute to this process; among these was a lawyer, Jytte, from the National Labor Market Authority who, a year later, would become involved in the drafting of the revised sickness benefit legislation as a result of the adopted *Action Plan on Sickness Benefit*. She remembered those weeks before Christmas 2007.

> *Jytte:* I had one good evening where, over a cup of tea, I made more than ten proposals. Little proposals. About a page long or so. I was able to do that because I have worked with this area for such a long time. I drew my inspiration from the de-bureaucratization [*afbureaukratisering*] report that Deloitte[17] had recently made which listed the municipalities' wishes and suggestions and they echoed the knowledge I have from having participated in Local Government Denmark's sickness benefit group. Furthermore, I have represented the Ministry in a Nordic collaboration and I had some good ideas from my time there too.

Among the suggestions Jytte took on from the de-bureaucratization report was the municipalities' wish to be able to refer recipients of sickness benefit to physiotherapists or psychologists, and in general be able to offer some kind of beneficial activity. During this interview with Jytte, which took place in May 2009, we spent most of our time discussing the controlled trial *Active—Back Sooner*, which had later grown out of this specific proposal and which by then had become the object of a great controversy, and causing lengthy debate in the media and Parliament. However, at the time of first drafting the proposal in December 2007, Jytte was responding to an overall wish that had long been articulated by the municipal caseworkers.

Towards the *Action Plan on Sickness Benefit*

When the Minister returned after the Christmas holiday in the early days of 2008 he set his civil servants to work again. He had liked the initial "gross catalogue," Lea said, but wanted a process that involved all the main interest groups, or as she put it; "the usual suspects."

> *Lea*: So in January, February, and parts of March 2008 we arranged to meet with all the employers' associations and with the employees' organizations. Separate meetings. Then we met with the patient organizations, for instance The Danish Cancer Society, Danish Patients, and the Danish Mental Health Fund. We also met with the municipalities—with representatives from the job centers and also from Local Government Denmark. Six different meetings in total, I think. What the Minister wanted was to hear their formulation of the problems and their own suggestions for possible solutions.

In the end the civil servants made a new elaborate "gross catalogue" where the individual proposals were assessed according to their estimated ability to reduce sickness absence. Some proposals were thought to have the possibility of directly reducing the sickness absence, such as the proposal that would turn into the project *Active—Back Sooner*, while some would be supporting initiatives such as campaigns to change the public attitude towards sickness and work; IT-systems and other tools for practically solving the tasks; brochures for communicating the initiatives, and so on. The proposals were also assessed in economic terms since, as Lea said, "some things might cost a billion and have little or no effect." Furthermore, the Minister wanted the civil servants to take seriously and strive to include what the interest organizations in each meeting thought most important and most effective. This, Lea told me, was how *Active—Back Sooner* was eventually included in the first collective and formal proposal for an *Action Plan on Sickness Benefit*.

> *Lea*: Many pointed out that what the job centers are able to do today is not sufficient. They want to be able to refer people to psychologists or physiotherapists and do many other things that the current law does not allow. And there is so much research that has indicated that we really need this.

The last assessment the civil servants made as they wrote their final recommendations to the Minister estimated whether or not the initiatives were likely to be implemented "at the other end," by which they meant the job centers, work places and among the general practitioners affected by the proposals:

Lea: We cannot force a hundred new rules upon them. The reform tempo is already high and there are limits to the extent to which you can change things and still expect them to happen in practice.

This precursory action plan was published by the Government in June 2008 under the heading "Sickness absence—a common challenge: the Government's action plan to reduce sickness absence" (Regeringen 2008, my translation). A further selection and augmentation of the proposals were later published as the "Conclusion paper on the action plan on sickness absence" (Beskæftigelsesministeriet 2008a, my translation), which the government had negotiated with the labor market parties—the Confederation of Danish Employers and the Danish Confederation of Trade Unions—on 29 September, 2008. Finally the action plan was adopted politically in November 2008 with support from the Danish People's Party (Dansk Folkeparti), Danish Social-Liberal Party (Radikale Venstre), and Liberal Alliance during the negotiations for the Finance Law (the public budgets) for 2009 (Finansministeriet 2008).

The Labor Market Commission

The stated objective of the *Action Plan*, which in its final form contained 39 different initiatives, was to reduce the collective sickness absence in Denmark by 20 percent by 2015 (Finansministeriet 2008: 102). The agreement called for new initiatives amounting to 170 million DKR a year (approximately £17 million) plus 240 million DKR (approximately £24 million) over a three-year period for an experiment with "clarification and work retention (*arbejdsfastholdelse*)" (ibid.). The effort to reduce sickness absence was aimed at freeing some labor power for an "already scarce workforce" (ibid.) and the conclusion paper therefore served as one method out of several in the Government's and the labor market parties' negotiations to secure the workforce.

As must be clear from this, the development of the *Action Plan on Sickness Benefit* and, along with it, the project *Active—Back Sooner*, were far from being developed in a political or economic vacuum. If the civil servants had worked on their analyses of the sickness absence largely unknown to the political level, from the moment the Government was re-elected, "sickness absence" became closely linked to the most central preoccupation of the re-elected Government for securing both the workforce and the public budgets (VK Regeringen III 2007). The demographic development in Denmark, as in the rest of Europe, tended towards more elderly people and fewer people in the active workforce (Bason 2010: 11ff.); paired with an expanding public sector this made the need for an increase in the workforce seem acute (Arbejdsmarkedskommissionen 2008a).

To reach this goal the Government, shortly after resuming office, appointed a group of independent researchers—the Labor Market Commission (*Arbejdsmarkedskommissionen*)—who would work under the slogan "more welfare requires more work" (Arbejdsmarkedskommissionen 2008a: 1, my translation). According to its terms of reference, the assignment of this Commission was to propose initiatives that would ensure an increase of unsubsidized labor power of 20,000 persons by 2015 along with "actions to maintain unchanged average working hours, that is, to counteract the negative impact on working hours from demographic changes" (Labor Market Commission 2010). In a press release issued by the newly appointed Labor Market Commission in April 2008 the challenges faced by the public sector in Denmark were described as follows:

> In Denmark we have been able to finance an ever increasing public sector for many years because the labor force—and therefore the tax—has gradually increased. The tax revenues have therefore been able to finance the growth in public expenses without a corresponding increase in the tax burden.
> This will not continue. The demographic development will reduce the collective labor supply measured in hours. With fewer people at the labor market there are fewer to pay the tax to finance the public sector. (Arbejdsmarkedskommissionen 2008a: 2, my translation)

In the press release it was estimated that if the Government program was to be financed, the public budgets were short by 14 billion DKR a year (approximately £1.4 billion). The Labor Market Commission defined three different ways of avoiding public debt. Firstly, the Government could raise taxes—a rhetorical solution since the liberal Prime Minister had made it his stated objective not to increase taxes further. A second solution would be to reduce the public expenses by cutting down on benefits and free services—an equally rhetorical solution as the examples mentioned would directly affect and be of concern to his key voters:

> To illustrate the extent of the challenge one could point out that 14 billion DKR approximately amounts to what is spent each year on benefits to families with young children [børnefamilieydelsen]. 14 billion DKR is a little more than is spent each year on the police, Prison Service and judicial system combined. (Arbejdsmarkedskommissionen 2008a: 2, my translation)

Finally, if the "tax burden" was not to be increased and the extent and quality of the public services not to be reduced there was but one option left:

> namely, that the Danes work more, so that—collectively seen—more earned income is created which will lead to more taxes paid ... The size of the challenge can also be illustrated by the number of Danes who—hypothetically—would have to move from passive, public support to normal, unsupported full-time work with a normal salary ... 50,000 people. (ibid.)

The Labor Market Commission had originally been asked to report their proposals to the Government by the summer of 2009 but as the lack of labor power had increased more than expected during the first half of 2008 (Arbejdsmarkedskommissionen 2008b: 1) the Government urged the Commission to prepare some preliminary recommendations that, along with the first public version of the *Action Plan on Sickness Benefit*, could be used in the tripartite negotiations between the labor markets parties in October 2008, which continued to focus on securing sufficient labor power in the long and short run. The Ministry's analysis report on sickness absence which the civil servants had been working on during 2007 (Beskæftigelsesministeriet, 2008b) was published in April 2008, the same month that the Labor Market Commission issued its press release stating that 14 billion DKR a year was missing from the budget, equivalent to 50,000 people that must be moved from "public support to normal, unsupported full-time work." The introductory lines of the analysis report on sickness absence read:

> The sickness absence in Denmark corresponds to a yearly loss of labor power of at least 150,000 persons in employment or about 5 percent of the labor force ... The sickness absence is estimated to cost society at least 37 billion DKR a year. (Beskæftigelsesministeriet, 2008b: 3, my translation)

Further into the first paragraph of the analysis report, lack of labor power and sickness absence were explicitly linked:

> The demographic development will henceforth pull more people out of the labor market than enter it. In order to ensure continuous welfare and prosperity there is a need to increase employment and the performed working hours [præsterede arbejdstid]. This too makes it interesting to look at the large potential residing in the reduction of sickness absence. (ibid.)

It seemed like a perfect plan had been crafted. Not only would the *Action Plan on Sickness Benefit* facilitate a quicker healing process for the sick, it would also assist them in retaining their connection to the labor market during long periods of illness. And finally, it would save the public budgets and secure sufficient labor power for the years to come.

Analysis: a container of discrete agendas

Peter Miller and Nikolas Rose (2008) encourage their readers to examine the circumstances under which certain categories of people come to be politically interesting and singled out as being in want of political intervention. They point to statistics as the origin of modern state craft (also Foucault 1991; Hacking 1991; Miller 2001; Porter 1995) and demonstrate how "particular devices of writing, listing, numbering and computing" (ibid.: 30) have the capacity to render an aspect of human existence "into discourse as a knowable, calculable and administrable object' (Miller & Rose 2008: 30). This dominant numeric approach to acquiring knowledge about the area of human affairs which one governs is far from neutral: as we saw in the second portrait a large political process was set in motion due to a deviation in a statistical module. When the old philosophical pragmatists referred to knowledge as "rules of action" (Peirce 1955 [1940]: 28) and "programs for more work" (James 1955 [1943]: 133) these were no mere figures of speech; a pivotal point for them was the notion that the way you conceptualize the world will afford and encourage particular actions—whether practical or mental—on the world. When the civil servants via their statistical modules conceptualized sickness absence as a sum total (150,000 people) and as an economic sum (37 billion DKR), the actions that presented themselves were reducing, moving, saving, increasing, and so on, and we have seen that these were indeed the actions that lay at the heart of the selection of those proposals that made it into the *Action Plan on Sickness Benefit*. The proposed actions had to be effective in "actually reducing the sickness absence," and also be "cost-effective," saving more money than they cost to execute. And vice-versa, we have seen that once it was decided that the action required was to reduce the costs, the knowledge the civil servants required was of a numerical nature.

The *Action Plan on Sickness Benefit* was enabled by techniques of numbering that directed the civil servants' attention to specific "groups" of the population (long-term recipients of sickness benefit), and the way in which the statistics rendered this group knowable (as a numerical sum, as an amount of money, as a length of time) influenced the responses the planners came up with (reducing the number of recipients, saving money, shortening the length of time spent receiving sickness benefit). However, once it was decided to make a plan, the plan became a platform where connections could be forged between all sorts of agendas, viewpoints, and interests. We have seen through the narratives of the civil servants in the Ministry of Employment and an analysis of a set of official documents how *Active—Back Sooner* became entangled in the Government's attempt to save both sufficient labor power and the public budgets. This entanglement was produced by way of "commensuration"; a calculative practice by which qualitatively different phenomena (as in this case administrative expense and individual illness) are converted into a "common metric where the difference between things is expressed as magnitude" (Espeland 2001: 1839). By converting the heterogeneous phenomena of, on the one hand, a group of people who had been absent from work due to sicknesses of various kinds and on the other hand, a set of challenges faced by the public sector into unequivocal numerical values, the *Action Plan on Sickness Absence* allowed for the possibility of performing mental actions like comparison, subtraction, and addition across the two fields and of presenting "sickness absence" as simultaneously a solution to and an explanation of "the lack of labor power" and the deficit in the public budgets.

This conversion of heterogeneous phenomena into unequivocal numerical figures was the central creative means by which the civil servants constructed the *Action Plan on Sickness Benefit* as a coherent policy document. However, the various agendas vested in the individual proposals remained discrete. At the municipal level the most immediate concerns for the caseworkers were to make their own work life meaningful and to be able to offer something helpful to the sick men and women who passed through their offices. *Active—Back Sooner* was therefore most immediately attractive in its capacity of projecting such a future in which the municipal caseworkers would get to "make a difference" and as a "thing" upon which they could hinge their dreams and their private wishes to "do better" and "make sense." Meanwhile, in the Ministry, *Active—Back Sooner* was important in that the trial embodied an ambition to work evidence-based and to experiment with conducting controlled trials. It was attractive here in its capacity to project a future where money would be spent wisely and where the effort to reduce the Danes' sickness absence would be based on initiatives with "documented effect." In these two first portraits, *Active—Back Sooner* has been portrayed on the background of the first portents of a strong force that would in time pull it apart both as a coherent policy document and as a set of governing principles for casework—the insistence that what one does or decides can be construed as sensible and purposeful. The ways in which such sense-making could be practiced and construed were, as we have seen the first discrete signs of, many. As the trial enters the hands of its implementers in the following portraits we will see how the policy immediately ceases to make sense and is torn apart upon its arrival only to be redesigned in multiple more or less coherent attempts to recreate the trial as a sensible endeavor.

Notes

1 My repeated use of the word "citizen" is a reflection of the vocabulary used in the job center. "Citizen" had come to substitute the word "client" which had been predominant during the 1990s. For a discussion of how the transition from a welfare paradigm to a neo-liberal paradigm had been paralleled by a shift towards viewing people as empowered citizens in society rather than as clients of the state, see Susan Hyatt 1997.

2 The specifics of the law and the way in which the exact numbers are calculated are far more complex than I make it appear here. I shall not pretend to completely understand the intricacies of the law but this rough outline will serve to give the reader a general idea of the importance of this benefit for both employer and employee.

3 I was told that the argument for this was that if they applied for a job, they would be considered ready to take a job, and if they were able to take a job they were not eligible for sickness benefit.

4 The law on sickness benefit is more nuanced and complex than this. However, since it was most caseworkers' clear impression that most recipients of sickness benefit either did not listen when they explained the law or forgot it again, these were the general terms in which the law was often communicated during initial meetings.

5 A "flex job" is a scheme where a person works at reduced hours or at reduced powers but still receives a full-time salary. The employer will be compensated by the municipality with (as a rule) half or two thirds of the minimum wage. This right was regulated by a different law, namely the Law on Active Employment Effort.

6 At the time, all cases were classified as belonging to one out of three "match groups." Ida's unit "team 1a" worked with the match groups 1 and 3 until they reached the administrative age of 26 weeks, whereas they referred match group 2 cases to their sister unit "team 1b." In match group 1 and 3 "follow-up" was only required every eight weeks (see Drost et al. 2006: 136).

7 A project targeting people with minor psychological disorders.

8 Sections of this portrait overlap with an article published as: N. Vohnsen (2013b), "Evidence-based policy: some pitfalls in the meeting of scientific research and politics." *Anthropology Today*: 29 (5), 3–5.

9 E.g. according to the *Journal of the American Medical Association* (Torpy 2010) the randomized controlled trial is used to determine a specific question about a given treatment—usually its effectiveness. It is important in such a study to ensure that the outcome of the trial is caused by "the treatment under study and not by other factors

that could otherwise influence the treatment assignment" (ibid.: 1216). Another key element in a controlled trial is the ethical review it has to undergo that assesses the risks involved, including the "adequacy of the informed consent" of the participants (ibid.).

10 In 2009 the Ministry of Employment was organized into a main Department of Employment referred to by the employees as simply "the Department" or "the Ministry." This department answered directly to the Minister of Employment. Below it in the organizational hierarchy were five authorities and directorates. Each administered a part of the labor market legislation and regulation. Under the authority of the Ministry of Employment was also a research center, NFA. This center was instrumental in supplying the Ministry with research into sickness absence.

11 The municipality comprising the capital area and responsible for a major part of the collective sickness benefit cases.

12 The municipal reform of 2007 had three key elements: a merging of the existing municipalities (a reduction from 271 to 98); a new division of tasks between municipalities, regions, and the state; and a reform of the financial (re)distribution (Indenrigs- og Sundhedsministeriet 2005: 5). This restructuring caused quite a bit of organizational turmoil in the municipalities. For an ethnographic analysis of the reform see Bjerge (2008: 93ff.).

13 The left- and right-wing parties are respectively referred to as "the red" and "the blue" block.

14 He refers here to the shift from a passive (merely informative) to an active (referral to activities and preventive offers) approach to intervention in cases of sickness benefit.

15 The reduction of sickness absence became part of the Government program after the elections on 13 November, 2007 (VK Regeringen III, 2007: 15).

16 "Professional" should here be understood as opposed to political. In Danish "faglig" refers to the reasoning inherent to a particular discipline or realm of craftsmanship. When she therefore speaks of a professional reason, she would imply a disciplinary reasoning (e.g. medical, economical, or judicial) as opposed to a strategic or ideological reasoning.

17 A consultancy company.

2

Mutations

The following two portraits portray *Active—Back Sooner* as "it" starts to disintegrate. They show how upon arrival in one of the municipal units charged with the implementation of the trial, the original project design is undermined and recreated by the multiple local concerns to which it must adapt or defer. What we will observe in the following is the circumstance that people's interests and intentions are situational; the goals they work towards might change significantly depending on the present task at hand. The text documents how contradictory decisions were being made from minute to minute, all generated by attempts to make the interventions sensible and purposeful. It concludes that when implementation fails, it does so because implementation is in fact a planning phase in its own right and one characterized by a high degree of instability.

Portrait 3: the trial mutates

My formal introduction to the municipal caseworkers took place at a meeting in Peter's office on 14 January, 2009. This meeting was also the first one of the "project group" which would be in charge of the local implementation of *Active—Back Sooner*. Before the political adoption of the *Action Plan on Sickness Benefit*, Peter had established a temporary group that worked on drafting a local version of the national project design, which they had submitted to the National Labor Market Authority when they applied to join the trial. On the morning of 14 January Peter explained to the attending caseworkers that this temporary group had been dissolved in favor of a new constellation of people who would "actually work with the project and have their fingers deep in the dough."

This new group consisted of a stable core unit of four caseworkers (Kirsten, Marie, Ida, and Klara)—and me on the side, the anthropologist who had permission to study the implementation of the trial "in whichever way I saw fit." When the group first met on 14 January, another local manager, Mette, and an internal development consultant, Helene, were also present. Peter opened the meeting by stating that they were already behind schedule, and that civil servants from the Ministry of Employment who were responsible for coordinating the multiple local trials around the country had expressed concern that this delay might impede the effort to draft 200 people into the control and intervention groups respectively. However, Peter did not share their concern. Set in a town of considerable size, he imagined their unit could round up the required 400 participants in a matter of a few weeks rather than the projected four months if they had to. He proceeded to discuss the practicalities of drafting.

> *Peter*: We need a description of how and when to select people for the project. In the document from the National Labor Market Authority it says that birth year determines whether a person goes into the intervention or control group. Since we have too many people and cannot include them all, we will select them by their birth date. My suggestion is that we begin by including the 01s ... everyone born on the 1st of any month.

Peter went on to do the math. With an average intake of 330 new cases a week—i.e. 330 new people on sickness benefit who each month reached the eight-week limit after which the Municipality was obliged to summon them to a meeting—to be divided by, say, 30 birth dates, he calculated that they would get around 10 people with birth dates on the 1st, to be divided between the control and intervention groups ... so five a week. Then, he reckoned, if they should turn out to be running short they could always fit in the 02s.

> *Peter*: We need to include the 01s in any case because refugees and immigrants who do not know their birth date get "01" when they enter the country.

Helene, the internal development consultant, now voiced her objection. Her concern was for the validity of the project:

> *Helene*: For that very reason the 01s ought to be left out altogether. They are not representative of our citizens.

In the Municipality the people whose cases they worked were referred to as "citizens" rather than for instance "clients," which was perceived to be a derogatory term associated with the employment policies of the 1980s preceding the "empowerment" paradigm.

> *Peter*: I completely agree but the documents specify the 01s must be included, so there is no avoiding them.

Having established the lack of representativity within the intervention group, Peter expected no further trouble related to the drafting of people into the project. Helene, nevertheless, cautioned Peter not to be too optimistic about the intake. In her experience from earlier projects it often proved difficult to reach the target number despite optimistic calculations based on their internal statistics. As the months progressed, Helene's caution would prove to be timely. Despite the prognosis, they later had to ask for the project period to be extended in order to reach the 200 participants for each of the two groups. However, on the day of the first meeting in the project group the most immediate foreseeable obstacle pertained to the definition of *when* a person could be said to have entered the project. Mette, the local manager responsible for the practical drafting of people into the trial, joined the discussion.

> *Mette*: Do I understand you correctly; do we not yet have an internal description of what we plan to do?

> *Peter*: No. That is what we are going to do now. To use a buzzword—we need to make a flowchart. But the whole procedure is totally straightforward. It is very comprehensively described here in the material from the National Labor Market Authority.

Vectors of concern

The procedure soon turned out to be not as straightforward as it seemed in the documents. The immediate problem was how to separate the legally required "introductory conversation" (to which everyone who had received sickness benefit for eight weeks was summoned regardless of their involvement in the trial) from the first "project conversation" during which a person would be informed that they had been drafted into the project's intervention group.

> *Peter*: One problem we need to handle is that our normal introductory conversation and the first project conversation *have* to be kept separate. And we have a maximum of one week from our first meeting with the people in the intervention group until we conduct our first project conversation. For various reasons it is unwise to wait. For instance, it would be unwise to say to a person "you have been drafted into a project which we will tell you about some other day." It makes no sense. So, despite the two conversations having to be kept separate, most municipalities have, like we have, decided to have them the same day. This makes most sense.

> *Mette*: But how will that be done in practice?

Marie had been part of the former group Peter had dissolved in favor of the new group in charge of the implementation. She had, therefore, been involved in drawing up the initial response to the Ministry's call for participation. She took over to speculate on the practicalities of drafting, while Peter seemed to be thinking hard about something while he reread the documents from the National Labor Market Authority.

> *Marie*: Well, I imagine we begin with our normal introductory conversation. We do what we normally do except we are attentive to how the information we get fits into the project. And then when we reach the point where we would normally say, "Listen, we have this project called *Back to Work*, or we would mention the Back Pain Clinic or other offers, we say instead "Listen, you have been drafted into this project and here is a letter from the National Labor Market Authority explaining it."

She imagined people could then go and drink a cup of coffee while reading it and come back afterwards. That way, she reasoned, it would be two separate conversations while to them it would seem integrated.

> *Marie*: I think we should avoid confusing people

Regarding the daily summoning of people to the obligatory consultations in the Municipality, Klara now joined in:

> *Klara*: Well, people probably couldn't care less about the fact that somebody has decided these conversations should be separate. What would matter to them is if they were asked to come in here twice instead of once. They wouldn't like that.

With these comments from Peter, Marie, and Klara, offered less than a quarter of an hour into the first meeting of the project group, a tension began to arise between what the project design "required," what would be "wise," what would "matter" to the people, and how best to "avoid confusion." These tensions unfolded as the discussion progressed.

> *Marie*: The problem is if they report "fit for duty" [i.e. say they are ready to return to work].

She had put her finger on what had been worrying Peter. He looked up from the documents. What if, he speculated aloud, having been drafted into the project by virtue of their birth date and year, people came to the meeting and it turned out that they were about to go back to work? The problem was, Peter explained, that the Municipality was paid 7,500 DKR (approximately £750), for each of the 200 people in the intervention group. This money was paid out in connection with the first project conversation, meaning that a person would be registered as part of the project the moment the caseworker informed them they had been chosen. Peter, Marie, and Helene all found this approach problematic:

> *Peter*: Now, I would imagine that just telling people they are part of a project must have some effect research-wise. I mean, surely it ought be interesting for the National Labor Market Authority to see whether telling people they have been drafted for a project that requires them to be active for ten hours a week while they are sick has some effect on the frequency of reporting fit for duty. But they have specifically chosen not to look at this variable and this means that if a person reports fit for duty during the introductory conversation they are *not* part of the project and we do *not* register them.

As opposed to Peter, whose work was of a strictly administrative nature, Marie was handling the introductory conversations on a daily basis and questioned the straightforwardness of his reasoning. In her experience it rarely happened that people showed up with a set date on which they planned to return to work. Usually, she explained, they would say something vague like "I plan to return to work within the next couple of weeks." Would they then be in the project or out?

> *Peter*: They are in. That is, unless they sign a fit-for-duty certification with a specific date on it immediately. If you have already begun informing them of the project then they are definitely in.

> *Helene*: And what if *after* having been informed of the project they decide they would rather go back to work?

> *Marie*: Then they are still part of the project.

> *Peter*: The problem is that there is a fundamental issue with the project design regarding the timing of when they report "fit for duty" versus when we begin informing them of the project. Regardless of Marie's arguments for letting the two conversations progress as one, I think we need to make a break. Perhaps it is enough simply to let the person sit alone for five minutes and read the letter from the National Labor Market Authority. It all comes down to a question of showing consideration for the person versus showing consideration for the case-worker and the project design. I think it is important that we are able to clearly distinguish one from the other.

On that very first day in the municipal life of the project *Active—Back Sooner*, in a remark soon passed over by the general discussion, Peter had named the three vectors of concern which would proceed to push the project in conflicting directions throughout its continuous planning and implementation: the concern for the citizen, the concern for the caseworker's ability to best manage the collective workload, and the concern for the validity of the project. These three concerns continued to appear at a meeting the following day. During this meeting the case-workers responsible, Marie and Ida (Kirsten was on leave and would not return for another four weeks), proceeded to plan how they would separate the two conversations in practice.

Their first idea was to ask the drafted person to go back to the waiting area, read the letter and then return after 15 minutes. But what would Marie and Ida do meanwhile? Both of them had a lot of work just managing their normal cases, and 15 minutes waiting for each project participant to read a letter could not be spent doing nothing. They briefly contemplated spending the time entering the participant's details into the electronic registration system which had been set up for the benefit of the trial's quantitative evaluation. But against this option weighed the fact that the longer they let the participant spend reading the letter, the longer the subsequent citizen would have to await their turn in the waiting room. They wondered whether they would have enough time to conduct the next introductory conversation while the first participant read the letter; but that would mean they could not allow the second conversation to last very long, which was not desirable if the case proved one of the more complicated ones. Perhaps the solution was to spread the five people across two hours rather than one? That way the three of them (they factored in Kirsten who would later join them) had no more than one "project person" per hour, and if they had time to spare they could always complete some normal introductory conversations.

The problem escalated when Ida did a quick calculation and found out that if they drafted five people into the project a week, as they had decided to do the previous day based on Peter's calculations, it would take 40 weeks to reach the 200 participants whereas, according to the official project description, the time available was 17 weeks. This, however, they imagined could be solved by conducting less normal introductory conversations and by increasing the project intake. During the meeting, Marie and Ida continued to encounter and overcome such small hypothetical obstacles. Critical comments were offered and evaluated, and practical obstacles dealt with as their plan gradually improved. They would, they decided, conduct the introductory conversation, then leave their offices and let the participant sit there for a shorter period of time to read the letter while they themselves went to the toilet or to get a cup of coffee or to find some documents they envisioned they might need. They would not waste time this way since these were all things they would have spent time on anyway.

Once the "action" began, what eventually made them abandon their plan and conduct the two conversations as one regardless of any arguments raised by Peter and Marie herself, did not relate to the concerns raised and overcome in these preliminary discussions. What they had not foreseen was the fact that many people did not understand the letter, were done reading it before Marie and Ida could leave the room, or responded to the message that they had been drafted for a project with numerous anxious questions. Some broke down and cried. All the considerations that had gone into the planning phase (being able to distinguish clearly between the legally required conversation and the project conversation, not wasting time, not letting people wait unreasonably long, ensuring more time was given in the case of complicated cases, and so on) were set aside in favor of the practical realization that all that happened when they left the office or asked the person to leave it was that the multitude of anxious, curious, frightened, or angry questions got postponed.

The heterogeneous nature of "local practice"

Returning to the first meeting on 14 January, such problems continued to crop up as Peter, Mette, and the caseworkers continued to draw the flowchart. If local concerns were several and some of them incompatible, "local practice" was not a straightforward phenomenon either. What was referred to in the project design as the "normal intervention" against which the effect of *Active—Back Sooner* was to be measured, was marked by the presence of other "controlled trials" such as *Back To Work* and of other local offers such as referrals to the Back Pain Clinic, where professional physiotherapy was offered. In the local description of the project elaborated by Peter and Marie for the National Labor Market Authority's approval a month earlier, they had suggested that these other ongoing projects would only be offered to the control group. However, the National Labor Market

Authority had insisted they changed this so that the two groups would be given the same intervention apart from the "extra" that would be offered as a result of *Active—Back Sooner*. This was in order to ensure a shared so-called "baseline intervention," but choosing this course of action did not make the related problems disappear:

Ida: So we *can* refer the intervention group to the *Back to Work* project as well?

Peter: Yes.

Ida: As something extra or as part of *Active—Back Sooner*?

Peter: Er ... well ... I would say it is an "activity," so I guess it *could* be part of our project ... But then we run into the big problem we anticipated when we originally decided only to offer it to the control group ... namely that we would then be offering the same intervention to our intervention group as we do to our control group.

Ida: But what if people from the intervention group from *Active—Back Sooner* end up in the control group for the *Back to Work* project? Then it would not be an active offer.

Peter: Er ...

Marie: No it would not. I am very fond of the *Back to Work* project as well but what we should do instead is see if we can find something similar elsewhere to ensure that the intervention group is in activity.

Helene: But if you refer them to *Back to Work* then we cannot be sure they'll get ten hours of activity a week. Can we demand that *Back to Work* give them at least ten hours a week?

Peter: Then we will have to mix it with another activity. We can mix as we want.

Mette: But *Back to Work* is really just an occupational health assessment. We can buy that from the private employment agencies.

Peter: Well, I guess we need to think differently. What we need to think is this: normally we would have chosen *Back to Work* but in this case we have an extra door open and we can offer people *anything*. *That* is why we do not choose *Back to Work*. Do you follow me? The important thing is that the ten hours can be put together however we want. Two hours of preventive bits and pieces, a fitness card and four hours of offers regulated by the law on active employment effort.

During this first meeting, where the attention shifted away from the crafting of a national project design and onto the elaboration of a practical course of action, the clear-cut distinction between the intervention group (receiving the "project intervention") and the control group (receiving the "normal intervention") began to dissolve. The project design required base-line comparability between the two groups (to facilitate later evaluation), but some of the methodological require-ments they had to operate by were questioned locally: they had to ensure ten hours of activity, yet the "intervention group" could end up in another project control group. There was Helene's objection that the insistence on including "the 01s" undermined the representativity of the project, and there was Peter's puzzle-ment over the design's disregard for registering those who decided to go back to work as a result of being informed of the project.

Illegibility and "local knowledge"

Weeks before the official start of *Active—Back Sooner*, during the regional launch-ing seminar on 17 December, 2008, it had become clear that most of the partici-pating municipalities had no "active offers" ready. The Municipality that Marie, Ida, and Peter belonged to had just concluded a large procurement process result-ing in a number of "framework agreements" with private employment agencies. It was to this group of private employment agencies that Marie, Ida, and Peter planned to refer those participants in *Active—Back Sooner* who were not able to go back to work part-time. When the project group met on 14 January they still had no active offers ready, despite planning to draft the first people into the project only a few days later.

Marie, Ida, and Kirsten, the caseworkers who would be responsible for imple-menting *Active—Back Sooner*, had until then worked exclusively with "early intervention"—i.e. cases of less than 26 weeks of administrative age. Their job had consisted primarily of informing people of their legal rights and obligations as recipients of sickness benefit and of helping people return to work part-time if possible. If they caught a more "complicated" or "heavy" case they had until now been obliged to transfer it to another team. In this capacity they had never dealt with the private employment agencies before. As team leader, Peter's knowl-edge was limited to what he had picked up from the caseworkers who worked with applications for early retirement pension and professional rehabilitation in other units. When they therefore discussed the attractive alternatives to the highly successful *Back To Work* project and "the extra" they would be able to offer the participants within the framework of *Active—Back Sooner*, it remained a purely speculative discussion. To make up for this, Peter asked Marie and Ida to read up on the private employment agencies and meet again the following day to shortlist a number of private employment agencies which they would then try to make arrangements with.

Marie and Ida each had five years of university studies behind them, as had the three other caseworkers who would eventually be involved. Trained in the humanities or social sciences, their analytical and reflective skills were manifest in their approach to the project. However, they had no formal training within the realm of social work in which the private employment agencies dealt. It was new and unfamiliar territory. After the meeting on 14 January Marie had read through a brochure that contained a description of the offers and specialties of the different private employment agencies. She had also taken time to discuss them with a colleague who was a trained social worker and who frequently dealt with the private employment agencies. Yet, despite her best efforts, Marie did not feel very enlightened when she met with Ida and me the following day in order to select the private employment agencies that would, in time, be used as suppliers of the "activity" required by the project design:

> *Marie*: What I mean is … OK, for example this one … they *also* have a "special focus on recipients of sickness benefit" … they write: "We are particularly skilled working with blind people; people with substance abuse; people with stress and depression; people with psychosomatic disorders and lifestyle diseases; with young people without education; with immigrants and refugees who need to learn Danish; with criminals and former inmates; with citizens who need job training." They basically claim to be particularly skilled in everything!

The descriptions in the brochures left the caseworkers with very little clarity on what kind of activities were actually carried out by the different organizations. This was a feeling they would continue to complain about throughout the project and even after the revised legislation during the autumn of 2009 had made referrals to the private employment agencies a stock part of their job. Marie said at one point that the private employment agencies all knew the most recent discourse and the right buzzwords but she had little if any idea of what they actually did. On the day when they had to decide which private employment agencies and which "active offers" to use in the project, the discussion therefore never went beyond general and structural issues: how to keep track of who was in the project and who was not; how to separate the introductory conversation from the project conversation; what to do if the participants applied for professional rehabilitation or early retirement pension (in both cases they would normally have transferred the cases to a specialized team, since Ida, Marie, and Kirsten had never handled such applications); what to do with the legal requirement for follow-up which ran alongside the project intervention; on what grounds they would exempt people from the project; what they should say to the people who they would in a few days draft into the project when they themselves still did not know which activities to offer.

Finally a large question remained: the project design obliged the caseworkers to conduct weekly meetings with each individual participant in the intervention group, but structurally, how could this be done (with three caseworkers handling the 200 citizens they would need to conduct between 60 and 70 individual meetings each week) and what would they talk about? That was a question they had discussed with Peter on the meeting on 14 January.

> *Peter*: We now come to our absolute largest unresolved business. The Central Administration has signed a framework agreement with a number of private agencies. We are kind of bound by these agreements to buy some specific "packages." Our idea so far has been to make more or less concrete deals with three of

these agencies to collaborate with us on this. The difficult part of this is that we are actually going to ask them to do something they—according to the framework agreements we have just signed—are not obliged to do.

What they would have to ask of the employment agencies at first seemed banal: they needed them to report back on the citizens and keep the caseworkers informed about whether and when they had held weekly conversations with *Active—Back Sooner*'s intervention group. What Peter thought might prove a problem was the firm agreement between the Municipality and the private employment agencies that all communication should take place in monthly "progress reports." These progress reports were of a more elaborate nature than the information Peter imagined they would need for the project, but they would need the information on a weekly, rather than on a monthly, basis.

It had been the intention that Marie, Ida, and Kirsten would be responsible for all contact with the participants in the projects themselves. This was exactly the close involvement in each case that they had dreamt of and which had made them want to join the project to begin with. Yet already on the second day of planning the intervention locally, it became obvious that they would not have the time. The new plan was therefore to hand over to the private employment agencies the responsibility both for these conversations as well as for carrying out the "active offers." This meant that the caseworkers' involvement in cases where people could not return part-time to work would be limited to the first "project conversation" and a brief conversation every four weeks as required by law (and not as part of the trial). In this regard the actual implementation of *Active—Back Sooner* was in practice handed over to the privately employed social workers and job consultants in all cases where part-time return to work was not possible.

The chronic lack of time under which they already worked was, on the one hand, what had given rise to a strong hope that things could be different (and would be in this new project), while on the other hand, this organizational condition would undermine any chance of fulfilling these hopes. From the very beginning it led to two competing sentiments within the project group, as we can see expressed in Marie's very contradictory remarks offered during the two planning meetings on 14 and 15 January respectively:

Marie: [On 14 January, to the project group] I have chosen to be a part of this project in order to try out some of the things that we have dreamt about as caseworkers and which we might be able to do in this project.

[On 15 January, to Ida] Initially, when we wrote our local project description, I guess we thought it would be more "project-like." But we have moved towards what is compatible with our day-to-day business. So what we decide now has to be do-able in the long run.

On the second day of adapting *Active—Back Sooner* to the local reality in the job center, the perfect plan elaborated in the hallways of the Labor Market Authority had slowly disintegrated in the offices of the municipal job center. Bits and pieces had been incorporated into a new *Active—Back Sooner* which were compatible—in theory still—with the municipal reality.

On the Friday before the Monday when the first citizens were supposed to be drafted into the intervention group, Klara stopped by Marie's and Ida's offices to let them know that no citizens registered as being born on the 1st of a month had been summoned on the Monday and only one on the Tuesday. However, on the Tuesday that person did not show up. So it was the end of January before a "red case" finally appeared in the stack of case-files on the coffee table in the reception. To make sure none of the other caseworkers took on an "active citizen" by mistake, Klara had put the usual yellow-brown cardboard file into a red plastic folder while the "control citizens" were put in blue plastic folders so that the caseworkers not involved in the project would remember that a special registration sheet for the purpose of baseline comparison would need to be filled in on these citizens. The caseworkers who were not part of the project were asked to specify such things as diagnoses (many had several, such as back pain *and* depression) and whether or not they would imagine exempting the person from the project had they been part of it. Later an intern would type the information into the National Labor Market Authority's registration system. The plastic folders were slippery and were soon substituted by red and blue tape which made them less conspicuous in the stack of files. However, on that morning at the end of January when a red file finally appeared in the stack of files in the reception area and could be seen from afar, everyone involved in the project, myself included, was excited. Ida and Marie had decided to handle the first couple of project conversations together to work out a common routine. The normal "introductory conversations" were kept separate from the "project conversations" by a brief break during which Ida and Marie went to the coffee area while the citizens were given time to read the introductory letter from the National Labor Market Authority. I met them during this break in the coffee area where they were nervously pacing the floor:

> *Marie*: This one we will not have around for long.

> *Ida*: No, he definitely hadn't counted on "activity." I bet he will not be bothered to be on sick leave now.

I left Marie and Ida in the coffee area and walked past the office in which they had left him waiting. The man was standing with his hands folded behind his back looking out the window while the letter sat on the table.

Portrait 4: satisfying needs

Due to teaching obligations at my department I had to leave the job center for three weeks just as the project finally began. When I returned at the end of February 2009, Marie and Ida already felt much more confident about the project and I was invited to sit in on any meeting or conversation they had. At this point in time, Kirsten had joined them: she felt less comfortable with my presence during the actual project conversations but willingly shared any reflection she made with me. In early February, Peter, Ida, and Marie had made agreements with the three private employment agencies they had chosen and they had begun referring people from the "intervention group" to "activity." To summarize, the specific goals were, in order of priority, firstly to have citizens return to work for ten hours a week, or secondly for them to return less than ten hours a week in combination with an "active offer," or thirdly to accept an "active offer" of at least ten hours a week. In practice this became, in the job center, a question of either returning to work at least ten hours a week or being referred to one of the three private employment agencies' "sickness benefit packages." These packages were originally developed in response to the Municipality's public tender on offers targeting recipients of sickness benefit who were possible candidates for professional rehabilitation, "flex jobs" (reduced work ability jobs), or early retirement pension. The content of the packages will be the topic of portraits 7 and 8, which moves the account partially to one of the three private employment agencies.

A project conversation

I attended the first "project conversation" on the day I returned to the unit. The first "red file" in the stack of case-files that day was a female artist who had lived abroad for some years. She had recently returned to Denmark to work a 20-hour job as a pedagogue in a day care institution. She seemed full of energy as she entered the office and sat down in the soft blue chair opposite Ida. Her case seemed straightforward: she suffered from back pain and was not sure she was getting the proper physical rehabilitation and she could not wait to go back to work. Also, she had regular contact with her employer and colleagues. However, as the conversation progressed it turned out that her problems were of a less straightforward nature. She bled heavily at random times throughout her menstrual cycle and she felt drained and "emotionally unstable." On top of that she was feeling increasingly stressed by doing nothing.

> *Ida*: Did you feel stressed before you got sick?

> *Woman*: Yes, it was there before. Long before. And then the back pain started. I do not know if it might be connected ... No, I actually do not think so. I have become increasingly stressed since I've been on sick leave. I worry that my manager might fire me. Then I won't be able to support myself. She was not the one who originally employed me and she makes a point of mentioning this every time we speak. I get very nervous. I am lucky to even have a job with no education and all. It has been a while since I have had a job ... I do not know if that might be it. Perhaps I cannot handle that all of a sudden people are making demands of me.

In a sense the woman's case exemplified the scenario *Active—Back Sooner* had been designed to address. Here was a case of somebody who, despite the odds (the unemployment rate was high among artists and the woman had no professional training), had acquired a job that she liked and wanted to return to. As predicted by a psychiatrist who participated in an "experience-gathering seminar" she felt increasingly stressed and insecure about not being at work, particularly since her most immediate manager did not seem to be too happy about having an employee on sick leave and she might therefore be in danger of being fired. Furthermore, since the woman had not been able to afford physiotherapy she did not attend any physical training for her back. When Ida proceeded to tell the woman that she had been drafted into a project due to her personal identification numbers and birth date she did not have any trouble "selling" the intervention to the woman; when she mentioned that the project gave her the opportunity to refer her to an "active offer" by a private employment agency that employed both physiotherapists and psychologists the woman happily accepted:

> Woman: I would like to see a psychologist as well because quite frankly I feel very, very bad ... and you know that when women begin to bleed at random times throughout the month it is not a good sign.

As mentioned earlier, in order for Ida and her colleagues to fulfill their role in the project they would have to identify a "need" which they could match with an offer. However, this was not always as easy as in the case above.

Negotiating need

If we forget for a moment that Ida and her colleagues (especially the two new members of the project group) had only the vaguest idea what took place at the private employment agencies, the match between the woman in the first example and the project was, in theory, perfect. Perhaps not surprisingly, those who reacted most positively to the news that they had been drafted into a compulsory project were the ones who were able to see how they could benefit from it, either because the project could be argued to address some concrete "need" that was currently unsatisfied or because it could be seen to pay for services (such as psychologist, physiotherapist, or access to fitness center) that the citizens so far had paid for themselves. Had it not been for the project, Ida told me, she would have had to inform the woman in the case above that her right to sickness benefit depended on her compliance with (within reasonable limits) the treatment her doctor had prescribed and that she therefore was obliged to attend to and pay for physiotherapy if she wanted to maintain her right to sickness benefit. Instead, Ida was able to offer it for free and, as something extra, provide access to a psychologist as well. Nevertheless, not all people reacted positively to this. Quite a few of those who were drafted into the project were confused about the fact that "the public sector" (det offentlige), constantly complaining about a scarcity of money, would spend money on things they were gladly paying for themselves or for which they felt no need. In such cases the compulsory aspect of the project stood out despite the caseworkers' attempts to present the project as an attractive bonus:

Man: You had me confused there for a moment because I thought you said it was an offer. So it is something I am forced to participate in?

Marie: Well, you are actually ... perhaps I should have mentioned that. But you have to look at it as if we are giving you something extra.

Man: Oh ... Then maybe I should not join the fitness center anyway ... or start swimming as I had planned ... I mean, if I have to participate in your activity. I would not want to overstrain myself either, right?

When Marie and her colleagues downplayed the obligatory aspect of the project to the citizens it was not out of ill will or neglect but based on the simple realization that the moment they mentioned the obligatory aspect of the project many people seemed to acquire a mental block against it. As Ann, one of two additional caseworkers who joined the project in March put it:

Ann: It is a delicate balance because on the one hand they need to know it has consequences if they do not participate, on the other hand we have to see that this does not end up being all about resistance against pressure because then they surely won't benefit from it anyway.

The caseworkers therefore sometimes overplayed the "meaningfulness" (*meningsfyldte*) of the project to make it seem more attractive. That these attempts to "sell" the project might not have a long lasting effect was not lost on the caseworkers. Here Sara, the other new caseworker, explains:

Sara: Sometimes I feel a bit like an ...er ...

Nina: Like a second-hand car dealer?

Sara: Exactly. I sit here and "sell" (*sælger*) something that doesn't really exist. It makes me feel bad about myself. I'm selling this "activity" that doesn't exist. I tell them it's a super offer and all the while I just know that this specific person will not fit into it. And at the same time I do not think what this private employment agency offers is any good. It leaves a bad taste in my mouth. But then you just have to hope for the best.

Often it was not possible for the caseworkers to find something concrete to offer the people who had been drafted into the intervention group. On the one hand, the concrete "needs" the recipients of sickness benefit had were often unfulfilled for very good reasons, such as long waiting lists or the lack of effective treatment options in the health care system; on the other hand, not all "needs" could be accepted as legitimate needs—for instance the need to be left alone and to have some peace and quiet. Furthermore, in many cases people's needs were already being met since most were very actively engaged in trying to get well and were already flanked by general practitioners, physiotherapists, psychologists, chiropractors, and the like, for which they happily paid themselves. The "offer" in these instances, of physical exercise or a number of consultations with the private employment agency's psychologist, had more to do with providing an—often happily received—economic relief than with providing some "activity" which ideally would bring people closer to the labor market.

In instances where the caseworkers did not have the possibility of offering something the recipient found of value, in terms of either finances or health, a negotiation began. In these cases the responses to the information about the compulsory project were not limited to happiness and bewilderment. Many people broke down and cried or were furious at the prospect of having to spend time (most commonly between 10 to 25 hours weekly, depending on the assessment of the individual caseworker) attending activities they thought of as useless, irrelevant, or even damaging to their health and attempts to return to work. They often pleaded with the caseworkers to exempt them or they raged against "the system." The caseworkers dealt with this "resistance" in different ways. Marie, for example, sometimes had luck reasoning with the resisting person that they should at least "give it a try." If it then turned out that attending the course made people feel worse she would have explicit grounds on which to argue for exemption. It was in these cases that the caseworkers had to draw on all their creative resources, and also the times in which their attempt to make the project appear meaningful was most threatened.

Creating demand

One illustrative discussion took place sometime after the National Labor Market Authority had changed the criteria for exemption from the project due to the preliminary feedback from the municipalities and criticism raised in the press. This news had not, however, reached Ann and had only a gradual, if any, impact on the caseworkers' practice. During a meeting in the project group, Ann brought up for discussion the case of a woman who persistently refused to be referred to activity. Ann had spent the four-week period they had available before "activity" had to commence according to the project design, trying to persuade the woman that a referral to a private employment agency was sound:

> *Ann*: She suffers from stress and maybe a bit of depression. And she refuses to be referred to activity. So I have spent these weeks preparing her for the referral. We have talked about it, demystified it a bit. I hope I get to refer her this week. Originally, when I told her she had to go into "activity" she started crying. Her whole world broke down. And till now she has simply been wasting enormous amounts of energy resisting this project. I think it would be easier for her to just be at work ten hours a week. She invests so much energy in resisting it.

> *Marie*: Yes, well, I feel a bit sorry for her.

> *Ann*: So much energy resisting and the offer *is* probably useless for her although there would be things she might be able to benefit from. So it has been nice for me to have these weeks to prepare her.

Marie: But I mean ... of course it would be good if you could reach an agreement of a kind. I have sometimes said to the citizens that I think they should just try it out. And then just limit it to ten hours or perhaps twenty hours ... and we *are* allowed to exempt them now down to just a few hours a week. Let her try it and then arrange a meeting where you follow up on how it was, immediately after. But if people downright refuse there is nothing we can do about it.

Ann: That is kind of the problem ... We have now got to the point where I have told her we will try ten hours and that the next time I call her we will make a concrete plan.

Marie: Have you tried asking her what she thinks she would benefit from?

Ann: Yes. Peace and quiet.

Marie: OK, fair enough. Maybe she is right.

Ann: Probably.

At this point in the conversation the caseworkers turned to discuss the new criteria for exemption from the project and whether these criteria could be used as grounds to exempt this woman. According to an official memorandum from the National Labor Market Authority issued on 12 March, the caseworkers could exempt from participation in the project those people who had a fixed treatment or physical rehabilitation plan with a fixed date-of-return to work if "the treatment / physical rehabilitation is of such a nature that the job center's contribution clearly cannot support the individual in a partial return to work" (Arbejdsmarkedsstyrelsen 2009a, my translation). It also established that the weekly follow-up could now be conducted over the phone rather than in person if the caseworker judged this would be most "expedient." In the specific case Ann was dealing with at that moment, however, these adjustments did not seem to help her.

Marie: I'm not sure it could be argued that she had a "fixed treatment plan." Maybe if we do not think she will benefit from it at all?

Ann: The thing is I am sure she will be able to benefit from this. She suffers from stress and she will be going back to the same work as before. She has worked three years, day and night. She doesn't cook. Only eats take-away. So I *do* think she could benefit from learning how to plan her work-life better.

Ida: [Joking] Offer her a cooking course.

Ann: You might think it sounds stupid but it would not be a bad idea. I don't think she *can* cook anymore. She has not cooked for three years. OK, that's irrelevant, but she could use some reflection on how she will manage to return to work without going down with stress again.

Marie: Is she having any treatment?

Ann: She sees a psychologist.

Marie: Then why don't you tell her you can buy her an individual series of meeting with a "coach?" A few hours a week and then if she likes it there [at the private employment agency] she can participate in the other activities. Write to Marianne at the private employment agency and tell her what you would like.

Much of the work of implementing *Active—Back Sooner* was about creating a need for the project's offers where, most of the time, there was none. Eva, one of the experienced lawyers I would later meet in the National Labor Market Authority, was particularly attentive to such mechanisms, since at a time where saving money was a growing concern for the Government the introduction of new public offers was something to be wary about. One of her colleagues, a lawyer who had been involved in some of the stages of crafting the *Action Plan on Sickness Benefit*, had had that particular critique to direct against *Active—Back Sooner*.

> *Lawyer*: My personal opinion about this project is that it is rather fantastic that we now want to give all these people offers even though they don't need them. It goes against everything else we try to do. One should only give people offers [give en indsats] based on a concrete assessment and in the case of a need. We are an employment system and our purpose is to bring people back to work as soon as possible and help them keep the job they have. We should not do anything that is unnecessary. It is a waste of resources. [Pause] ... I am sorry ... I think I lost the thread.

The lawyer felt she had spoken out of turn by offering this critique. I have chosen to include her views anyhow because her comment went to the heart of the problems that the municipal caseworkers experienced. How were they to argue that the men and women who were already doing everything they could to get back to work should cancel these activities in order to join the municipal offer of "activity" about the content of which only little was known?

The problematic absence of "need"

The moment the fact was introduced that people had been drafted into a controlled trial which they were obliged to be part of was usually a moment of significant change in the interaction between the caseworker and the sick man or woman. The conversation below was typical in the sense that it illustrates both Ida's attempts to explain the project's logic and the citizen's failure to see the point. I have included this particular meeting because it was a conversation Ida and I would often return to discuss because it illustrated how much of a bother the project could be in an individual person's work life while seeming to be simple enough. The conversation had begun well. It was the case of a young policeman who had broken his leg and who now, despite having had to wait an extraordinarily long time in the waiting room, was in a good mood that was infectious. Ida apologized for the long waiting time.

Man: No worries. I brought a book!

He leaned cheerfully back in the blue chair in Ida's office and folded his arms behind his head. He was only a few days away from having the splint that stabilized his broken foot removed and would return part-time to his job where he and his team manager had agreed he would start with some administrative tasks and phone tending until he was ready to "get back out on the street again."

Man: There are plenty of people who can use a living voice on the phone. I just cannot wait to get back to work again!

This was exactly the attitude the civil servants hoped to achieve with *Active—Back Sooner* and the *Action Plan*. As Ida went on to explain about the project and the weekly conversations they were obliged to hold the man leaned forward in the chair and began to frown:

Man: Well this would really be a bother. This seems silly. I'm in close contact with my employer and my doctors …

Ida: Yes, well the purpose of the project is to examine if a close contact with your municipal caseworker and returning part-time to work will help you get back to work sooner.

Man: But I am already on my way back to work. How would it help me to speak to you? I'm sure it's a fine project you have there, but I kind of don't fit into your box, do I?

Ida: Well, it is important that we document the cases when it does not make sense as well.

Man: Well, if you think it helps me.

Ida: I think we should do it. In your case where you have already returned to work part-time it simply means that we will meet here once a week until you are working full-time again.

Man: But what on God's earth do you want us to talk about? If we aren't doing anything worthwhile I honestly couldn't be bothered to be part of this. I'm sorry, I didn't mean to sound harsh but I'm not doing this just for the fun of it. OK? It is a bloody waste of both your time and my time. Can we at least just keep it to the phone then?

Ida: Well, I'll summon you for a meeting here when you get your splint removed. Then we can talk about it. Also I would like you to fill in a short diary about your daily progress.

Man: [Smiles to himself and shakes his head.] Whatever …

Shortly after the meeting a decision was made in the Labor Market Authority that the caseworkers could now choose to hold the weekly conversation over the phone rather than as a physical meeting and Ida was relieved and happy to inform the policeman that the only implication of being part of the project would be a weekly phone conversation. However, the man and his employer found these disturbances of his work so annoying that the man called up Ida and explained that his boss had offered to pay his full salary during the remaining illness period and not ask for reimbursement from the Municipality if this meant that they would stop calling him at work. Embarrassed on behalf of the project Ida decided to exempt him from it. In this case she had really tried to explain the project; at other times she would be blunt and simply say:

> *Ida*: We cannot give you any treatment that will shorten your period of absence from work, but we have to find a way to plan your illness period so that it fits with the project's demand for at least ten hours of activity a week.

Sometimes people were happy to be offered what they saw as a gift ("I cannot believe the public sector wants to spend all this money on me"), other times they went along with it ("OK, if you think so?"). Those who were in fact most averse to the project and remained so throughout the course of it were the men and women who were already doing everything they could to get well. The interesting thing to remember here is that the project was born out of an overall concern for saving money on the public budgets and getting people back to work as soon as possible, yet now it seemed that the project was encouraging and in some cases even demanding a substitution of self-paid, professional rehabilitation with publicly paid "treatment-like" offers.

I would often hear this concern repeated by the citizens, both during the project and after the revised sickness benefit legislation was enforced. The following interaction between the project's participants and one of the privately employed physiotherapists took place some months later at ENGA where I had moved my research by then:

> *Woman*: [Directed to me during "physical exercise"] I feel this "offer" slows me down. I was meant to go to the gym on Friday. I have a list of exercises from my physiotherapist that I go through there. It helps me so much. Instead I have to come here and sit in a classroom. It is so deeply frustrating. Take the lot of us down here in the gym. All of us do exercise regularly already. ... [Directed to private employment agency physiotherapist] I would really, really just like to follow the program my physiotherapist made me. It helps me a lot. But I simply cannot find the time for it now that I have to be here all the time. I am just getting more and more stressed by the day.

> *Private employment agency physiotherapist*: Try to see this as a supplement to what you already do. And you are also very welcome to use our machines here and do your program.

Other woman: [Directed to private employment agency physiotherapist] Excuse me ... I think maybe I should probably just take part in relaxation exercises? I already exercise half an hour a day and I am afraid to overstrain myself.

People like these two women in the example above and the policeman whose case Ida kept returning to already lived up to the overall goal of being "active while sick." Yet early in the process of implementation they were attributed the role of being "problematic." At the midterm seminar held on 1 April one of the civil servants from the National Labor Market Authority would sum up a group discussion stating that the general impression was that the most difficult group of people were the ones that "think they are in control over what they are doing and do not think they need any help."[1] While the verb "think" allowed the civil servant to place the fault of not benefitting from *Active—Back Sooner* with the individual participant, one of the municipal caseworkers stated more plainly during the discussion that in her municipality they did not know what to do about those "who already live up to our criteria for success—those who actually already are active and in a lot of treatment."

Analysis: vectors of concern

"The ultimate purpose of strategy in a democracy," writes Geoff Mulgan in his book on public strategy, "is to meet public wants and needs" (Mulgan 2009: 37). Mulgan's credo can be seen as an encouragement of what Nikolas Rose has called "to govern in an advanced liberal way" (Rose 2006: 155). As central to this form of governing Rose has identified the tendency to regard citizens as "costumers" or "consumers" of public services (ibid. 158). The Danish Government's 2002 strategy targeting the labor market area, *More People in Work* (Regeringen 2002a, my translation) might be read as an effort to govern or strategize in such a way. In the document issued upon political agreement (Beskæftigelsesministeriet 2002) it is specified that the central element in the effort is the insistence that the individual citizen must be placed at the center of the employment effort, their needs determining the nature of the effort, and even stressing that "the system must be adapted to the individual not the reverse" (Beskæftigelsesministeriet 2002: 1, my translation).

This strategy was meant to signal a break from the "mass activation" (*masseaktivering*) and "clientization" (*klientgørelse*) that had come to be associated with the various interventions directed at the Danish recipients of social benefits up through the 1990s despite continuous attempts to counter this tendency (see Bjerge 2008: 78ff.). For instance, in *More People in Work* it was stated that "No one shall be placed in pointless activation anymore. There shall be less activation, but with better results" (Regeringen 2002a: 13, my translation) and in a governmental discussion paper preceding the political agreement to adopt *More People in Work* it says that "The activation factory must be shut" (Regeringen 2002b: 1). A stated aim of the strategy and the subsequent political settlement was (just as in the case of *Active—Back Sooner*) to focus the labor market-directed interventions on the individual needs and preconditions of the recipients of public benefits. Some legal scholars who had been closely following the employment area found it strange that with the adaption of the *Action Plan on Sickness Benefit* (Beskæftigelsesministeriet 2008a) new policy was made and legal revisions planned to ensure principles which were already supposed to be foundational to the Danish labor market efforts. Why were individual needs and preconditions not already at the center of every decision made within the employment system?

There seems to be universal agreement in the central administration and in much of the public debate too that if people on social benefits keep being subjected to inexpedient referrals and "offers" it is not at the policy level the problem lies but at the municipal administrative level. And indeed, without pretending to understand the employment legislation or even the sickness benefit legislation I write about more than at a superficial level, I venture to claim that the legislations governing the labor market area are carefully crafted exactly to avoid pointless referrals. Indeed their recurrent revisions seem to be governed by the repeated attempts to make it ever clearer that individual needs and preconditions must be at the center of the administrative decision-making. Thus part of these recurrent revisions includes a continual reinvention of different mechanisms (most often economic incentives) to ensure this is done.

So here we hit upon the main theme of the implementation literature: why do implementers distort the policy they administer? In this literature the implementers' (also referred to as street-level workers, front-line workers, street-level bureaucrats, etc.) disregard for, or misapplication of, rules and directives are typically ascribed to a particular set of concerns which distinguishes them, as a group, from their managers and from those who craft the official policies. Benny Hjern and David Porter (1981), for instance, argue that people who participate in inter-organizational program implementation pursue a "program rationale" and tend to adjust their organizations to the needs of the program they are implementing (ibid.: 216), while their managers adhere to an "organizational rationale" and do the opposite (ibid.: 215). Michael Lipsky (1980) describes street-level bureaucrats as preoccupied with making their excessive workload manageable, while their superiors are concerned with organizational results. James Scott (1998) shows how local implementers tend to act in such a way that their own interests are furthered. These interests are, in his examples, in contrast to the interests of the policy-makers from a higher administrative level who are preoccupied with the most recent management trends and scientific developments. For Steven Maynard-Moody & Michael Musheno (2000), street-level workers are defined in opposition to "elected and other top government officials" in that "they do not see citizens as abstractions but as individuals" and also that their "relationships with these various citizen clients are personal and emotional, rarely cold and rational" (Maynard-Moody & Musheno 2000: 334).

So in this literature the 'implementers' who are charged with the responsibility for policy failure or distortion are most usually described as a group of people with clear-cut identities and with a certain set of concerns and preoccupations which distinguishes them as a group from other professional groups. Yet in the preceding portraits the whole thing is less straightforward. The caseworkers in this book cannot be confined to one such identity: one minute they are advocating the project like true politicians, while the next moment they are criticizing it much in the style of detached academic scholars. They are deeply involved in drawing up a workable project design one day, while ditching the design in favor of individual common sense approaches the next. One moment they resemble Maynard-Moody and Musheno's emotionally involved citizen-agents (their hearts go out to the individual person they have to involve in this trial), while the next moment they ship all the subjects off to the private employment agencies with one grand administrative gesture. They are devoted to the overall requirements of the trial in one situation, only to make contradictory decisions in the next. They are interchangeably the trial's planners, implementers, administrators, and underminers.

Accepting this will shed a different light on the difficulties faced by Peter, Marie, Helene, Ida, and Mette. Rather than being on the recipient end of policy-making, that is rather than being presented with a plan devised centrally on the basis of concerns which are different from their own, they are co-planners faced with a plan, partly of their own making, which, having passed its first test and been approved by the National Labor Market Authority, now faces the task of being put to work locally. Note that none of the team leaders or caseworkers in the job center are put out or even surprised by the fact that their initial plan appears impossible to implement. They simply proceed to change, adapt, and completely alter it so that it fits the task they now face. *Active—Back Sooner* in the guise of the policy document we knew from Chapter 1 is pulled apart by the three initial local concerns to which it repeatedly had to be adapted: firstly, the concern that it should make sense to the sick people and inconvenience them as little as possible; secondly, the concern for managing the entire corpus of the caseworkers' responsibilities (of which the implementation of *Active—Back Sooner* was just one among many); and thirdly, the concern for living up to the demands of the project design itself.

These concerns might at first appear partially overlapping with the oppositional pairs found in the implementation literature mentioned previously: Hjern and Porter (1981) operate with an organizational versus program rationale (ibid.: 215–16); Lipsky (1980) sees a concern for results versus a concern for managing the workload (ibid.: 18); Maynard-Moody and Musheno (2000: 334) describe street-level workers relating personally and directly to individual citizen-clients, in opposition to their managers and to politicians who relate abstractly to the citizens as a generalized group. However, the caseworkers' discussions, as presented in these implementation portraits, challenge these oppositional pairs. In their street-level planning they must employ a tripartite consciousness. Here concerns do not belong to people in different parts of an organization, but rather to particular problems, and are pursued in turn by all involved. Concerns, then, are not internal psychological drives but rather external and dynamic perspectives which have to be juggled and weighed against each other on an hourly basis. I propose we call these dynamic perspectives "vectors of concern" to capture exactly the capacity of such concerns to pull a policy apart and out of course.

Further blows to the original policy are dealt as the complex inter-organizational and social realities that characterized the cases of the recipients of sickness benefit undermined the hypothesis on which *Active—Back Sooner* was built; namely, that it would be and could be helpful. Rather than merely satisfying needs, the caseworkers therefore had to negotiate, create, and sometimes invent needs. The result was that *Active—Back Sooner* disintegrated into individual decisions— little ad hoc plans—all of which were directed towards satisfying one or more goals the caseworker was subjected to, although far from all working towards providing the recipients with an offer that would help them get back to work.

In Tania Murray Li's critical study of the mentality she calls "the will to improve," she states that a key practice of development work is "identifying deficiencies that need to be rectified" (Li 2007: 7). Experts' claim to expertise, she writes, "depends on their capacity to diagnose problems in ways that match the kinds of solutions that fall within their repertoire" (ibid.: 7). In Li's case the solution comes first. It is a nice trick to reverse the order of things; it has the appeal of the counter-intuitive. And is it not what I have just shown? That referral to a private employment agency is the solution and the caseworkers (*Active—Back Sooner*'s experts) diagnose the recipients' needs correspondingly? Yet my hesitation to adopt her explanation is that it skips over the confusion and bypasses the crucial steps through which both "problem" and "solution" ("need" and "offer") are matched, negotiated, or sometimes invented. No part of what takes place is stable. Not the problems, not the solutions and most definitely not the link between the two. It is the instability I have wished to highlight in these portraits. Sensible decisions are made in response to concrete situations in which they must be taken by caseworkers who are aware that the "sense" they have produced is of a fleeting nature.

What the empirical findings in this study would imply is that when policy is invariably distorted by implementation this is because implementation happens hand in hand with street-level planning; a second, highly unstable planning phase which occurs in the hands of a group of people who must continuously plan and redraft the policy along the vectors of a set of local concerns. What drives this separation between the official policy design and the local policy design is not the local project group's opposition to the official project design. *The coherence disintegrates because the assumption that there are such things as stable and unambiguous local organizational environments in which to implement policy is an illusion.* The "local practice," which in the project design is called the "normal intervention" was already marked by the presence of other "controlled trials" and of other local initiatives such as the Back Pain Clinic. At the same time, the project design's requirement for comparability between the two groups (to facilitate later evaluation) was rendered impossible by specific methodological requirements; for instance, they had to ensure ten hours of activity; the two groups were not allowed to get the exact same intervention; the "intervention group" could risk ending up in another project "control group," and so forth. The local concerns changed depending on the problem addressed at any given moment, even at the preparatory stages.

Note

1 In Danish, 'dem som mener de har styr på det selv og ikke mener de skal hjælpes.'

3

Multiplications

The following two portraits will explore how the temporarily united interests and viewpoints that had found a common ground in the proposal for the trial continued to live on and produce new versions of *Active—Back Sooner*. Portrait 5 portrays *Active—Back Sooner* as its methodological requirements put it on collision course with national employment policy, legal principles, and local organizational attempts to ensure the quality of the general casework. Through attempts to rectify counterproductive or inexpedient practice the trial's purpose begins to multiply. In portrait 6 *Active—Back Sooner* is portrayed against the backdrop of the legal controversy that the official trial gave rise to in the spring of 2009. Here we see that the continuous planning that *Active—Back Sooner* was subjected to was not restricted to the municipal job center, but rather that the trial continued to be designed and planned centrally in the Ministry too. The chapter documents that all these diversions from the initial plans were generated by highly sensible decisions and attempts to make the interventions meaningful, and further, that these attempts were what in turns tore *Active—Back Sooner* utterly apart or inflated it beyond recognition. It concludes that the recognition of the absurdity of the labor market effort rather than being a mode of ridicule in fact offers a holistic analytical position from which to appreciate the sum total of the labor market effort.

Portrait 5: the purpose multiplies

I return now to late February, four weeks into *Active—Back Sooner*'s active phase. This morning I sat in on Ida's conversations and in between them she would reflect aloud on her decisions for my benefit. Having accustomed herself to my constant asking "why?" she preempted my asking by explaining most things she did. At present she was unsure, she told me, whether or not to make a referral to activity for a woman who planned to return to work four weeks later. She decided to postpone the decision for a while. In compliance with the project design she could choose to wait four weeks until the "activity" should be started and she now contemplated whether she should use this opportunity to do "nothing" in the case. Had the woman not already had a fixed date for returning to work, Ida said, she would have referred her to activity straight away because it meant she could avoid the weekly meetings she was obliged by the project design to hold.

> *Ida*: From a purely egoistical point of view [laughs apologetically] I cannot be bothered with these conversations. I mean, what is it I am supposed to talk to them about?

However, it was not a purely egoistical point of view. Ida was troubled by the fact that she had to ask people to travel the sometimes long distance from home or from work to the job center (for some it could take up to an hour each way) to talk about essentially nothing. At the time, these conversations seemed so trivial and void of content that I failed to record any of them. The concrete change of wordings in the example below is therefore my stereotypical reconstruction of such a conversation based on my own memory and on the memory of recipients of sickness benefit I interviewed later:

> *Caseworker*: So how have you been since last week?
>
> *Citizen*: Well, the same, pretty much.
>
> *Caseworker*: You don't feel better?
>
> *Citizen*: No. I mean, it's only been a week.
>
> *Caseworker*: You don't feel ready to work more hours?
>
> *Citizen*: I don't know. I guess ten hours is fine for now.
>
> *Caseworker*: Have you thought about how you will increase the amount of hours you work per week?
>
> *Citizen*: If I take it easy for now I think it may be next week.
>
> *Caseworker*: When do you plan to be able to work full-time?
>
> *Citizen*: I don't know. This is a lot for now. I'll try to work more hours next week.

If such an exchange of words seems harmless, this was not how it was experienced by the citizens. In fact, as one young woman who had been drafted for the trial commented to me, the conversations were something she anticipated with anxiety. The fact that she had to report her "progress" to her caseworkers every week made it seem to her as if there was no progress at all. She was trying to return to work while suffering from stress-related depression, and although she could see how far she had come in terms of "getting back on her feet" in the course of months, from week to week she felt no different. This became such a source of stress for her that, in order to demonstrate "progress," she began to increase the amount of hours she went to work from week to week. This resulted in a relapse and under reproaches and instructions from the health care personnel involved in her case she had to reduce the number of hours drastically; something she experienced as a massive failure and which for a time "knocked her out."

While Ida and Marie had initially had ideas about how they would get the recipients of sickness benefit to fill in diaries about their weekly progress at work or at home, it was soon clear that there was nothing much to write about or talk about from week to week. As the months progressed and more and more citizens were drafted into the project the weekly conversations increasingly became a logistical problem. At one point Kirsten realized that before long she would, apart from her regular casework, be responsible for 40 citizens with whom she would have to fit in weekly meetings and it dawned on her that, were they to stick to the project design, none of the caseworkers involved in the project would be able to take Easter holidays or go on summer vacation. Thus when some weeks later Sara and Ann joined the project group, they were introduced to the work with these words:

> Refer people as soon as you can in order to get rid of them. I know this sound bad but considering the fact that I have to find time for six conversations about essentially nothing between our team meeting tomorrow morning and our meeting at the private employment agency around noon you can see where I am heading. The fewer cases you keep for yourself the better.

Going back again to that day in late February, Ida brought me up to date with her experiences from the past month when Marie and Kirsten came by. While I had been back at the university, Kirsten had come back from vacation and joined the project group. From the beginning her motivation for joining the project had been different from Ida's and Marie's. Knowing that this would most likely be the way they would all be working once the new act on sickness benefit had been approved she had wanted to get a head start. Unlike Marie and Ida, Kirsten joined the group less than enthusiastically. She was uncomfortable with the underlying premise that activity would lead to quicker return to work and was particularly troubled by the compulsory aspect of the project. With Kirsten and Marie hovering in the doorway to Ida's office, Ida brought up the question of whether or not to refer people to activity if they planned to return to work before the twelve week limit for referral was up. So far she had not done it in any of her cases, judging that it would be a waste of time, money, and everybody's (especially the citizen's) energy to begin an activity only to stop it again after a short period of time. Marie and Kirsten, on the other hand, had made referrals for such brief periods of time, reasoning that the citizens might as well learn something for future use while the project offered the opportunity.

A conversation that took place on the following day added to the picture of the lack of clear-cut goals. I was sitting in on Marie's conversations that morning and as the first hour of "intake" ended we met Kirsten in the hallway on our way towards the coffee area to make coffee. Kirsten was recounting a meeting she had just had to Caroline, a caseworker who was not part of the project group.

Kirsten: I have just had a very uncomfortable conversation with a citizen. She was very upset about being drafted into the project. She is suffering from a stress-related condition and already does everything she can to get back to work. She sees a psychologist and a physiotherapist and she goes to the gym regularly. She talks to her doctor once a week ... She did not want to be referred to any "active offer" and she felt that I coerced her into a part-time return to work even though neither she nor her employer think that she is ready ... nor do I for that matter. But she refuses to be referred to activity.

Caroline: What is the purpose of that project again? It cannot be to interfere with the good work people already do?

Kirsten: The worst thing about it is that in terms of the project this will look like a success. She can be pointed out as one of the good examples because she goes back to work to avoid being referred to activity and the project thereby lives up to its goal of making people go back to work sooner.

Marie: This might end up becoming one of those "revolving doors projects" [*svingdørsprojekter*] where people return to us after a brief period of being back to work. I am not sure we can actually see if that happens from the way the registration system is set up.

Once a recipient of sickness benefit had gone back to work full-time their case was closed. If they later reported sick again a new case would start and another eight weeks would pass until they would again be summoned to an "introductory conversation." Marie would often return to this circumstance, unsure whether a person's exit from and re-entry into "the system" would be discernible in the future quantitative evaluation of the project.

Registration

The mismatch between the caseworkers' qualitative experience of the project's effects and the data they typed into the registration system was a recurring concern for them. Earlier that day Marie had stopped by Ida's office to discuss the criteria for exemption from the project. She had just had a meeting with a citizen who suffered from cancer and who was in chemotherapy. The person in question had been happy to join the project so Marie's concern was of a more general kind. Was it acceptable to exempt people with cancer more often than people with other kinds of illnesses? It would not look good in the statistics. This concerned her because one of the other participating municipalities had just been asked by the National Labor Market Authority to do something about the fact that they exempted significantly more people from the intervention group than from the control group. In Marie's opinion it was quite natural that deciding whether to refer a person to a concrete offer of activity as was the case of the intervention group would lead to more exemptions than to merely hypothetically contemplate doing it as in the case of the control group. Nevertheless, the message she read

from the communication was that for statistical reasons the participating municipalities should hold back on exemptions in general.

Back in the corridor that day these problems were only just beginning to arise.
No one responded to Caroline's somewhat rhetorical drawing of attention to the
conflict between the project's overall "purpose" and the "activities" meant to bring
about the fulfillment of this purpose ("*It [the purpose] cannot be to interfere with
the good work people already do?*"). Although fundamental questioning did take
place throughout the implementation of *Active—Back Sooner* of how the "activities" related to the purpose of getting people back to work, such considerations
had to make way for practical problems of a more immediate kind and to which
the caseworkers were sometimes able to come up with solutions. At the moment
it was Kirsten's case that caused trouble and called for a response. The woman
had been drafted into the project and was not "unwell enough" (*dårlig nok*) for
Kirsten to consider exemption, so somehow she had to be kept active ten hours a
week. The caseworkers were soon busily engaged in discussing how they might,
in her case, combine the practicalities of living up to the project design's demand
for activity with something that at least did not "add insult to injury" (*gøre ondt
værre*). I too participated in the discussion and brought up a question that had
also been discussed at the local planning phase, namely the discussions about
whether or not activities initiated by people themselves could count as an "active
offer."

> *Nina*: Why is it again that you cannot include the things she already does in the
> ten hours?
>
> *Kirsten*: You cannot register it.
>
> *Nina*: Why not? It can't be more difficult than showing the receipt from a psy-
> chologist or getting the physiotherapist to sign a piece of paper indicating they
> have been there or getting a note from the gym and so forth?

A brief pause followed in which my suggestion was considered, despite having
been considered and dismissed before. During the first planning meeting back on
14 January, Peter had argued that the ten hours could be put together in whichever way they saw fit. The example he had given was "two hours of preventive
odds and ends [*ting og sager*], a fitness card, and four hours of offers regulated
by the law on active employment effort [*LAB-tilbud*]." On 15 January, when it
was just Ida, Marie, and I who were discussing the project, we had talked about it
again. The problem identified in the discussion then—as now—was the issue of
registration. Could they oblige a fitness center (obviously not part of the public
sector and no "partner" of theirs) to register people's coming and going? And in
the case of the Back Pain Clinic (with which they did have agreements of collaboration), rather than put extra work on the staff there, was it not better to find a
private employment agency that had training facilities and employed physiotherapists and whom they could therefore pay for the extra work? Furthermore, if

they pieced together an offer of ten hours of "odds and ends" they would have to conduct the weekly project conversations themselves—something they wanted to avoid due to time constraints. The willingness to include people's own activities and to use a combination of different "offers" got stalled every time on administrative obstacles. However, this time my concrete proposal to "count" time spent by privately funded psychologists and physiotherapists got blocked on a definitional matter:

Marie: I don't think we are even allowed to count treatment.

Caroline: [Protest] But we *do* refer people to treatment now [referring to the MPD project and the *Back to Work* project].

Marie: No, those are treatment-like offers [*behandlingslignende tilbud*] because we would get into trouble with the health care sector if we began referring people to treatment. ... On the other hand, if it is ultimately the same psychologist it is a rather academic discussion.

Here Marie was simultaneously reminding her colleagues of the legal distinction (only medical doctors can refer people to treatment) and acknowledging that sometimes it seemed a purely analytical distinction. However analytical it was, though, in this case it was an obstacle to counting the hours spent in private pursuit of healing as "activity," even if it had been possible administratively. The National Labor Market Authority had already, unknown to any of us, considered this very question, in a memorandum dated 19 January, 2009, which I read much later. Here they established that only activity initiated by the job centers as a result of the controlled trial could be "counted." Parallel and similar activities initiated by the participant's medical doctors or other parts of the municipalities could not be included (Arbejdsmarkedsstyrelsen 2009b). If at any point the controlled trial could have been said to be a testing of whether "activity" versus "no activity" would lead to a quicker return to work, the decision to exclude (or in some cases substitute as was the case) the treatment and privately sponsored or initiated activities in favor of the courses at the private employment agencies put an end to this ambition. As Ida stated at one point, in reality the project was not an investigation of the usefulness of being active while sick but an investigation of people's ability to benefit from whatever happened to take place at the private employment agencies.

Experience-gathering seminar

No solution was found to the dilemma Kirsten was facing that day in the hallway. She eventually persuaded the woman that her best option would be to return to work ten hours a week. Kirsten told me that in such cases where she pressured people into returning to work or accepting an "offer" of "activity," she was convinced she was doing harm by adding to the source of people's illness (stress, in this case) or possibly prolonging their course of illness. Kirsten was not alone with her preoccupations. If at the trial's launching seminar most municipal case-workers and team leaders had been concerned with questions of the implement-ability of the trial, by the time the National Labor Market Authority hosted an "experience-gathering" seminar the primary concern shared across the participat-ing municipalities was the fact that participation in the trial was compulsory. Back in Ida and Marie's unit in the job center many of the caseworkers were averse to having to ask all the sick people in for the obligatory "introductory conversations" to begin with, and the thought of now furthermore having to refer people suffer-ing from stress, anxiety, or depression, for instance, to a yet unknown offer of at least ten hours' activity a week seemed to many contrary to what they thought of as beneficial to the healing processes of the sick men and women whose cases they worked.

This discomfort had been foreseen by some of the civil servants in the National Labor Market Authority. When they invited the participating municipalities to join them for an "experience-gathering seminar" on 26 January 2009, they had allied themselves with a psychiatrist whose job (according to the program) was to talk about the "experiences with activation[1] of persons with stress / mental con-ditions." Peter encouraged me to accompany Ida and Marie to the seminar which was held in a large meeting room in the National Labor Market Authority. Before inviting the psychiatrist to speak, the Vice Director said:

> V.D.: These people ... a lot of them are not sick because you cannot measure it. They are not sick because you cannot give them a diagnosis. What is wrong is they lack job satisfaction and they feel bad about themselves.[2]

She continued to argue that "really this was no job for the health care sector" and that what was "really missing was solidarity between colleagues." Encouraging people to go home when they were sick was "doing them a disfavor" (gøre dem en bjørnetjeneste). The psychiatrist picked up on this theme:

> Psychiatrist: Where the general practitioners go wrong is when they make the mistake of believing what their patients tell them. You must not make the same mistake because self-devaluation is part of their mental condition.

The day after the "experience-gathering seminar" I met Marie in the coffee area where she was talking to a colleague about the psychiatrist's remark. She turned to me and said in an ironical tone of voice:

> Marie: Is it not true, Nina, that if you have depression it is part of your mental condition to underestimate your own abilities to work? So we shall just exert maximum pressure.

The reason for her irony was, as she had pointed out during the seminar, that this placed people with depression in a catch-22 situation in which their insistence that they were too ill to participate in the trial would just serve to confirm the assumption that they ought to. There was, if the views of the psychiatrist were accepted, no way out as even the general practitioner was not to be trusted. Throughout the planning stages until the beginning of February 2009, by which time few municipalities had had anything but scattered experiences with the project intervention,[3] the tiny Danish adverb "*jo*" (best translated into the English "*after all*" or "*do*" in the sentence "we *do* know") had found its way into most conversations about the project: from the consultant from Danish Industry who said at the "launching seminar" held in December 2008, "after all, it is good to get back to work if you suffer from depression or stress," extending to the caseworkers' own embracing of the exercise agenda: "If it's the back, you benefit from exercise. If it's the psyche, you benefit from exercise. *After all*, it is all connected,"[4] and culminating in the Vice Director's address to the municipalities during the "experience-gathering seminar":

> V.D.: They are not sick after all. They are just really sad. And it is, after all, not a doctor they need but the community. After all, they are not sick but are just going through a rough time. But, after all, that is not the task of the healthcare system.[5]

The tiny adverb *jo* (after all) was forceful. Apart from presuming a shared understanding between the speaker and the listener it erased all doubt about the evidence of the statements and established the assertions as self-evident premises for further discussion. Having spent a couple of weeks alternating between sitting in on the normal conversations in the unit and dealing with the local practicalities of preparing for the project, it was a significant change of registry to listen to the Vice Director of the National Labor Market Authority as she began her address to the municipalities:

> V.D.: Every day 150,000 people stay at home because they are sick. It corresponds to shutting down three municipalities entirely every day … It is expensive for society to have this many people walking about sick and we would rather spend the money on something else.[6]

Gone were the patients with anxiety, depression, or a broken leg, for whom the caseworkers struggled to find a suitable "active offer" and present were again the hypothetical 150,000 people from the Ministry of Employment's analysis report (Beskæftigelsesministeriet, 2008b: 3, my translation), whose return to work would save the public budgets. Here they were cast as a passive resource to be activated in order for money to be spent more wisely. At a discursive level something interesting happened during these hours. It was no longer clear what the purpose of the project was. Was testing whether activity during sickness leads to a quicker return to work the issue? Was it saving the public budgets? Was it collegial solidarity? The gradual discursive multiplication of the project's purposes became even more apparent later in the meeting when the participants split up into groups to facilitate the sharing of preliminary experiences, which were scarce. In the group I joined, one caseworker shared her enthusiasm for the project by telling a story about how she had "overcome the opposition" from one of the participants in the project. It was the case of a young man who had broken his wrist.

> *Caseworker*: He told me he thought the resources in this project would be better used on someone else. He just needed his wrist to heal, he said, and then he would go back to work. But during the conversation he had told me he liked to sing. So I told him that since he liked to sing he might as well spend the time he was on sick leave at a nursing home singing to the elderly.

In this anecdote the purpose of the project seemed to be self-referential. This case-worker's understanding of the purpose seemed to be to get the man into "activity" irrespective of whether this activity would speed up his healing process or whether it was a "preventive or clarifying offer" such as had originally been stated in the *Action Plan on Sickness Benefit*'s proposition 32[7] (Beskæftigelsesministeriet 2008a). In another municipality the caseworkers attached to the project had been trained in "coaching," a popular management trend at that time, and one of the caseworkers, a middle-aged woman, anticipated that the project would be a great opportunity for her to develop her "professional skills."

Competing goals and purposes

With its scientific aspirations the trial was allowed to overrule both the intention in the political agreement *More People in Work* from 2002 (a key policy of the Government), in which it was stressed that any public offer must take into account an individual's needs and preconditions (Regeringen 2002a, my translation), and the overall purpose of the sickness benefit legislation that the municipalities are obliged to assist the person on sickness benefit in recuperating their work-ability as fast as possible. The caseworkers' attempts to maintain the trial's methodological integrity would continue to put it on collision course with a number of other efforts as the months progressed. In April and May, despite Peter's optimistic calculations back in January, it soon became obvious that the 200 people they needed in the intervention group in order to end the trial was a hard number to reach. During these two months, where Ida and Marie were assisted by Sara, Ann, and Klara, therefore, the intake was speeded up. This effort to reach the target size of the intervention group came to overrule both new directives from the National Labor Market Authority and a local organizational effort to improve the quality of the general casework in the Municipality. Firstly, after extended critiquing of the project in the press and Parliament, the Labor Market Authority had in March changed the criteria for exemption. However, as the months progressed and several municipalities lagged behind and had to ask for an extension of the project period, the Labor Market Authority had put pressure on the participating municipalities to finish. As the trial was such a source of stress for the casework-ers this meant that they held back on exemptions in general (and regardless of the exemption criteria) to reach this goal sooner. Secondly, the caseworkers in Peter's teams did in general have too many cases to be able to work them properly. Some had twice the number of cases other municipalities recommended as the maximum any caseworker should work. This was recognized by Peter and also by the Central Administration who, after Ulla had put pressure on them for a long time, had signed a contract with a private employment agency to transfer 2000 cases to them. These cases had to be "new" cases. However, none of the cases assigned to either the control or intervention group of *Active—Back Sooner* could be transferred. Unfortunately the effort to reach the intervention group's target number coincided with the signing of the contract and the caseworkers were unable to transfer the scheduled number of cases which was meant to buy them time for proper casework.

Portrait 6: the productivity of controversy

On 1 April, 2009 I arrived at the trial's midterm seminar in the company of Sara. A large meeting room on the ground floor in the National Labor Market Authority was set with six long tables placed perpendicular to a wall on which two large identical power point shows were blown up. "Well, I'll be damned," said Sara and raised her eyebrows as she read the words on the screen closest to us:

PRESS COVERAGE
DR P1 Orientation accuses the controlled trial of:
- being illegal and without basis in the law
- sanctioning recipients of sickness benefit without legal basis
- being against the European Human Rights Convention

"DR P1 Orientation" (the accuser in my translation of the power point slide) is a daily, independent analytical radio program characterized by extensive background stories on contemporary national and international questions. The legality of *Active—Back Sooner* had been questioned by several legal experts through a series of the program's radio features, the first of which was aired 5 March, 2009. The features were part of a series of critical programs, all looking at the Ministry of Employment, and were made by a reporter from Danish Radio's Program 1. The reporter thought of the programs as "constitutional radio," by which he aimed to examine the Minister of Employment's relationship to the "separation of powers"[8] (*magtens tredeling*) (Tynell 2009: 2). A few months later, this series of programs helped him win the highly prestigious Danish prize for critical journalism, *Cavling Prisen*. When I interviewed him about his involvement in the legal controversy a few weeks after the midterm seminar, he told me his persistent interest in the legal basis for carrying out an experiment such as *Active—Back Sooner* was due to a "democratic instinct." There had been a significant change, he had observed, in the way public debates were carried out.

> *Reporter*: It is no longer a place where you discuss what you mean or what you think is right. It has become a claim game about who can describe reality in a convincing manner. And often, when you have your description of "reality"

the solution follows naturally. If I claim in a convincing way that some research shows that "this" helps, then it appears evident that we must also do it.

What resulted from this tendency, he had observed, was that politicians had stopped arguing for their particular politics. As, for instance, in the case of the recipients of sickness benefit, they no longer took their time to explain why they thought making demands of them was a good idea, they merely pointed to "evidence." This became a democratic problem, he thought, because most people did not understand the "evidence" and so were cut off from participating in the public debate. This was where he saw his role as a reporter and "watch-dog of democracy."

> *Reporter*: The political arena has been substituted—as I see it—by evidence battles. Who can document what? ... So I feel it is my job to sort out the technicalities. What do we know? What don't we know? Where is there doubt? And then I leave it to other people to discuss it.

If discussion had been his objective, he had certainly achieved it. At the midterm seminar the National Labor Market Authority had dedicated the opening address to a summary and subsequent rejection of the points of criticism that had been raised by the legal experts in his broadcasts. His programs had also been the subject of much discussion back at the job center.

The critique

The first mentioning of the critique of the project at the job center had taken place a good three weeks earlier over a beer after work on Friday 6 March the day after the first feature was broadcast. A caseworker from one of the other units had said:

> I hear this crap about us being part of this crap project where sick people are being sent to work? I was listening to the radio last night and was thinking what a crazy idea it was. Then I come to work today to find out we're a part of it.

However, the first real discussion among the caseworkers in the project group took place some days later on 10 March. This was the day after the reporter informed listeners, in his second broadcast, that there was presently a majority in Parliament against the continuation of *Active—Back Sooner*.

In these first two features the issue the reporter addressed was whether or not the Minister of Employment had bypassed Parliament in launching an intervention for which there was (yet) no legal basis (there would be if the revised sickness benefit legislation was approved). A group of the caseworkers (Caroline, Jo, Marie, Kirsten, and Ida) met in the corridor outside Kirsten's office. Neither Ida nor Marie had heard the program while both Jo (one of the more experienced caseworkers) and I had heard the feature on the radio the night before. According to Jo, the issue had also been raised in the evening news and we tried to recount the critique as best we could. When announcing the controlled trial the Ministry of Employment had referred to a paragraph in the Law on Active Employment Effort as their legal basis. Since the people involved in the project were only subject to the Law on Sickness Benefit this was a problem: it is not legally possible to argue for the legitimacy of an intervention based on a paragraph in a law that does not regulate to the area you are addressing. The objections raised in the features were, therefore, firstly that the project was illegal; secondly, that the Minister of Employment was behaving as if the revised sickness benefit legislation had already been approved and thereby in effect was bypassing the Parliament.

The timing of the critique was particularly interesting since the revised law on sickness benefit would be formally introduced to Parliament on 12 March, two days later, and a parliamentary rejection of *Active—Back Sooner* could be a forewarning that the three obligatory readings the legislation would have to go through before it could be adopted would not go smoothly. The National Labor Market Authority was quick to recognize the problem with the legal basis and issued a new "promulgation"[9] [*bekendtgørelse*], this time finding its legal basis in the Law on Sickness Benefit. This, however, did not put an end to the questioning of the *Active—Back Sooner*'s legality. A highly esteemed lecturer of law who specialized in the Law on Sickness Benefit argued that the paragraph which they now used to argue for the legality of conducting a controlled trial had originally been added to the Law on Sickness Benefit in order to pave way for experiments with digital administration and for municipal following-up in the cases. Experimenting with referral to activity of the kind involved in *Active—Back Sooner*, he argued, was too far from the law's original intention to allow for its legality. A professor in Social Law furthermore pointed out that a project that experimented with people's entitlement to public benefits, such as sickness benefit, and discriminated between citizens based on objective criteria such as their birth year was not only without legal warrant but was, furthermore, in conflict with the European Human Rights Convention.

Kirsten too had heard the features on the radio and told her colleagues that she had asked Peter for permission to leave the project group. She had had her doubts about the project all along and now that its legality was being questioned, she no longer wanted to be part of it. In the corridor on 10 March the discussion continued. Jo and Caroline were puzzled about the whole affair.

> *Jo*: How come they [the National Labor Market Authority] haven't checked this already?

> *Caroline*: One would think that when you launch a project of this kind—and surely they must have been able to foresee the criticism it would invite—that they would make dead sure they had their legal basis straight.

Throughout the discussion Ida had been quiet, leaning against the brick wall. She was distraught and later commented that this was the kind of thing that made her feel like a mere "foot soldier."

> *Ida*: You don't question every single thing you are asked to do. You assume that
> when you are asked to do something things are in order.

Kirsten's pending exit from the project group and other colleagues' overtly expressed criticism of the intervention made the situation uncomfortable for Ida and Marie. It foregrounded the worry they had had all along that they were pressuring people to return to work earlier than was good for them. They worried, once again, that they were forcing people to take part in activities they did not feel ready for at the threat of losing their income. Now it seemed that what they had done did not just feel wrong but was possibly illegal. Marie took a quick decision later that day and went to Ida's office where she and I were currently discussing the situation. They would not, Marie said, force anybody into the project after the message that Parliament was uncertain about the legality. It would not be good for those citizens who might have heard the radio programs and it would not be good for Ida and Marie and their peace of mind either. However, they would not simply stop working on the project.

> *Marie*: What we will do is benefit from the project while it is still running and
> only make referrals in cases where people might *actually* benefit from it and are
> themselves interested.

I left the municipal offices early that day and returned to my office in the capital for a meeting. In the afternoon, I ran into Lea, the civil servant from the Ministry of Employment, who had been in charge of the coordination of the *Action Plan on Sickness Benefit*. She asked me if I had heard the news and shook her head in amazement that things were not in order legally. She had herself not been closely involved in the writing of the legal promulgation of the project and concluded that in the future they (the Department of Employment) would have to monitor the work they did in the National Labor Market Authority much more closely. (Indeed, about six months later when I spent time in one of the offices in the National Labor Market Authority and the information spread that a new, and in some respects similar, project was being prepared, the civil servants from the Department of Employment were on the phone to the National Labor Market Authority immediately to make sure they would run all legal paperwork past them.)

That afternoon in March when I spoke to Lea, I asked her about the probability that the project would be closed since this was the current concern in the job center. Despite the features on the radio and in the evening news, Lea found it hard to believe that there would really be a majority against the project in Parliament. The support had been "broad" when the *Action Plan* had been approved and she could not imagine that the coalition partners (most specifically, the Danish People's Party) would bail out just before the law was about to be presented to Parliament:

> *Lea*: I imagine that as we speak they are in a crisis meeting. The Minister has most
> likely summoned his coalition partners [*forligsparter*] in an attempt to reach an

agreement. I cannot imagine they will stop the project altogether ... perhaps what they will do is drop the part about sanctioning.

Had the participation in the controlled trial become voluntary, Ida and Marie would have welcomed it. Marie often said that the obligation to participate undermined the entire purpose of the project; the moment people realized they were forced to participate most, as Marie put it, "acquired a mental blockage." While they waited for the National Labor Market Authority's response to the critique in the days following the initial features, Peter decided that Marie's course of action was the proper one: they were not going to penalize anybody who refused to participate by cutting off their sickness benefit until there was absolute clarity about the question of the legality of the project. Usually Peter received what he referred to as a "steady stream of emails" from the Employment Region, which was the organizational arm of the National Labor Market Authority through which communication with the municipalities passed. Recently, Peter said, they had been "conspicuously quiet" and he interpreted this as an expression of uncertainty about the legal basis of the project on their behalf. A week later he finally received an email in which the National Labor Market Authority established that the project would continue, that the existing legal framework was sufficient, and that the caseworkers should sanction against (stop the sickness benefit of) people who refused to participate in the project.

If the civil servants in the National Labor Market Authority had hoped the debate was over they were wrong. The reporter was driven by what he described, when I pressed him on the reasons for his deep involvement in the case, as "a feel for the logical flaw." He was not convinced by the National Labor Market Authority's reasoning and felt that something did not add up. Over the following month and a half he produced five more features in which he meticulously picked apart the civil servants' answers and (later) the arguments of the Junior Counsel to the Treasury.[10] The latter became involved when the National Labor Market Authority requested that they investigate whether or not the caseworkers could issue sanctions against those who refused to participate in the project and then later whether the project in itself was legal.

The multiple lives of Active—Back Sooner

The spring of 2009 was a period that would later be remembered with anything but fondness by Jytte, the lawyer from the National Labor Market Authority who in December 2007 had written ten little proposals over a cup of tea, one of which had in time evolved into Active—Back Sooner. It became her job to respond to the critique and rectify what her recently employed Head of Office, Henry, described as a "foot fault" [fodfejl]. When I spoke to him in a break during the midterm seminar, Henry commented to me that he and Jytte had been working around the clock to keep up with the extra work that this "foot fault" had caused. Half a year later, in the autumn of 2009, when I was allowed to follow the work in his office, he remembered the period as follows:

Henry: Back in the spring so many employees here in the office were sick. Eventually the only lawyer left was Jytte. I had to plan each day hour by hour every morning and step in and work it out myself as best as I could. I negotiated deadlines with the Department [of Employment] every day. It was a tough period. I was so afraid of losing Jytte—that she would quit or simply break down.

When I interviewed Jytte at the end of May, the day before the law was about to go through its second reading in Parliament, she summed up the period thus:

Jytte: It was really, really, really expensive. I have no idea how much it has cost us economically but we are talking several hundred thousand kroner [100,000 DKR ≈ £10,000]. I would get sick if I were to calculate how much time we have spent correcting these errors. There has been evening work, weekend work, and work during the Easter holidays. We had two inquests [*samrådsspørgsmål*] and one acute inquest [*hasteforespørgsel*] in Parliament, and numerous questions from Parliament, and we have had to deliver material to the media [*pressen*] as well. Enormous amounts of work ... And I did not know at what moment I would simply break down.

According to one of the civil servants in the Ministry of Employment, the original "promulgation of the project" (*forsøgsbekendtgørelsen*) had been "a potboiler" (*venstrehåndsarbejde*). There had been little time to write it and it had not been given priority. The same went, according to some, for the law itself, the first version of which had been sent to "public hearing"[11] (*offentlig høring*) in December 2008. One of the civil servants attributed the hurry with which it had been written to the fact that the Labor Market Commission's recommendations—which had been hurried along for the sake of the tripartite negotiations in the autumn of 2008, and which had been the subject of great political anticipations—"collapsed like a house of cards." This was because many of the recommendations lacked what they referred to as "political saleability" (*politisk gangbarhed*). One such was the Commission's recommendation that in order to secure the labor force the politicians would have to restrict the right to early retirement benefit. "The law was written very quickly," one civil servant commented, "they [the politicians] needed a success and they needed it quickly."

At the midterm seminar on 1 April, Sara and I sat down by one of the long tables. Some weeks earlier she had been substituted for Kirsten as a member of the project group, along with another colleague, Ann. The Vice Director of the National Labor Market Authority opened the day by offering her assessment of the critique as "a bit of harassment and lots of politics."[12] She went through the critique point by point while I took notes as fast as I could. According to these notes, she ended her address as follows:

V.D.: As I said, this is about politics. The most recent suggestion is that it [the trial] is against human rights. It is so far out. It does not even border on the question of human rights and when I went to inform the Minister and some of the political spokesmen they did not take it especially seriously.[13]

Nevertheless, many of the municipal caseworkers did. The coffee break was buzzing with disapproval of the Vice Director's handling of the question. One caseworker called it "unbecoming" (*uklædeligt*), another "condescending" (*nedladende*), a third "unprofessional" (*useriøst*). Marie (who had come to the meeting a bit late and joined me and Sara in the break) was provoked by the V.D.'s approach to the legal issue, and summed up her assessment like this:

> *Marie*: Much of what she ignores as "politics" is legislative questions. She stands up there and laughs at the critique. It is disrespectful to our citizens.

What allowed the Vice Director of the National Labor Market Authority to treat the critique more lightly than did Marie and some of the other caseworkers from other municipalities was the fact that they were no longer talking about the same intervention. The Vice Director was talking about an evidence-based effort carefully designed to assist people in going back to work through individual offers that addressed their specific needs. Marie was talking about a practical reality in which she had to force people to participate in activities that bore no resemblance to the sort of interventions described in any of the formal designs. The version of *Active—Back Sooner* which the Vice Director knew was the one she had herself participated in constructing on paper, and which now existed only in the formal project design. The version of *Active—Back Sooner* that Marie, Ida, Ann, and Sara knew was one that sometimes helped people, sometimes served to substitute people's individual plans with a municipal generalized offer, and sometimes seemed to hurt, stress, and violate them.

The dissolution and multiplication of purpose

At the midterm seminar the Vice Director proceeded to make clear that due to the criticism in the press, and the preliminary findings of a phone survey conducted among the caseworkers by the consultancy company Rambøll Management, some adjustments had been made to the project design pertaining to the content of the intervention. In the case of the weekly conversation with those who had returned to work partially it would now be possible to conduct the conversations over the phone instead of in person. People who planned to return to full-time work within two weeks of the first conversation could be exempted from the project altogether. Finally, those who had a clear treatment plan could be exempted. If the local version of the controlled trial had been undermined in practice by the logistic difficulties back at the job center during the planning meetings back in January (for instance by the absence of any homogenous "normal intervention"), it was now undermined officially in theory by the inconsistency in the given "intervention." One of the civil servants from the National Labor Market Authority expressed her regret:

> What a controlled trial like this one can be used for is to bust some myths and make us cleverer. If we think this makes sense then we must test it and dare see

that it might not make sense. I therefore regret that these adjustments have been made.

A further, semantic change occurred during the meeting and it seemed that the purpose was no longer to see *if* activity was beneficial, but to examine *how* it was beneficial. On one power point slide from the midterm seminar it read:

> The experiment has as its purpose to examine *how* recipients of sickness benefit can return to work quicker. (My translation and italics.)

If the purpose seemed to have changed, it had not done so once and for all, as will be clear from the following. I had been puzzled about the relationship between the controlled trial and the revised sickness benefit legislation before but it was only at the midterm seminar that the realization really sunk in that the revised sickness benefit legislation was actually due for its first reading in Parliament two days later and most likely would go through the required three readings and have been approved long before the project was completed. I had been momentarily confused about the order in which things took place before, but by now it was as if the whole purpose of the project began to escape me. I was not alone in being confused. The following exchange took place during a coffee break at the midterm seminar:

> *Caseworker A*: How come the law is being been sent to Parliament before the project is over?

> *Caseworker B*: I have been thinking about that too. It is rather peculiar.

The political opposition in Parliament was quick to catch this apparent flaw in the logic. During one of the interpellations caused by the reporter's broadcasts the Minister was asked to clarify this by a member of the opposition, Line Barfod:

> *L.B.*: It is … difficult to believe that the purpose of the controlled trial [*forsøg*] is to consider whether to adopt the legislation because in that case you would have delayed the law. So my … question is how the Minister's argument—that this is a controlled trial with the purpose of considering the legislation—corresponds with having already initiated the legislative work and with the fact that this will most likely be approved before the controlled trial is over and the results of it are known. (Arbejdsmarkedsudvalget 2009: 4)[14]

The Minister of Employment did not answer this question, which was raised by Line Barfod at four different instances during the interpellation. However, he did make it clear that he regarded the purpose of the controlled trial as answering two central questions:

> *M.E.*: If we make a more intensified intervention does it then save more people from being ostracized from the labor market and, secondly, of all the different tools we have can we then deduce if any work better than others? (ibid.: 33)[15]

It was as if the purpose had simultaneously dissolved and multiplied. Line Barfod's question could not be answered because it assumed a coherence that was nonexistent. *Active—Back Sooner* was not and had at no point been an unambiguous intervention. The project was born out of several hopes and considerations that had guided the crafting of the *Action Plan on Sickness Benefit*. There was the caseworkers' dream of a meaningful work life, the politicians' need to secure sufficient labor power and save the public budgets, the Minister's will to craft a plan that was endorsed by as many of the affected parties as possible, and the Permanent Secretary's ambition to work in an "evidence-based" manner. If these agendas had seemed for a moment to find a common ground in the *Action Plan* and in the project design for *Active—Back Sooner*, the concerns had not merged into a homogenous effort but continued to coexist and pull the intervention in different directions.

As if that was not enough, *Active—Back Sooner* had continued to take on agendas long after it had been approved as proposition 32 in the *Action Plan*. Considerations for legal and scientific consistency and administrative practicalities had been added to the forces that pulled *Active—Back Sooner* apart and caused it to multiply. During the month of March the various memorandums produced in response to the criticism raised in the media had furthermore led to a multiplication of the official formulations of *Active—Back Sooner*'s purpose. A few examples to illustrate this are given. The first is from the original politically adopted *Action Plan on Sickness Benefit* (29 September, 2008). The purposes of the experiment are:

> To *test how the usage of active offers* according to the law on active employment effort and individual offers of a preventive and clarifying nature ... *can further work retention* and a quick return to work.
>   To *provide knowledge about* which interventions work. (Beskæftigelsesministeriet 2008a, my translation and italics)

The next line is from a memorandum from the National Labor Market Authority to the Minister of Employment concerning the background and practice of *Active—Back Sooner* (10 March, 2009):

> The purpose of the experiment is *to bring the individual back to work sooner*. (Arbejdsmarkedsstyrelsen 2009c, my translation and italics)

Already with these three purposes it is hard to fathom a single intervention which could deliver. Testing *how* rather than *if* active offers could be beneficial already calls for a much more explorative intervention than what is possible within the framework of a controlled trial. Providing knowledge *about* which interventions work would ideally require a desk review of a number of controlled trials and finally, if the purpose was to simply bring the individual back to work sooner, then an anything-goes approach would most likely have been more effective. However, more purposes were soon added to the intervention. The following line is from the Junior Counsel to the Treasury's official answer to the question regarding the legality of sanctioning, on 12 March, 2009:

The project is a controlled trial, which shall *make it possible to measure the effect* of an active intervention, including preventive and clarifying offers. (Kammeradvokaten 2009: 3, my translation and italics)

According to an excerpt from a memorandum from the National Labor Market Authority to the Minister of Employment (on 16 March, 2009) regarding the legality of *Active—Back Sooner*, the purpose of the experiment is:

objective and well-founded [*sagligt og velbegrundet*], namely to secure the recipients of sickness benefit's [*sygemeldte borgeres*] connection to the labor market. (Arbejdsmarkedsstyrelsen 2009d)

A memorandum from the National Labor Market Authority to the Minister of Employment (17 March, 2009) concerning the European Human Rights Convention and its relationship to the "sickness benefit trial" (*sygedagpengeforsøget*) arguing for the legitimacy of the intervention's purpose stated:

The purpose of the experiment is to *test how an intervention can be planned* more concretely so that it, in the best way possible, supports the recipients of sickness benefit's [*sygemeldtes*] return to work.

The experiment must ... furthermore *provide knowledge about* which offers and which active intervention will assist the work retention of the recipient of sickness benefit.

The experiment must furthermore *contribute to increase the quality of the municipal follow-up* in sickness benefit cases for the benefit of the recipient of sickness benefit, the companies and the society as a whole. (Arbejdsmarkedsstyrelsen 2009e, my translation and italics)

And finally, a memorandum from the National Labor Market Authority to the Ministry of Employment concerning the legal basis for economic sanction against those recipients who refuse to participate in *Active—Back Sooner* (31 March, 2009):

The purpose is *to document if* an early and more intensive intervention towards the target group can further the chances of returning [more quickly] to work. (Arbejdsmarkedsstyrelsen 2009f, my translation and italics)

The distance and irreconcilability between, on the one hand, the hypothetical and rather omnipotent *Active—Back Sooner* and on the other hand, the practical implementation of the local *Active—Back Sooner* expressed in the individual caseworker's decision-making can be illustrated by the juxtaposition between two explanations stemming from the spring of 2009. In the first quote the Minister is addressing Parliament; in the second, one of the municipal caseworkers is addressing a privately employed social worker at ENGA charged with the actual provision of the intervention's content:

Minister of Employment: [1 April] The intervention in this trial [*Active—Back Sooner*] is planned according to the individual's preconditions, the individual's need, the individual's health and the individual's resources. (Arbejdsmarkedsudvalget 2009: 14)

Caseworker to private employment agency : [4 May] It works like this: Unless this hurts the citizens or is completely hopeless and makes no sense at all we are bound hands and feet to offer them ten hours of activity a week for four months.

Through the ongoing productions of memorandums and public documents—meant to argue the case for the legality and feasibility of the project in response to the criticisms—the civil servants in the National Labor Market Authority had constructed a more and more all-encompassing *Active—Back Sooner*. It was the multi-tool of interventions: It could test how activity could further work retention and a quick return to work; provide knowledge about which of the interventions worked; make it possible to measure the effect of that kind of intervention; secure the recipient's connection to the labor market; test how an intervention could best be planned; increase the quality of the municipal follow-up for the benefit of society as a whole; and finally, it would document if such an intervention actually worked. It could do all these things at once because the *Active—Back Sooner* which had all these capacities led a purely discursive existence.

Analysis: absurdity is a perspective that appreciates the sum-total

In David Mosse's book *Cultivating development* (2005) he analyses the crafting and implementation of a central piece of UK aid policy. Mosse was himself one of the consultants who partook in the drafting of the policy which was for a time praised as a model example for how to design sound and scientifically based interventions. "As consultants" he writes, "we appeared to have done our job well, to have produced a singular knowledge system providing a coherent project analysis. In fact, there was no such system. We had no single view" (Mosse 2005: 34). As a text, Mosse argues, a policy must, in its primary stages, primarily meet the task of communicating a convincing argument that mediates the different interests and professions involved in its making (Mosse 2005: 35). A policy, he continues, might therefore most accurately be described in its design phase as a "site for coalition building." The "success" of a policy depends on its ability to win the support of as many of the stakeholders as possible and to find a phrasing that both embraces and conceals irreconcilable interests and points of view (ibid.).

Borrowing the words of David Mosse, if *Active—Back Sooner* had been a "site of coalition building" (Mosse 2005: 35) and had been able to mobilize political support, as we saw in Chapter 1, as a guiding star for practical decision-making it had proved slippery. If diverging interests had momentarily found a common ground in a formal project design for a controlled trial, they had proceeded to pull the project apart into separate versions that were adapted, stretched, or changed in response to the requests made of "it" in particular organizational environments or by the discussions "it" became involved in. Some of these versions could be expanded, as we have seen, ad infinitum since they operated in a purely discursive realm while other versions, by virtue of being confronted with circumstances or people who were impossible to ignore or resolve in speech, were adapted (momentarily or once and for all) or simply ignored.

Against the backdrop of the legal controversy it became clear that *Active— Back Sooner* never had been and never would be a uniform intervention. It was a controlled trial, an exploratory project, an attempt to be up front with the development, a source of distress for the recipients of sickness benefit and its planners alike. It was an occasion on which enormous amounts of money and man power were spent, yet it was an attempt to reduce public expenses. It was an attempt to make casework meaningful yet at the same time an occasion for the caseworkers to confront the meaninglessness of their work. Despite the caseworkers' persistent attempts to be loyal to the project design it was difficult—not only because of its irreconcilability with the organizational reality, or because its underlying assumption that something helpful could be identified and provided proved to be wrong, but also because of its official inconsistency: which of its multiple purposes were the caseworkers meant to work towards?

Less than a month into the trial's implementation phase a number of different ways in which the caseworkers could construe their decisions as meaningful and sensible had emerged. Seen from an economic perspective it could be a waste of money to refer a participant to activity when a clear date of return was lurking on the horizon, while from the point of view of "learning something" for future use it might be argued to be a sensible way for citizens to spend their sick leave. From an administrative point of view it would make sense to get rid of the cases through referrals as soon as possible to avoid the weekly conversation considered by all parties involved to be pointless. Yet in terms of what would actually help the recovery of the sick person the most, leaving them completely in peace might be the best course of action. Making people return to work at least ten hours a week was the top priority intervention-wise and would statistically be construed as a policy success. Yet if going back to work prolonged the individual's recovery it would work against both national labor market policy and legislation in force.

Despite the caseworkers' persistent attempts to be loyal to the project design this was difficult because the trial was in constant conflict with other political, legal, and organizational priorities and finally because the formulation and discussion of the trials overall purpose continued throughout the implementation phase: by late May the trial officially in circulation had no less than two sets of exemption criteria and at least eight different formulations of its overall purpose, some of which were mutually exclusive. For the caseworkers there was no clear hierarchy between these different ways of framing their decisions. This point is important because the absence of a clear goal or purpose hierarchy left the caseworkers disoriented and the sheer number of often contradictory and conflicting goals was exactly what led them to describe their work as meaningless, and to work harder to make their work seem sensible.

What we see here is that the empirical grounds for the individual's experience of "purposelessness," "lack of expediency," "meaninglessness," and that things "make no sense"—what I call with an umbrella term the experience of "absurdity"—has nothing to do with lack of purpose, sense, or meaning, and everything to do with an excess of it. What people do, then, when they describe their work as meaningless or purposeless is in fact that they step out of the flow of engaged decision-making, pause, and reflect upon the sum total of the organizational work they take part in. What the appreciation of absurdity may inform us about is therefore not the lack of internal logics according to which specific routines and processes are ordered. Rather, it tells us about the collective effects of all the organizational logics combined. We would therefore miss important insights about the working of complex inter-organizational implementation were we to regard this calling attention to the absurdity of things as primarily a mode in which people make ironic remarks, express dissent, or complain about their work. Rather we should regard it as a highly analytical mode of addressing the distortive effects of the work they are pursuing.

Notes

1 "Activation" is a word most often used in connection to political intervention targeting recipients of social security or unemployment benefit. It covers a vast spectrum of activities meant to assist and / or encourage recipients of these public benefits to go back to work and / or away from public benefits.
2 This quote and all other such quotes are from my notebook in which I scribbled hastily as people spoke.
3 During the "experience-gathering seminar" many municipalities were still in the process of finding "active offers" and their experiences were therefore restricted to weekly conversations as few had referred anybody to "activity" yet.
4 This quote stems from one of the interviews my research assistant Rasmus Kolding conducted with caseworkers who were involved in the implementation of *Active—Back Sooner*, in late January 2009.
5 From my notes taken during her address: "Det er jo ikke fordi de er syge. De er bare rigtig kede af det. Og det er jo ikke en læge de har brug for, men fællesskabet. For de er jo ikke syge, de har det bare rigtig hårdt. Men det er jo ikke sundhedsvæsenets opgave."
6 Address to municipalities by the Vice Director of the National Labor Market Authority, 26 January, 2009, private fieldnote.
7 Beskæftigelsesministeriet 2008a, *Konklusionspapir om Handlingsplan om Sygefravær.*
8 The separation of powers refers to the legislative, the executive, and the judicial powers.
9 Some laws entitle the Minister to make modifications in specific areas of regulation without having to go through Parliament. Such specifications are called promulgations.
10 The Junior Counsel to the Treasury is a privately employed lawyer who works as a solicitor for the State.
11 A public hearing is a consultative procedure through which a policy (in this case the planned law) is sent to a group of authorities and interested organizations (in this case, among others, the Danish Association of Social Workers, Local Government Denmark, the Confederation of Danish Employers, the Danish Confederation of Trade Unions, and the Danish Association for the Disabled, who are all encouraged to submit

their written responses to the policy. The authority responsible for the policy is free to ignore the submitted responses.

12 In Danish, "Der har været lidt chikane og meget, meget politik."

13 In Danish, "som sagt, så handler det som politik. Det sidste som har været fremme er, at det skulle være i strid med menneskerettighederne. Det er så langt ude på overdrevet. Det snitter jo ikke engang menneskerettighederne og da jeg var ovre for at orientere ministeren og nogle af de andre politiske ordførere tog de det heller ikke særligt alvorligt."

14 Line Barfod represented the Red-Green Alliance—a union of three former left wing parties. The original sentence in Danish was, according to the official minutes: "Derfor er det svært at tro på, at det her er et forsøg med henblik på at overveje, om man skal lave lovgivning, fordi så ville man have ventet med lovgivningen. Så det er mit andet spørgsmål, hvordan hænger ministerens argument om, at det er et forsøg med henblik på at overveje lovgivningen sammen med, at man allerede har iværksat lovarbejdet og regner med, at det bliver vedtaget før, at forsøget er afsluttet, og man kender resultaterne af det."

15 Original sentence in Danish: "Hvis man laver en intensiveret indsats, redder det så flere fra at blive udstødt af arbejdsmarkedet—og punkt 2—af de forskellige redskaber, vi har, kan man så udlede, at det er nogen, der virker bedre end andre." (CHF: 33)

4

The quest for meaning

Portrait 7 follows *Active—Back Sooner* to one of the private employment agencies. I have given this private employment agency the meaningless acronym ENGA to distinguish it from other private employment agencies. It was here at ENGA that the core delivery of the local version of the trial, the "activities" and the "close follow-up," were meant to take place. We follow here the privately employed social workers as they do their utmost to make something sensible take place in the face of what they find to be utterly pointless referrals from the municipal caseworkers. The final portrait, portrait 8, takes us back to the job center again and describes the time after the revised sickness benefit legislation is adopted and the central elements in the trial became obligatory in all cases. It portrays what happens when the caseworkers and employees are pushed to the limits of their personal capacities to make sense of what is going on and ultimately stop trying. The chapter concludes that the fundamental urge to make sensible decisions, driving the employees to rebel against local directive and agreements, is the very thing that creates the grounds for institutional absurdity while being in itself the only stable source of meaning.

Portrait 7: "bending" the rules and agreements

During one of the meetings between the municipal caseworkers and the private employment agency called ENGA, I had asked Marianne, the team leader of the "sickness benefit team," if I could follow the employees at ENGA who worked with the project. Permission was granted after a formal meeting with Marianne and her director and after the employees attached to the project had given their consent to my presence in their team. On a Monday morning, 31 August, I therefore met Marianne by the back entrance of ENGA where she was waiting for me while smoking and talking to her colleagues as they arrived. ENGA was based in a three storey building not far from the municipal job center, along a road with heavy traffic. The ground floor consisted mainly of practical "workshops" used by other teams who worked with recipients of different social benefits. These people had various problems which were seen by their caseworkers as preventing them from getting a job, and the employees at ENGA were to help overcome these "obstacles" (*barrierer*); some were homeless, some suffered from psychiatric conditions, and some were immigrants who did not speak Danish or had never worked outside their home before. One of these workshops—the central canteen where people received training in order to prepare them for (re)entry into the labor market—was situated on the second floor of the building. This was where Marianne took me when I arrived and where she introduced me to Sofie whose work I would follow the first day. Bypassing the elevator, Sofie then led me up two flights of stairs to the hallway where her office was situated, next to the seminar room where the "sickness benefit group" had most of their "classes." It was here that I had previously met some of Sofie's colleagues in meetings between the employees at ENGA and the municipal caseworkers Marie, Ida, and Sara.

An inkling

Sofie had already set the table with coffee, milk, mugs, sugar, and spoons. As we sat down next to each other at the table she said:

> *Sofie*: What you will observe in just a few minutes is that none of the people who are about to arrive have more than an inkling of why their caseworkers have referred them to us.

Monday morning was when the most recently referred people arrived and were introduced to the "sickness benefit package" to which their municipal caseworkers had referred them in the course of the previous week. However, only a small number of the participants in the "sickness benefit group" had been referred as a result of *Active—Back Sooner*. The "package" had originally been designed to answer the municipal tender on offers to people who were in the process of applying for professional rehabilitation, "flex jobs," or early retirement pensions. People who had been referred to ENGA in the previous weeks were in the gym on the ground floor where the physiotherapist gave classes in "relaxation exercises," and they could use the fitness machines available. While Sofie and I waited for the new participants to show up she told me a bit about her work:

> *Sofie*: Most people have been sick for about 52 weeks when they come here.[1] Their caseworkers have referred them to us directly without previous meetings so they often think we are the Municipality.

Therefore, Sofie told me, staff usually had to set aside some time to explain the difference between the Municipality and a private employment agency, and the kind of involvement and responsibility either organization had with regard to their case.

> *Sofie*: And most usually we do not know a thing about them when they arrive. We just know their name and the overall purpose of their referral. At the moment practically everybody in the "sickness benefit group" is here with the state purpose "to apply for jobs" and a few are here to "train for a stable attendance."

My hypothesis is that many of the newly referred won't show up today. This is how it usually goes.

At ten minutes past 9am, the scheduled hour of arrival, no one had arrived. Sofie got up and left me in the seminar room and went down to the reception to see if anybody had left messages with the receptionist. A few minutes later she came back up the stairs and walked straight to her office to return some phone calls from people who had not been able to attend. At a quarter past nine, a young woman, Nadja, arrived and Sofie returned to the seminar room to start the introduction:[2]

Sofie: So you have been referred here by your caseworker for six weeks.

Nadja: She told me four weeks.

Sofie: OK. In my contract it says six but I will check up on that. Is being here at 9am a problem for you?

Nadja: No … well usually I take the children to the day care at 9.30 so I have just got to change that rhythm. It won't be a problem.

Sofie: OK. Has your caseworker informed you why you are here?

Nadja: No, I don't know anything [laughs nervously].

Sofie handed the woman a document with her name on it and the purpose and period of her referral. The document contained no further personal information since it would later be put into a ring binder that stayed permanently in the seminar room and was accessible to all. The ring binder was a recent invention of the employees and had two related purposes. Firstly, employees at ENGA had found that the participants referred to the "sickness benefit package" repeatedly forgot why they were there and for how long: these papers were meant to remind them. The second purpose, in continuation of this, was to enable to the participants to work out/develop their own specific goals based on the overall purpose of their referral that was formulated by the municipal caseworkers and typed into the electronic contracts. These overall purposes could be, as Sofie had mentioned, "to train for stable attendance" or "to apply for jobs" or—as it turned out to be in the case of Nadja—to "find a place for an internship."

Having explained this to Nadja, Sofie now proceeded to tell her about the "sickness benefit package" in which she had been enrolled. When Sofie's introduction of the weekly program to Nadja was about to end she asked me if I had any questions. I did. Nadja had been referred to ENGA as a result of having been drafted into *Active—Back Sooner*. Ideally her referral should therefore have been the result of a match between what she needed and what ENGA could provide.

Nina: Did your caseworker tell you why she chose to refer you to ENGA specifically? Were you given options?

Nadja: No. She just said "you receive sickness benefit so you have to go there."

Nadja's experience would turn out to be representative of all the people in the "sickness benefit group" I spoke to at ENGA. None of them knew why they were at ENGA apart from in vague terms ("I guess they sent me here so that I will go back to work sooner"). They did not know why ENGA had been chosen or what the specific purpose of their referral was. This went both for people who, knowingly or not, were there as a result of having been drafted into *Active—Back Sooner,* and for those who were there for any other reason, for instance Irene, an elderly woman, who for various health-related issues could no longer work full-time:

> *Irene*: I thought I was being sent to a place where I had to work eight hours a day. I don't know why she [the caseworker] didn't just tell me what it was like. It is nice here. I was so afraid.

Irene's confusion was not a unique example. Later in the afternoon, during a session where recent and not-so-recent participants were united in one big group, Sofie asked them to evaluate the content of the "sickness benefit package" for my benefit. During the conversation a middle-aged woman, Louise, expressed her fear of the impending closure of her case which would mean she could no longer receive sickness benefit.

> *Louise*: It is nice being here but I can't help thinking what is it that is supposed to come out of it? How is it that the Municipality can decide that I have to go on social security [*kontanthjælp*]? I do not understand how the Municipality can decide that I am not sick. I know I'm ill and my doctor says I am ill. How can they just decide I'm not? I'm afraid they will just let go of me.

Louise's quote here was pregnant with confusion: She was terrified of "ending up" on social security (that is, on the dole). While sickness benefit was, by the recipients I spoke to, depicted as a public benefit one had a right to and which one had earned through long years of paying tax, social security was, on the other hand, regarded as "sponging off society." Loiuse did not understand why she had been referred to ENGA; while it was a nice place to be she failed to see how it would resolve her overall problem—namely that she was about to lose her entitlement to sickness benefit despite still being ill. She also did not understand why she was no longer entitled to sickness benefit, or the scenario of Municipal caseworker versus her GP in relation to her status as "sick."

Sofie, unlike many of the municipal caseworkers who referred people to ENGA, was a professionally trained social worker. Much of her time at ENGA, I gradually found out, consisted in trying to explain the sickness benefit legislation and the legal background for the Municipal caseworkers' decisions. In this case she tried to explain the criteria for prolongation of sickness benefit to Louise. I give below a simplified summary of Sofie's explanation.

> *Sofie*: If all possibilities for treatment are exhausted and there is no progress in your case then they cannot prolong it. They will not just close it [what Louise

had called "to let go" of her]. They will have to make an assessment of what will happen to you next.

Louise had received sickness benefit for more than two years without hearing from the Municipality. Clearly a mistake, since by law the Municipality was obliged to contact people after eight weeks of receiving sickness benefit. In the end she had contacted them herself and asked if they could help her. Normally, Louise would have lost her right to sickness benefit after 52 weeks unless her caseworkers had decided to prolong it based on the assessment that she met the legal criteria for prolongation. Since the case was more than 52 weeks old and no assessment of the prolongation had been made her case should have been shut long ago. However, in cases such as Louise's that had been lost in the electronic case management system the municipal caseworkers would, in recognition of their mistake of not having contacted the recipient within the stipulated time, make a so-called "administrative prolongation," which was not strictly legal.

Back at the job center, I had in fact been present when Peter informed the caseworkers during a team meeting that on 20 May, 2009, the National Social Appeals Board had published a report in which they described "administrative prolongations" as a nationally widespread practice and stressed that it was not in accordance with the law (Ankestyrelsen 2009: 34). This was a particularly problematic directive for the caseworkers since the local case management system was defunct and they struggled to keep track of the citizens during this period. Often they would have people come in for "introductory conversations" who, like Louise, had already received sickness benefit for more than a year. In this case they had referred Louise to ENGA so that she could be helped find a suitable work place where she could get a traineeship which would hopefully help her back into the labor market. If it did not work out her municipal caseworker would shut her case—this was Sofie's understanding—and Louise would be obliged to apply for social security if she could not support herself without any income.

The purpose of referral

As we know from the earlier portraits, sometimes the municipal caseworkers referred the recipients of sickness benefit to the private employment agencies in the hope that there would be people there who would take proper care of the cases which they themselves did not have the time to work on properly. This absence—in some of the cases—of any specific purpose behind the referrals did come through in the contracts ENGA received. To recapitulate, here is a brief dialogue from the Municipality where Ena was about to write the purpose of the referral into a contract with ENGA:

> *Ena*: And now I have to figure out what to write ... Oh well, they know him [Jens] already. I'll write: "clarification continues and Jens is expected to return to work by the end of the contract."

Nina: Do you reckon he will benefit from another four weeks?

Ena: No ... But he has applied for professional rehabilitation so until that begins ... I don't know ... He does not like it there.

Nina: Do you think it will help him return to work quicker?

Ena: No, I do not think so. Maybe if he does some physical exercise.

One day at ENGA I was sitting next to Marianne as she accessed the internet-based device through which the municipal caseworkers sent the contracts. She checked her computer three times a day to see if any new contracts had arrived for the "sickness benefit package" which was her responsibility. She could distinguish her contracts from those directed towards other groups and "packages" (for example, the "motivation package" or the "job search package") by a number attached to the heading of the contract. In order to demonstrate to me how the referral system worked, she opened a contract that had just arrived:

Marianne: OK let's see ... This is a classic, actually. Here is a contract where the only information they give us is "clarification." I mean, this person has already been here for three months without making any progress and now he has been sent back to us again with no directives but the message "clarification."

Nina: Why do you think that is?

Marianne: One explanation could be that the caseworkers have no idea what to do with the person in question. Or maybe the caseworker has just been employed recently and has no idea what we need to know.

Nina: Do you write back to them then?

Marianne: No, I don't, although I agree that it would be appropriate. But there is no device in this portal for communication between me and the caseworker.

Nina: Why don't you just send an email?

Marianne: Because the contract starts as of today and I know that Karen [a job consultant at ENGA] will keep an eye on this one. She knows him from before. I believe there might be a different offer that this person could benefit from and I think maybe we will try to get the caseworker to change the contract.

[Pause in which Marianne accepts the contract.]

Marianne: I will show you another contract which I declined earlier today. In this case, I can see that we have already got one contract going for this person. It is meant to run for three months but the person in question has yet to show up a single time. Why the caseworker then chooses to buy another three months is beyond me. However, in this case I will send the caseworker an email and suggest they wait. I mean, from an economic point of view I should just take it but I think a little decency is warranted here. I kind of have to do their work. They really should have checked this out themselves before they signed a contract.

[She opens the next new contract in the portal.]

Marianne: In this case you can see that the caseworker has written that the purpose of the referral is: "pain in back, loins, neck, and legs" ... And she has referred the person in question to a "package" which has four sub-groups which target distinct problems but she has not indicated which subgroup she intends this person to go into. ... OK. Here you can see, that she has set the entry date to a Wednesday which could indicate that she is thinking about a completely different "package." Our "job training package" begins on Wednesdays. Perhaps that is what she wants. I often have to sit here and guess what they want. And apart from the obvious problem of people being subjected to mistaken or unnecessary referrals, for us—as a private agency—it becomes extra problematic because we are being benchmarked against other private employment agencies on our ability to fulfill the contracts.

Marianne subsequently spent half an hour writing emails to the different caseworkers in whose cases she was unsure what had been intended with the referral. To the caseworker of the first contract she wrote "the information under the heading 'purpose' is scarce and it is difficult for me to see what you intend for us to do," and in the last case she requested more information and wrote "are you aware that package 96 is sub-divided into four groups?!" and "perhaps you were thinking of a work ability test, that being on the Wednesday in question?" Of the three contracts, Marianne only accepted the first—a decision she felt the need to explain:

Marianne: We have as an internal organizational goal that we accept all contracts on the day they are written and contact the recipients immediately. Furthermore, by our overall framework agreement with the Municipality we are obliged to do so. But if I had accepted these three contracts today we would have risked the citizens being referred to the wrong offers and they would have arrived here before even *we* know what the purpose of their referral is. That would not have been expedient [*hensigtsmæssigt*]. It would confuse them unnecessarily and would be a bad start.

Public procurements and tenders

The contracts were a recurrent problem for the employees at ENGA. It was not only a question of mistaken or poorly informed referrals. The strange formulations of purposes was sometimes a reflection of the circumstance that what the municipal caseworkers needed in a specific case and what they could book in the electronic portal did not necessarily match. The existing "package-structure" such as the "sickness benefit package" or the "motivation package" were the result of a tender ENGA had drafted in response to the Municipality's procurement from 2008 in which the execution of the labor market directed "offers" was put out to tender. Along with a series of other private employment agencies ENGA had won the tender and the "packages" had been included in the offers to which the municipal caseworkers could refer people from 1 January, 2009.

The commencement of this framework agreement therefore coincided with the beginning of Active—Back Sooner, which meant that Peter's caseworkers had, from the onset, asked the employees at ENGA to make exceptions from the agreements in order to match the requirement for activity in the controlled trial. If the referrals in connection to Active—Back Sooner amounted to a relatively small group (a total of approximately 70 were referred to ENGA) after the commencement of the revised sickness benefit legislation—which incorporated referrals to "activities" as a central principle—the referrals to their "sickness benefit package" sky-rocketed. And so did the requests to make exceptions from the "package structure" which had been designed to match an altogether different group of people with very different needs. I asked Jane, who had written ENGA's original tender, how the content of the specific packages had come about:

> Jane: There was no dialogue between the private employment agencies and the Municipality before the procurement was announced. Not as I recall. There were meetings but it was not my impression that we – the private suppliers to the Municipality – could have any influence on how the procurement eventually looked. The tender documents were narrow in the sense that they specified very clearly what they [the Municipality] wanted. It left us with very little room for being creative.
>
> Nina: So your tender was less governed by what you thought were actually needed and more by how to meet the municipal criteria?
>
> Jane: No, it wasn't that simple. It was more that when we wrote our tender we could see some big problems with the packages they wanted.

Jane and her colleagues at ENGA were experienced social workers; they had been in the field for many years and had seen unemployment rates go up and down and the labor market conditions change. What they found problematic about the Municipal procurement was that the requirements in it were shortsighted and symptomatic of the moment in which it was written, reflecting the acute lack of labor power which dominated public debate around the end of 2007 and early 2008.

> Jane: At the time of writing and responding to the procurement the financial crisis wasn't a fact yet but then when the offers began on 1 January 2009 the reality had already changed and we were facing increasing unemployment. And perhaps that is what happens when you produce a tender document that is so closely bound up with a current trend. The result is that the tasks we are given by the Municipality are different from the ones we were asked to respond to.

Nina: Does this mean that you are expected to behave as if there are jobs in abundance out there?

Jane: No. I think everybody would be very disappointed if we in fact stuck to the agreements we made when they accepted our tender. No, what happens is rather that our agreements are slowly bent. ... For example, the tendency I see now is that we are asked to make very extensive assessments of people—of psychological aspects, job potential, social problems, the whole lot. And that was one of the things they specified in their tender documents that they did *not* want. Because in the tender documents all they wanted us to do was to talk about labor marked directed initiatives.

One of the things that had, for instance, not been part of the framework agreements was any individual components in the "sickness benefit package" to which those included in *Active—Back Sooner* were referred if they could not return to their employment part-time. Yet *Active—Back Sooner* was founded on the assumption that the controlled trial's intervention group would be given an individual offer; the employees at ENGA saw this as a central methodological challenge. And not just in the cases of *Active—Back Sooner*. The employees felt there was an acute need for individual counselling or conversations with the bewildered people in the "sickness benefit group" and they therefore tried different re-arrangements of the weekly schedule:

Sofie: Thursday is hellish; I know they feel that way. They sit in the computer room all day long and just have to apply for work.

Nina: Why do you keep it on the program if it is this bad?

Sofie: First of all, it is the day when we talk concretely about applying for jobs and where they write applications.

This was the one of the "labor market oriented initiatives" which the Municipality had stressed in their tender and which was the corner stone in the Government's effort to lead an "active employment policy"; to move the attention in general away from people's problems and into facilitating the transition back to work. Therefore it was a politically and organizationally important part of the schedule. But there was another reason for keeping it which related directly to the effort of making space for an individual component:

Sofie: There is also a question about economy involved here. 1000 DKR [approximately £100] a week for 25 hours is not a lot to get by on. In principle we need to do everything in groups, so if we cut down on personnel on Thursdays then we win a little time for individual dealings with the participants.

I was surprised at the cost. In the job center the caseworkers had argued that if they referred the participants to a 25-hour course and only needed 10 hours then there ought to be plenty of room left in the budget for individual treatment of the person in question. Now it seemed this calculation was built on an assumption which proved to be a fiction—that staying away from some of the hours would somehow generate extra time. The fact that the 25-hour course could be converted into only one hour of consultation plus subsequent feedback with the in-house psychologist, which had seemed a bit excessive when discussed back at the job center, suddenly made sense.

Expediency

So to recapitulate, according to the framework agreements and the "package structure" there were no individual conversations involved in the "sickness benefit package." In theory, a recipient of sickness benefit who had unwillingly been referred to ENGA could go through a four-week course or several subsequent periods of four-week courses without ever having a one-on-one conversation with any of the employees. While this was a surprise and a frustration to the recipients of sickness benefit ("I have been here four weeks now and not yet had a personal conversation!") it was also a concern for the staff at ENGA who did not find their generalized offers at all suitable for meeting the purposes of *Active—Back Sooner* or the purposes of the referred people in general. Therefore, they would try to create room for informal, individual conversations.

Sofie and her colleague Kate, for instance, spent a considerable amount of time each week providing social counselling to people whose questions were left unanswered by their municipal caseworkers. Sofie and another colleague Karin, had furthermore doubled their presence during Tuesdays despite the fact that the economy of the "sickness benefit package" could be balanced only with one employee attached at a time. By doubling their presence on Tuesdays they could, and did, take turns taking people aside to make individual plans for how their stay at ENGA would best contribute to the fulfilment of their specific purposes. I brought up this observation with Joan, who was the coach attached to the "sickness benefit group":

> *Joan:* I want to commend them on their extreme flexibility in this sense. Because it is not a part of what the Municipality pays for. It is not a job they have been asked to do but if we don't do stuff like that then how are we to endure this work? In this sense we are autonomous and we run faster and we conduct individual counselling sessions which we are not paid for and we work longer hours than our contracts says because we can see that this is what it takes. If we don't do this then the rest does not matter.

Many of the employees at ENGA felt that if they could only be allowed to do what they deemed to be relevant, from a professional point of view, they would be able to be of much more use. Peter was one of those who reflected on this question; he was a trained psychologist who was not officially a part of the "sickness benefit team" but had given a few sessions on stress and stress management because the psychologist who normally took the classes had some days off. I interviewed him after one of the sessions.

Peter: I come across many people here where I can see something specific is needed but I might not be involved in their case. My working hours are bound up in other tasks. If I am asked by the municipal caseworker to make an assessment then of course I do. But by now the courses we offer are so cheap that for us, as an organization, it has become a question of internal resource management: Do we choose to involve the psychologist—despite not being paid—or not?

Peter touched on a sensitive spot. It was easy for the employees at ENGA to see that what took place was not expedient (*hensigtsmæssigt*) in the formal sense that it did not serve the purpose it was legally meant to, namely assisting people in getting back to work. Unlike the caseworkers at the municipal job center who might occasionally reflect on the purposelessness of what they were instigating—as we have seen throughout their dealings with *Active—Back Sooner*—the employees at ENGA were faced with the lack of expediency and purpose every day through weeks and sometimes through months.

It was rare that employees at ENGA got a chance to speak to the caseworkers at the municipal job center, and that was one of the things *Active—Back Sooner* helped. In the course of running *Active—Back Sooner* the involved employees from either organization met in person a couple of times. In these more informal situations, where the municipal managers were not present it was easier to speak bluntly and reach agreements. One such meeting between on the one hand Ida and Marie, and on the other hand Marianne and Kate took place early one afternoon in the seminar room used by the "sickness benefit class." Kate brought up a case she wanted to discuss with Ida, who was the caseworker of Martin, the man in question. Kate told Ida that Martin (who had recently lost a son and furthermore suffered from severe back pain) would come to class two hours a day to reach the ten weekly hours of presence requested by Ida in her referral. Usually, Kate said, he would spend these two hours interchangeably sitting down or walking around with tears running down his cheeks.

> *Kate*: I think two hours is a lot to demand from him. I told him I would be seeing you today and would talk to you. I will be very honest with you now and confess to you that I am at a point where I feel like telling you that he has been here ten hours no matter how long he is actually here.
>
> *Marie*: [Interrupts] If he is in this much pain we need to assess whether it is reasonable to ask him to be here ten hours at all. We can exempt people from the demand for activity down to one hour a week. Those are the new guidelines. In your opinion, what would be a reasonable requirement to make of him?
>
> *Kate*: I would exempt him altogether. He is in great pain and I do not think he benefits from this in any way. Not least because he has to make great efforts even to understand what is going on. Most of his energy is with the language—trying to understand what is said.
>
> *Ida*: Is there nothing here he can benefit from at all? I feel this way: he has been referred here, after all, and if there is anything he could benefit from we might

as well get that out of it. He needs to find a job at some point. Could he perhaps benefit from talking to the job consultant?

A lengthy discussion followed about how this could be done, contract-wise. Marie suggested that the way forward would be to cut the required activity down to one or two hours a week, which could consist of a consultation with the job consultant; alternatively, he could be exempted from the project altogether. "It was actually the point that this should help him get better, not that it should torture him," she felt the need to remind herself and Ida.

As mentioned earlier, the employees at ENGA rarely had this opportunity to meet and discuss the actual cases with the municipal caseworkers. However, many of these informal dialogues across the two organizations resulted in attempts to make up for the mismatch between what the caseworkers wanted for the individual citizens and the formal "package structure." The management at ENGA was aware of this and asked their staff to stop this flow of informal communication. On the one hand they were full of understanding for their employees' wish to cut the specific deals they felt would be sound and expedient in concrete cases; on the other hand, they needed the municipal management to recognize that what they had requested originally in their procurement was not what they now persistently asked for. When their employees continuously went "the extra mile" and in various ingenuous ways made up for the lack of the framework agreements, they inadvertently deprived their managers of the proof they needed to argue for better working conditions.

Minus-cases

At the municipal job center, Peter experienced similar problems with getting the caseworkers to follow orders. In the spring of 2009 the municipal town hall decided that it should be an administrative priority in the job center not to have "minus-cases" (*minussager*). A minus-case was a case in which the municipal caseworker had not contacted one of "their" citizens within a set period defined by law. The first time I heard about a minus-case was one Tuesday in March 2009 when I overheard a conversation between a caseworker and Peter as I passed them in the hallway of the Municipality. The caseworker, Frank, was clearly upset and, it seemed to me, on the verge of tears:

> *Frank*: But she risks getting fired if I do not hurry with this decision.

> *Peter*: If you ask me why I tell you to give priority to the minus-cases it is because we are obliged to abide by the law. We have to comply with the requirement for punctuality. By the end of this week we can have no more minus-cases. However you prioritise your work.

I was walking next to Marie as we passed them and she whispered to me that in such cases you should never ask your boss what to do because "what else can he tell you but to follow the law." Later in the day, as the term minus-cases kept coming up in all conversations between caseworkers, I asked Marie again about the incident.

It turned out that the reduction of minus-cases had become a political focus and thereby a matter of administrative concern. Not that it was ever *not* a concern, Marie said, but now it had been decided that all minus-cases should be eradicated within the week. This meant that Peter had had to ask all the caseworkers in the two teams he managed to prioritze getting rid of minus-cases—first their own and then their colleagues'—before doing any other work. In the case of Frank's team this meant they had to stop working on all applications for flex jobs, professional rehabilitation, and early retirement pensions in which they had not already exceeded the time-limit set by the law until they had cleared all minus-cases. Marie understood that the caseworkers from Frank's team would be upset about this because people in their cases were unable to move on with their lives until the caseworkers had processed their applications. In her own cases the follow-ups seemed less acute. In the afternoon one of Marie's colleagues popped into her office to ask about the minus-cases and Peter's announcement that they were to get rid of them within the week:

Merete: So I hear we are getting rid of the minus-cases this week?

The "this week" in Merete's remark was a "so what it is this week," which expressed her lack of admiration for the management she was exposed to. She would often complain about the lack of consistency and soundness of their directives. Marie gave her a summary of the meeting in which they had been informed about the decision to tackle the minus-cases.

Merete: So what are we not to do then?

Although her remark was offered in a sarcastic tone of voice, it did touch upon something that concerned many of her colleagues. Sara, for one, often wondered if anybody paid attention to or kept account of the effects of what was *not* done whenever it was decided that they should do more of one thing or another. It was not, Sara stressed, as if they had all this empty time where they sat around and did nothing in which the new initiatives could be carried out. Marie, however, did not take Merete's bait and neutrally replied.

Marie: We are not to touch any cases that are not "in minus."

Merete left and Marie turned to me:

Marie: Well, I have some project meetings booked Wednesday, Thursday, and Friday already.

Nina: But you just said you weren't allowed to work on anything but minus-cases.

Marie: I know, but I bloody have to follow up in these cases from *Active—Back Sooner*. We have to if the project is to make any sense. It is not like we can choose to cancel it for a week.

Portrait 8: the end of meaning

Initially, *Active—Back Sooner* had been anticipated as the possible solution to the meaninglessness of the general municipal casework—what in the project design of the controlled trial became defined as the "normal intervention." As the many organizational and ethical problems related to the intervention became clear to all but a few die-hard supporters in the National Labor Market Authority, the revised sickness benefit legislation which was adopted in the summer of 2009 did for a while become something towards which the caseworkers and civil servants could look as a kind of redemption.

> *Lawyer*: A difference between the proposed law and the controlled trial is that, contrary to the controlled trial, in the law it is the "need" that must be addressed. The law will allow the municipalities to make offers and the offer must be adjusted to the individual's precondition and needs; and also his or her health and resources. This is stated in paragraph 15, piece 4. As long as the municipalities give such an offer, which may be down to just one hour a week, they are reimbursed by the State. But this is just between the State and the municipalities in order to give the municipalities an incentive to make such offers. They are still not allowed to refer a sick person to an offer if there is no need. And such a decision requires a concrete assessment and the recipient of sickness benefit can lodge an appeal if they think that what they are being exposed to is not reasonable.

However, as 2009 drew to an end, most such hopes had faded considerably in the job center and at ENGA. After having spent a month in the National Labor Market Authority in the autumn of 2009 I returned to the job center to find the caseworkers in a state of chaos. In the National Labor Market Authority the civil servants had long ago moved on to new tasks and new projects that had to be prepared. "Oh, are you still looking at the implementation of the law?," one of the civil servants had said in surprise. "But that is all over." It seemed that with the approval of the new law in the summer of 2009, as far as they were concerned, the project and the law were matters of the past. Yet, in Ida's and Marie's unit back at the municipal level the law was as overwhelming a presence as could be.

I returned to the Municipality on 2 November, 2009, sometime after the caseworkers had begun to make systematic referrals to "activity" in most sickness benefit cases when part-time return to work was impossible. The revised sickness benefit legislation had, as of 6 July, allowed for the referral of recipients of sickness benefit to "activity" by the private employment agencies normally used in cases of unemployment. "You have returned to Ragnarok,"[3] said Ian when I met him in the coffee area, alluding to the chaos that seemed to reign in the unit. That did indeed sum up my impression: unfiled cardboard folders piled up on the shelves in all offices, some of the caseworkers had themselves become recipients of sickness benefit due to stress conditions, and when I stopped by the caseworkers' individual offices to say hi on the day of my return, I noticed that several of them had stuck A4 print-outs onto their walls, which spelled out, in large type, the Serenity Prayer typically associated with the 12-step rehabilitation programs used by Alcoholics Anonymous and Addicts Anonymous: "God grant me the serenity to accept the things I cannot change, courage to change the things I can, and wisdom to know the difference." In Denmark, religiosity is a very private thing and you rarely, if ever, see people sticking up prayers on the walls—in public offices such as the job center it would be considered highly inappropriate. The act of putting up such a prayer signaled an ironic although seriously felt commentary on what was going on in the unit at that time. Despite the hope and strength the prayer is ideally supposed to install in the person who prays, these caseworkers seemed on the verge of despair and the atmosphere was, in general, tense. The weekly team meetings were no longer marked by the light humor with which Peter had earlier run them, but had become sites of confrontations and arguments:

Peter: Right now I can see that 3 of you have more than 110 cases on your case management sheet.

Jo: Try 130! That's what I've got.

Peter: You are not allowed to have that many cases.

Jo: Well, what the hell do you want us to do when the waiting room is stuffed with people?

Ann: There were more than the normal 40 citizens summoned for the first hour last Tuesday.

Peter: We only summoned 40. I can see that on the numbers.

Frank: Well, we already told you that the numbers do not reflect the reality. You cannot say that we each take 2.8 citizens an hour. Some might take only 1 or 2 because the person is crying and is completely miserable. Then somebody else will have to take four that hour. You cannot do this by averages.

Jo: We are also dealing with extended requirements for record keeping. Qualitatively that means that I can do half the number of cases I could before.

Peter: If we look at the numbers we reach our goals.

Ann: But your numbers do not match our experience.

Peter: I cannot argue for more resources when we actually comply with our goal curve ... and we do more than that, actually.

Laura: We are doing factory work here. The numbers might look good but we do not do a proper job.

The busyness and lack of time had been a topic since I first set foot in the unit but the tone had changed from when I was last there. In the early spring of 2009, the caseworkers had complained, as they did now, about having too much to do, arguing that the management made the wrong decisions by focussing too much on numbers rather than on the qualitative movement of a case. Then I saw irritation, anger, and sometimes tears, but this time it was despair, resignation, and irony. The few people who expressed their dissatisfaction during meetings ("we are doing factory work") were silenced by their colleagues ("nothing good comes from sitting here complaining").

That the disposition of the section was split was quite obvious. One part were resigned ("I understand the frustration but I can't take any more complaining") and retreated into irony ("when even Jo can't find the time to shut the cases then you can tell where we are heading"). The other part were in despair, many contemplating quitting ("I am asking myself whether I wouldn't rather be unemployed than work here"), attributing whatever good work did happen to a private crusade against the Municipality ("I see myself as the citizen's person rather than the Municipality's person, trying to make this a good experience rather than some shit we put people through"). Some people took it out on the management:

> *Ena*: Imagine this—a unit that works with sickness benefit in which the bosses do not understand that stress is something people get sick from. And who are we to direct ourselves to? We are more or less told that we seem to report sick whenever we feel like a day off ... You only survive here if you are absolutely indifferent to your work .... if you do not care that the citizens are in a mess ... if you do not care about doing a poor job.

Some took it out on each other:

> *Frank*: As long as some people [unspecified colleagues] insist on chitchatting with the citizens the rest of us will have to run all the faster if we are ever to empty the waiting rooms.

Some took it out on themselves:

> *Sara*: You need to change your personality because you are under so much pressure. One incident that alerted me to how I have become was when a woman sat in my office and told me how her husband beats her regularly. I just cut her off and said: "So you mentioned you have a problem with your arm." I felt sick with myself. I was the caseworker from hell ... cold and inhuman because I could not take any more. I have had to numb my empathy. Some days I talk to twelve people in a row. I am wrecked after such a day.

What had changed with the new law was that as a result of extending the content of the conversations the record-keeping was extended as well. As Jo had said during the team meeting, she could now do half of the conversations she did earlier. To save time a series of short cuts had been invented: many had stopped informing the citizens about the law and the specific rules that applied to them as recipients of sickness benefit (or cut it down to the very basics) because it "took too many words to explain it properly" and because it "confused people more than it enlightened them."

> *Ida*: We don't talk so much about rules anymore. Mostly we just talk about how to "be active."

Another time saving strategy was to copy-and-paste a lot. An internal consultant had elaborated a set of template formulas covering the most used journal entries in which the caseworkers could just alter the name and type in the specific papers they had handed out in a case.

> *Ena*: They regularly update the template we can use for a standard journal entry so that it matches with the current requirements for a conversation. We just copy-and-paste it and fill in the specifics.

> *Nina*: Do you change the way you handle your cases according to the template then?

> *Ena*: No, just what I register.

> *Nina*: Did you always copy-and-paste your journal entries?

> *Ena*: Yes, that was the way I was taught. Like when we have to state our reasons for the category we place people in. I copy-and-paste it from the webpage of the National Labor Market Authority. I assume that is why they make them accessible.

I had seen the copy-and-pasting done often before. On the one hand it had the effect that the journal entries could state that a given citizen had been informed about his or her legal rights and obligations when in fact they had only been handed a folder; on the other, I too had seen citizens doze off during these summaries of their rights and obligations. It was not as if they lacked things to talk about during the meetings with the recipients of sickness benefit—it took a long time to explain to people why they had to be referred to activity and what would be done by the private employment agencies. Especially since it was the case—as it had been during the trial's implementation—that many of the caseworkers were not sure what the content in the courses was. To make up for this they had begun inviting the private employment agencies to come around and present their courses at the weekly team meetings. At one such meeting Marianne, Karin, and Birgit from ENGA came around to present the current content of their "sickness benefit package."

> *Karin*: It is a very mixed group of people you refer to us these days. People have all kinds of diagnoses and they have been ill for quite different periods of time.

Being the only known face, Karin asked me to help her pass around a photocopy of the timetable of the sickness benefit package. I noticed there were now two days allocated to the "job club" as opposed to one. The "job club" was the day Sofie had described as the "hell day." It did not escape the attention of the caseworkers.

> *Jo*: [From job center] Are there no alternatives to the "job club"? I mean for people who already have a job?

> *Birgit*: [From ENGA] They are most welcome to use the training facilities. We have a fully equipped gym.

> *Frank*: [From job center] Our problem is that we sometimes have to find some activity for those with broken legs; those cases where really there is nothing to do but wait until the plaster comes off.

> *Karin*: [From ENGA] Er ... You can always book fewer hours?

> *Peter*: [From job center] It is really a pity they miss two days just because there is nothing suitable on your program.

As is hinted at in this exchange of words, the caseworkers were concerned with what they exposed the citizens to. Yet many felt they did not have a choice but to refer people to activity. As Frank told me:

> *Frank*: The message is that we have to refer people to activity unless there is a very good reason not to do so. And it is so difficult to refer people to activity when you just know it makes no sense. That you have to just because the system says so. And we have been in such a state of chaos that we have no time to look at the feedback from the private employment agencies, so people just sort of "hang there."

As with the record keeping which the caseworkers struggled to keep up with, other parts of the casework had also been subjected to routine. In some instances the caseworkers seemed to be on autopilot. If Jo managed to keep her spirits high as always, others seemed not to have the surplus energy to engage in the meetings with the citizens. One day I sat through such a series of conversations with Ena. In this meeting recounted below she and the citizen, a young man, had agreed that he would be a likely candidate for professional rehabilitation since he had gone through several operations on his knees and had worked as a manual laborer. None of them therefore thought it likely that he would be able to return to his former position.

> *Man*: The criteria for professional rehabilitation, what are they?

> *Ena*: I don't know but I will forward your case to the team that deals with applications. Meanwhile, according to the new law, I need to refer you to an "active offer" run by one of the private employment agencies we work with.

Man: Will that be one of those places that are paid to push me into some ridiculous activity?

Ena: No, I cannot imagine that.

Man: It was no part of my plan to be subjected to some kind of silly "offer." I mean, what do they actually do?

Ena: [Hands him a piece of paper describing the "activity" at ENGA, clearly irritated.] You can read this if you want.

Man: [Skimming through paper.] Is it something I am forced to do?

Ena: No. You can say no if you do not want to.

Man: OK then. I do not want to. I mean, I do not see where it fits into my plan about professional rehabilitation? How would it fit in?

[Pause ... Ena does not answer.]

Man: Are there any statistics about the number of people whose applications for rehabilitation are accepted?

Ena: I do not know.

Man: [Reads description of ENGA.] I just don't see how it fits with the general plan. How will this help me get back to work?

[Ena does not reply.]

The incident made an impression on me because it was atypical of anything I had observed before. It would, however, turn out to be typical of what I would observe with greater frequency in the remaining weeks I spent at the job center. Ena did not even pretend to care about explaining to the young man what the law was about or what the purpose of a referral would be. She was irritated and did not bother to hide it. In a sense, it was an honest interaction: Ena did not answer because she did not have an answer. She had no idea how it would fit into the man's plan to return to work and she could not summon the energy to make up a reason. The next citizen that day was a man from the Middle East who worked in a pizzeria. In this case Ena did not bring up the demand for activity but exempted him without further ado:

Ena: [To me after the conversation] This is utterly pointless. He wouldn't even understand what they say at ENGA. I ought to contact his employer but I cannot be bothered. It's too big a project and I am too tired. I don't believe anything useful would come from it.

The third conversation I sat in on made the extent of Ena's resignation clear as she wound up the meeting with a woman:

> *Ena*: I will call you in four weeks' time.
>
> *Woman*: Why?
>
> *Ena*: Because I am obliged to by law.
>
> *Woman*: OK, but what do you want us to talk about?
>
> *Ena*: Yes, that is the heart of the whole affair. What indeed? I am sorry, but I have to.

The unit seemed to be in a state of crisis. Peter had suspended all following-up in the cases because the caseworkers had a hard time just keeping up with the intake. This in reality cut the caseworkers' job down to "introductory conversations" and the subsequent record-keeping and answering emails and phone calls. Despite this, the piles of unfiled case folders grew taller by the day. Some put in a lot of extra time to keep up but did not manage anyway. Against this background it was a strange experience to sit in on a general staff meeting hosted by the job center's manager Ulla and her recently appointed deputy manager. Ulla presented a range of statistics to the collective of caseworkers that all showed how the caseworkers complied with the numbers they had promised to deliver to the Central Administration. Among other things Ulla had noticed that they received far less complaints about their work from citizens.

> *Ulla*: I take this as a sign that the quality of our work has improved significantly during the past year. And your job satisfaction has increased too. It is higher than ever. It is higher than anywhere else in our entire administrative area.

After this talk the deputy manager addressed the fact that despite the documented high job satisfaction, in the job center they currently expected the average of days lost due to sickness to reach 20 days per employee by the end of the year.[4]

> *D.M.*: You need to change your attitude to work. You *can* go to work even if you are not feeling on top of things.

Later in the meeting Ulla chimed in:

> *Ulla*: We really need those hands that are bound up in sickness absence, I mean for the sake of the wellbeing of the rest of us. And we know this has nothing to do with either recognition of your work or with the amount of work you have to do—we can see this from the survey. You have told us yourselves.

One of the caseworkers mumbled quietly in the coffee break that the survey had been conducted during the quietest month that summer before the law had been revised but nobody challenged Ulla's interpretation at the meeting. Thus when I left the Municipality at the end of November to spend the remaining part of my fieldwork at ENGA it was a disheartened unit I left behind.

At ENGA the staff found their classrooms flooded with people who were about to go back to work and who saw no purpose in their referral. When I had last been there, three months earlier, Sofie had shared her office space with Kate but now they had separate offices: As the number of referrals had escalated after the new law had been passed a few months earlier Sofie's case load had exploded. Kate had moved out of their shared office because their work was frequently interrupted by the people who came to see either of them. After Kate moved out, Sofie had remodeled the office so that she now sat at the back of the room facing the wall instead of facing the big glass window towards the hallway as she had done earlier. This window was situated so that everyone who came in from the stair well and onto the floor where the staff associated with the "sickness benefit package" had their offices would look straight at her. Many of the participants from the "sickness benefit class" had therefore made a habit out of dropping in on her or Kate to ask about decisions made by their municipal caseworkers or about letters received which they did not understand, wanting their advice and help in understanding "the system" and "the law" they were subjected to at the moment.

Instead of signaling a *welcome* as she used to, Sofie had therefore consciously rearranged her office so as to signal the opposite by now facing the wall rather than the window. She told me she thought of this as a personal failure but as absolutely necessary for her own survival, health-wise and work-wise, in the unit. There was more confusion among the people in the "sickness benefit class" and less time to deal with it. The groups were three times the size of what they had been earlier, and the strategies that Sofie and Karin had previously pursued in order to make space for individual conversations were now absolutely unviable. The caseworkers tried to confer the responsibility of making the referral tolerable onto the sick people themselves with only little success:

ENGA employee: Well, what would you like to get out of your time here?

Woman: I did not ask to come here. I do not want to be here. I am beginning a new education course in four weeks and I do not think it is my responsibility to make this purposeless referral appear meaningful.

On the day of my return I stopped by Karin's office on my way to a meeting with Marianne. Marianne joined us a few seconds later. We had seen each other just recently during the meeting at the job center so the conversation naturally began there.

Nina: They liked your presentation.

Marianne: They did? We do receive an enormous amount of contracts. But those who come here are confused and have no idea why they have been sent here. ...

I rather thought many of the caseworkers were rather uncompromising [*stejle*] when we were over there. I mean, critical about the fact that we ought to be able to offer something which would make sense for everyone.

Nina: I think their frustration is that many of them have no idea what it is they are referring people to. They are worried about those who have quite simple cases and about how they can benefit from what you have to offer.

Karin: But do they think we should be able to invent something meaningful in every instance? Do they think we are an evening school?

Evening schools in Danish are self-financed, open to anyone, and offer a broad cat-alogue of courses ranging from physical exercise to specialized language courses, training in different forms of handicraft and courses on politics or opera. They are generally thought of as leisurely pastimes. Several of the employees at ENGA were puzzled why—if *any* kind of activity could help *any* person as the ideology seemed to be—they did not allow people to choose a course at an evening school.

If the employees were puzzled about the fact that people seemed to be referred to them for no apparent reason, so were the people who were referred there. There was a lot of mumbling and complaints in the hallways and in the canteen.

Man: I am not benefitting from this. Jesus, how could I possibly? None of us has had a one-to-one conversation with anyone since we came here three weeks ago.

As we know from the previous portrait, the "sickness benefit package" had never included individual sessions and with a classroom filled with sometimes more than 20 people it was difficult to find the time to make the individual's partici-pation seem meaningful. The dissatisfaction erupted again and again during the classroom sessions. I sat in on a session with the psychologist Birgit one day. She had recently returned from a period of leave and was trying to figure out how to tackle the large groups. Questions and complaints were flung at her:

Man: I have been here four weeks and I haven't been "clarified" yet.

Woman 1: I have no idea what it is I am supposed to get out of being here, but I guess I'll get something or other out of it.

Woman 2: I've got two weeks left and I have not had a conversation with anybody yet. Will there at least be a conversation in the end?

Birgit: No. This is a different kind of course.

Woman 3: It is not particularly meaningful to sit in the computer room during the "job club." I have no idea what I am supposed to do there.

During the class, Birgit tried to answer each question clearly but as opposed to when I was last here it was primarily those who spoke up who got attention and the employees were not so forthcoming anymore.

Man: I would really, really like an individual conversation with you, Sofie, so I can get a proper plan for how I get back to work.

Sofie: It is not part of your referral. I cannot do it.

As 2009 drew to a close the staff at ENGA met to evaluate the year. Jane, the local top manager, addressed the staff with a summary of the economy and of the job situation. I was invited to join in and this is what I wrote down from Jane's talk:

> *Jane*: Our economy is just balancing. Even though we have run as fast as we have there is no profit. This means we cannot allow ourselves the luxury of declining any contracts. We have not got the economic possibility of declining contracts! On top of that you will have noticed that the job center is extremely busy refer-ring people to us because they have to do it before Christmas if they are to receive the full economic reimbursement from the State. As you have observed this means that people are being referred to "packages" more randomly. So, apart from the fact that we are extraordinarily busy we are dealing with a lot of people who are mismatched to what we can offer. And we know very well that you bend and stretch and work beyond the things we are paid to do but you must stop this! And we know this is tough. But you will have to be firm with the job center and not do all kinds of things we are not paid to do.

But Sofie could not help herself. After the incident above where she had declined to help the man, she had second thoughts. She did not go to lunch but remained in the classroom and spent her lunch break assisting the man in drawing up a plan for his return to work. I saw Karin, Joan, and the other employees do similar things. They did not have the possibility any more to do it in a systematic way and those people who kept quiet could easily spend four weeks at ENGA without ever knowing why they had been sent there. Meanwhile the employees continued to do their best with the available means. As Joan said:

> *Joan*: If we don't put in the extra hours, the ones we are not paid for but without which the rest is utterly pointless, then I will never survive in this job.

Later I learned that Sofie went through a long period of sick leave suffering from stress—a great cause of humiliation for her. Her colleagues attributed her condi-tion to the fact that she had worked well beyond the hours in her contract for an extended period of time to make up for the insufficiency of what she felt she could deliver with in her normal working schedule.

Analysis: they rebel, they do not resist

In the Danish National Center for Social Research's investigation (Winter et al. 2008) of the implementation of *More People in Work* (Regeringen 2002a), a series of dichotomies figures. In Winter et al.'s report the caseworkers involved in implementing the central Government policy are either "oriented towards rules" or they are "flexible." Here orientation towards rules is linked with formality and compliance with the law, while flexibility is linked with kindness, understanding, and result orientation (ibid.). This theoretical opposition between abiding by the rules and achieving results was one that had been embraced to some extent by the caseworkers and the employees at ENGA, who would often present their actions as "bending the rules," "finding a hole in the law," or just plain "disregarding the rules." I will not pursue here the questions of whether they *actually* broke or circumvented the law and local rules and agreements. Some lawyers have, in private conversations, alerted me to the fact that what in some cases in my material was described as "bending the rules" or "breaking the rules" were in fact completely in accordance with the law. Instead then, what I will discuss here is the individual caseworker's or employee's *experience* of rebellion against directives.

My understanding of rebellion will depart from Glenn Goodwin's article "On transcending the absurd: an inquiry in the sociology of meaning' (Goodwin 1971). Goodwin argued here that the rebellion against "institutional absurdity" in itself was a source of meaning for students and for blacks of all ages in the USA at the time of his research in the 1960s. To his understanding it was in the reaction to absurdity which he defined as "the inevitable contradictions in life" (Goodwin 1971: 838) that human beings could find meaning. Goodwin's article was a parallel publication to Stanford Lyman and Marvin Scott's *A sociology of the absurd* (1970). Whereas Lyman and Scott argued that human existence was characterized by being devoid of purpose and that this was the root of the absurdity of human life (Lyman and Scott 1989: 8), Goodwin understood absurdity to result from conflicting meanings. Therefore, it is Goodwin's understanding of the rebellious act that resonates with my material: where Lyman and Scott viewed the rebellious act as a way of achieving the non-absurd—that is, of creating meaning where before there was none (Lyman and Scott 1989: 194), in Goodwin's understanding rebellion is a quest for clear-cut meaning in a context too full of contradictions—that is, for a singular meaning in the face of too much meaning (Goodwin 1971: 837).

The rebellious acts I have written about in these two portraits relate to everyday routines: deliberately disobeying managers' directives to stick to the plan; prolonging the sickness benefit beyond what the law allows; disregarding agreements made or decisions taken at higher administrative levels. Perhaps it seems that "rebellion" is too grand a word, that perhaps "resistance" is a more accurate description? In Michael Lipsky's classic book on "street-level bureaucrats" and their relationship to their managers he describes "resistance" as the means whereby lower-level employees can hamper their managers' efforts through refusals to carry out particular kinds of work, refusals to take short cuts through department regulations in order to achieve results, or by insisting on following the rules too rigidly (Lipsky 1980: 24f.). In Goodwin's understanding, "rebellion" is the reaction to contradictions in which something new is created—i.e. singular meaning or singular purpose—while in Lipsky's understanding "resistance" is the subordinates' refusal to contribute to the realization of their managers' plans. Therefore, to speak of resistance would imply a refusal or reluctance on behalf of the municipal caseworkers and the employees at ENGA to engage with the tasks they were presented with by their managers and this, as we have seen, was not the case.

Departing from Goodwin's and Lipsky's observations I will argue the following: rebellion implies that the person who rebels *wants to achieve* something and move beyond the present; resistance implies that the person who resists will *not* do something. Thus, if resistance is a refusal to participate, rebellion reworks what it means to participate and surpasses what has been requested. Rebellion is an action on the present directed towards the future; resistance remains with the present and precludes the present from establishing a link to the future. When I therefore retain the word rebellion it is because it does justice to the commitment which the caseworkers devoted to the tasks in hand, taking decisions that established links between what took place in the present with what they wanted to take place in the larger scheme of things. When the employees at ENGA, like Sofie, Karen, and Joan, chose not to follow their managers' request that they stick to the plan and not provide services beyond what had been formally agreed, their disobedience might at first glance make it difficult for their managers to achieve their goals; however, when they put in extra time and extra services they did so to fulfill the overall purpose of their job (to help people return to the labor market). Likewise, when Marie deliberately disobeyed Peter's orders that only the "minus-cases" may be worked with, as we saw in an earlier portrait, or when the caseworkers in general prolonged sickness benefit illegally, an understanding that these actions are directed towards making the employment effort meaningful in the larger scheme of things lends more credence to their engagement than a perspective that views it as mere resistance and failure to comply with the law.

In James Scott's *Seeing like a State* he observes that a planned city, village, or language is likely to be "thin" in the sense of offering but a sketchy framework for the real-life "thick" cities, villages, and languages that are characterized by being constituted of "inexhaustibly complex activities" (Scott 1998: 261). As a consequence, he continues, planning will generate an unofficial and "far more disorderly and complex" reality (the real "thick" city) that will sustain and fill in the inevitable gaps in the plan and, in fact, make it (the planned "thin" city) work (ibid.). In the previous portrait, I presented just such an "unofficial" reality that, de facto, made the "official" reality work: employees at ENGA put in extra hours and went beyond the requirements of the plan and we saw that, when possible, the caseworkers at the Municipality went along with their suggestions. They too tried to cut deals that bypassed the agreements between their two organizations or prolonged the sickness benefit beyond what was legally possible in an acknowledgement of the practicality of doing so.

Goodwin found contemporary American society anno 1971 to be characterized by institutional absurdity and by a high degree of recognition of this absurdity on behalf of the members of the same institutions. The result, he found, was a quest for the non-absurd—i.e. meaning—coexisting with the recognition that institutions unmarked by contradictions cannot be. The act of rebellion against meaninglessness, he argued, became in itself a source of meaning in an absurd institutional or social structure in this context (Goodwin 1971: 838f.). This point is important. Note that all the caseworkers' and privately employed social workers' rebellion—i.e. the attempt to make sensible decisions—did not result in a purposeful or expedient labor market intervention. Nor did it necessarily result in a sensible outcome for the subjects of the interventions. Rather, the rebellion *in itself* became the source of meaningfulness for the employees when faced by the overall absurdity resulting from the implementation of the various coexisting labor market directed policies and organizational initiatives. And it was this very quest for a meaningful and purposeful intervention which sustained what they all experienced as the overall meaninglessness of the effort. The municipal caseworkers and the employees at ENGA refused to simply let the plans fail. So strong was the impetus for doing something meaningful and for improving the faulty plan they had been handed that only at the verge of individual human breakdown—resignation—did they allow the purposelessness to be exposed.

Notes

1 52 weeks was the limit for receiving sickness benefit unless the recipient met one of the multiple criteria for prolongation. As always, when I attempt to summarize the law it is a gross simplification but will serve to give the reader a general idea.
2 I introduced myself and my research focus (studying the employees' work) as I would do repeatedly throughout the week as new people joined the group.
3 Ragnarok is the great final battle in Norse mythology, in popular use more often used to describe situations of total chaos than to indicate any finality.
4 According to the analysis report elaborated by the consultancy company, Mploy, the national average among the working population was 1.16 weeks per year (Arbejdsmarkedsstyrelsen 2008: 24).

How implementation works

[no cause] has the power to define how it will cause [and nothing has] the power to determine how it will matter for others. (Isabelle Stengers 2009: 40).

I want to begin this chapter with a premise: *Policy implementation is doomed to fail, if by failure we mean failing to deliver the desired result in the prescribed way*. But we must not despair, for if policy invariably fails to achieve the planned results, it fails to do so in predictable ways and for predictable reasons. And it does so in ways full of effects. In this chapter I will build on the analyses from the previous four chapters and answer the question I raised at the beginning of the book: *How might we understand the self-generative character of bureaucracy? And what might we learn about how implementation works in general based on a discussion of this specific ethnographic study?* In this chapter then, I will present five theses on how implementation works, which I propose can be observed in most if not all cases of policy implementation—be that national policy or international development policy. I realize this is a grand claim but since I have chosen to reclaim implementation studies for the humanities I will proceed by the principle of abduction and present the best possible theorization of the nature of implementation, meaning by "best possible" a theorization that does not contradict but rather incorporates previous insights in a general explanatory—perhaps even programmatic—framework.

Thesis 1: interventions always have effects beyond their scope

"Failure" was my crude summary of the conclusions of the quantitative evaluation (Rambøll 2010) which established that *Active—Back Sooner* had failed to make the recipients of sickness benefit less reliant on public benefits (ibid.: 1), failed to provide knowledge about how or which "active offers" might lead to a swift return to work (ibid.: 21), and failed to save money in that the intervention proved more costly than the "normal intervention" it had come to substitute (ibid.: 2). Yet it would be a mistake to regard such conclusions as satisfying or correct. They do not even begin to exhaust what happened in the course of implementing *Active—Back Sooner*, nor the effects the intervention had. Development schemes and political interventions such as *Active—Back Sooner* have effects that go far beyond what can be accessed through evaluations that measure "effect" against pre-defined criteria for success. Were we to restrict our interest to such a narrow field of outcome, all we would do is test the ability of our hypothesis to manifest itself in practical action (and in order to believe in the narrow set of data this would generate we would have to kid ourselves into thinking that what we hypothesized was identical to what actually took place). We would remain ignorant of the majority of the effects political initiatives have and of the ways they are achieved.

One way of exploring the outcome of policy implementation is, as James Ferguson suggested (Ferguson 2005: 272), to pay attention to the effects a policy is instrumental in bringing about; such an approach will tune our attention to the *actual* rather the hypothesized impact of policy. Portrait 6, *The productivity of controversy*, which examines the legal controversy the trial gave rise to in the spring of 2009, might be read as one long series of unplanned successive and parallel effects of the circumstance that the civil servants in the National Labor Market Authority had referred to a wrong paragraph in the wrong law when they first issued the promulgation for the controlled trial. We might regard the reporter's engagement with the official policy documents and legal texts which earned him a prestigious prize for critical journalism as another effect. His engagement was, furthermore, instrumental in occasioning a huge amount of overtime and expenditure in the National Labor Market Authority who were tasked with producing answers and responses to the myriad questions raised by the media, Parliament, and the Minister of Employment. This work was, and this is the central link, instrumental in producing a series of conflicting formulations of the purpose and guiding principles of the project, which led to further blurring of the caseworkers' understanding of what they were working towards. All of this was unplanned, none of this can be seen in the evaluation, yet it had tangible effects which were instrumental in shaping the implementation of *Active—Back Sooner* locally in the Municipality: Kirsten quit the project group, and Ida and Marie struggled to mediate between their overall understanding of the purpose (to see if activity would help people get back to work sooner) and the increasingly explicitly formulated demands that the "active offers" should be useful and beneficial (in which case the project could only ever have a positive outcome).

In the seventh portrait, *"Bending" the rules and agreements*, we see how the caseworkers' attempts to be loyal to the official project design of *Active—Back Sooner* were in conflict with parallel local attempts to reduce the number of cases overdue for administrative handling—i.e. to comply with the legal requirements for punctuality. That the caseworkers' attempts to comply with their managers' directives were directly instrumental in undermining the fulfilment of the *purposes* of these directives is most clear in the final portrait, *The end of meaning*. In this portrait the analytic focus is shifted from the implementation of *Active—Back Sooner* to the effectuation of the revised sickness benefit legislation that subjected *all* cases in the unit to assessment for referral to activity or pressure for part-time return. Here we saw how the stated intention—that each and every case would be subjected to thorough assessment and, if possible, referral to beneficial activity—

blew the casework out of proportion and was instrumental, locally, in effecting the suspension of all follow-up in the sickness benefit cases, leaving little if any time to actually work them. Such nitty-gritty details of daily office life might appear petty. After all, we are interested in learning about the outcome of nationwide large scale interventions. But I must insist: these instances of human interaction and decision-making were much more potent in shaping the implementation of *Active—Back Sooner* than the official project designs. The scope of the impact the trial had went far beyond anything projected in the policies or captured in the evaluations. If this observation is banal, consider nevertheless the amount of public funds spent on quantitative evaluations which just like the one conducted in the case of *Active—Back Sooner* assume an unproblematic relationship between project design, activities, and outcome. If it is a story often told, it has yet to have impact, so we must keep telling it.

Thesis 2: policy-makers project their "sites of intervention" as blank slates

The implementation literature is replete with examples of how development initiatives and political interventions end up working against or undermining the very future outcome they project. A classic example of such a study is Jeffrey Pressman's and Aaron Wildavsky's *Implementation* (1984 [1973]). Here they analyse an urban development scheme which, during the 1960s, sought to preempt racial unrest in Oakland, California, by generating jobs in some of the city's poorest neighborhoods. One of the initiatives which initially excited both constituents and Congress members was a business loans program which would support the growth of new local enterprises in order to generate long-term jobs (ibid.: 73). However, when it came to implementing the program the same people who had initially supported it turned to critique it, since it soon became clear it would end up subsidizing some companies and not others and thus in reality would result in State sponsored competition to existing enterprises already struggling with low demand. In other words it would create jobs for some by taking jobs from others (ibid.). As a result of these concerns the official criteria for getting a loan were changed, eventually making it next to impossible to get a loan. In the end only eight loans were approved and of these only three companies generated any jobs (ibid.: 80). Pressman and Wildavsky cite the *Oakland Tribune's* headline conclusion from 1969: "U.S. invests $1,085,000 to create 43 Oakland jobs" (ibid.: 82). More recently, in Tania Murray Li's (2007) analysis of the international development community, *The will to improve*, she describes an NGO's (non-governmental organization) efforts to improve the livelihood of the farmers of Lore Lindu National Park in Sulawesi, Indonesia. She points out how, in their preparation of a rural development program, which aimed at persuading the local farmers to improve their agricultural production, the NGO workers failed to take into account that the farmers were already experimenting with different crops and cultivation techniques and needed no persuasion; in fact, with the intervention they ended up being economically worse off than before (2007: 129). What these two analyses share is that they are examples of interventions where the policy-makers seem to have forgotten that the implementation of their plans does not take place in social or organizational voids but in highly complex and dense socio-economical settings.

This forgetfulness, I want to argue, is—ironically—tied less to sloppiness than it is to a drive towards perfection inherent it seems to planning. To understand the scope and potency of this "drive towards perfection," consider the work of anthropologist Maj Nygaard-Christensen. In her research on international nation building she documents how the consultants in the UN international development community imagine and speak of their sites of intervention as places where they can build, from scratch, the kind of society or government they have dreamed up (Nygaard-Christensen 2011). In her material from East Timor, Nygaard-Christensen notes how, after the country gained independence from Indonesia, the international development community began speaking of East-Timor as "a laboratory case," as somewhere the UN programmers could build an infrastructure "from scratch" and even "institutionalize from scratch" (2011: 8). The irony of this approach to planning is that it might be considered a holistic approach sensitive to the importance of context: the problems these types of development schemes are designed to overcome are being addressed from a variety of angles and underpinned by numerous supporting initiatives. As such they resemble the genre of societal planning detailed in Thomas More's *Utopia*, in which the governmental structures and their roles within the wider society are incredibly well thought out and demonstrates a nuanced understanding of human nature. Yet, just as in the case of More's *Utopia* the schemes are built on the premise that there is nothing already with which they will interfere—what the economists like to refer to as "all things being equal" and of course, outside the worlds of spreadsheets and models, things are *never* equal.

Active—Back Sooner was, on a smaller scale, entangled in exactly such an attempt to create, "from scratch," a perfect reality. Viewing the recipients of sickness benefit as people who passively awaited their healing (pottering about in their apartment or slouching on their sofas in solitary confinement as the Minister would have it) made them simultaneously the perfect site for (re)constructing the perfect labor market asset and the perfect tool for (re)constructing societal economic equilibrium. In portrait 2, *The perfect plan*, we saw how quantitative and abstracted data allowed the civil servants and those who crafted the research and analyses to perform hypothetical work on this image of the passive recipient of sickness benefit whom they discursively molded to fix the holes in the public budgets: leaving people alone was doing them a disfavor; it was not good to be passive; physical exercise would help most beneficiaries; sitting alone on a couch all day was unwise. Of course, when it came to fulfilling the needs of the actual men and women who wound up in the intervention group they often turned out to be not so alone, passive, and isolated as imagined. In the fourth portrait, *Satisfying needs*, we saw that those who challenged the project the most were exactly those who already embodied the behavior the project was meant to encourage. Had the overarching purpose of *Active—Back Sooner* been to establish whether or not activity (and which kind of activity) during an illness period would lead to a quicker return to full-time work it might have been relevant to meticulously note and register the strategies and "activities" used by these people. Instead, they became a problem and the caseworkers were eventually allowed to exempt them from the project.

The built-in assumption that there would be *some* sensible activity to offer the participants in the trial caused the caseworkers to creatively identify, invent, and match "needs" with "active offers" and it led, in some cases, to a substitution of self-financed and specialized treatment and exercise with a generalized offer paid for by the public sector. This was yet another tangible effect of local attempts to implement *Active—Back Sooner* which had definitely not been planned or foreseen. This fundamental misconception of the people and the social area the intervention targeted was not the only "blind spot" the National Labor Market Authority had been operating with in the design phase. They had failed to take account of the fact that the municipal context was already marked by numerous projects and initiatives which made it impossible to speak of a "normal intervention" shared across the municipalities. In portrait 5, *The purpose multiplies*, it is described how the trial's methodological requests alternately overruled and were overruled by other local and parallel attempts to improve the quality of the casework. This meant that despite the fact that the National Labor Market Authority changed the criteria for exemption much to the liking of the caseworkers, they did not implement these changes. As we learned in portrait 6, *The productivity of controversy*, implementation of the new criteria for exemption would work directly against the methodological requirement that they include 200 citizens in the "intervention group" within the month of May. The pressure to reach the target group and "finish" the project thus over-ruled the application of the new criteria for exemption despite the fact that the caseworkers in the job center all found these new criteria to be much more sound than the original.

Thesis 3: "local knowledge" is always situated and contradictory

This brings us directly to the conception of "local knowledge and practice." With the introduction of the innovation agenda in the Danish, British, and American governments, there has been a growing emphasis on the productive role of involving street-level workers in formulating new policy (e.g. Bason 2010; Behn 1995; Eggers & Singh 2009; Hill 2003; Patterson et al. 2009). This is because they are presumed to possess useful insight into what people need, and valuable experience in how to provide it. This idea can be found, for instance, in Catherine Durose's analysis of how the role of street-level workers has changed since New Labor set out to reform the British public sector's service provision (2009; 2011). She argues that in this new type of governance, street-level workers' jobs have shifted from the bureaucratic role described by Michael Lipsky (1980) to what she terms "civic entrepreneurship" (Durose 2011: 979): a role enabled by street-level workers' privileged "local knowledge," stemming from their "lived experience" (Ibid.: 985). This knowledge enables them to "work to reconcile policy priorities with community demands through community-centered strategies" (Ibid.: 979).

The idea that a certain group of people, by virtue of their lived experience, should be particularly resourceful in policy-making is not a new idea spawned by the public sector innovation agenda. "Local knowledge" has long been a stock concept in international development literature, where is it seen as an important driver of viable policy. One classic example is James Scott's book *Seeing like a State* (1998), in which he examines, among other cases, the implementation of a Tanzanian policy to promote settlement in model villages. Scott attributes this case of failed implementation, as he does generally in the book, to the centrally placed policy-makers' disregard for local knowledge and practices (ibid.: 227). He advocates listening to and taking account of local experts and their knowledge in order to make sustainable policy. *Active—Back Sooner* in fact offers a good example of such bottom-up policy-making. The intervention initially came about as a result of a need identified by municipal caseworkers across the country. They had been involved in the trial's planning and crafting from the very beginning; caseworkers and managers such as Marie and Peter had taken part in the drafting of the various local versions of the overall design; Marie and Peter thought the plan was comprehensive, sound, and that it "made sense." Yet it did not take more than a few hours of concentrated drafting of local guidelines for the controlled trial to dissolve and a new project to emerge that fundamentally undermined it. Why, if the policy's crafters had listened to the "local experts" and been attentive to the local knowledge and practice did this happen?

Li (2005) problematizes Scott's argument by pointing out that even when local knowledge is mobilized and factored in it does not sit easily with planning: in fact, local knowledge makes it more difficult to make clear recommendations by which to "rule" (ibid.: 389; also Boden & Epstein 2006). Also, she points out that by recognizing the full extent of local knowledge planners might find that they have nothing to add and that their interventions are unwanted (ibid.: 390). While being valid points, my contention is that Li, like Scott and Durose, operates with too high a degree of consistency on behalf of "planners" and the "knowledge" or "intentions" they possess. Their analyses of "local experts" (Scott 1998) and "street-level workers" (Durose 2009; 2011) imply a cumulative view of knowledge; if some locals or street-level workers know more than others, it is because they have longer experience working with the area building up the particular skills that go with a job or profession. And of course this is partly so. In this present study we saw this perhaps most clearly when the caseworkers ventured into unexplored territory and began working with private employment agencies. They took decisions more or less blindfolded, since they had but the vaguest idea of what took place in the various courses offered by the private employment agencies. Yet there is more to this than a lack of knowledge which may be compensated for by accumulating more knowledge, as Durose (2009, 2011) and Scott's (1998) arguments would imply. We know from chapters 2, 3, and 4 that "local practice" is a tricky phenomenon; that local concerns are multiple and often contradictory; and that one person may interchangeably inhabit the position of planner, underminer, and implementer. If people inhabit contradictory positions and work to satisfy contradictory concerns it becomes difficult to uphold the idea of "knowledge" as a coherent body of insights that slowly grows and may be harvested for the purpose of sound policy-making.

The analytical value of the "vectors of concern" metaphor I introduced in Chapter 2 is that it helps us to see that what one person holds to be of importance in one specific situation is not necessarily what the same person might attribute importance to in a different situation—in other words what people *know* to be of local relevance in one situation might be different from what they *know* to be of local relevance in the next situation. We saw in portrait 3 *The trial mutates*, how during the first project meeting the project design initially appeared to Peter as straightforward to implement and then, in the course of a few sentences, as ridden with internal contradictions. We saw how Marie's interest in the project on 14 January was highly idealistic, while on the following day she spoke to Ida about the need for the project to adapt to the daily running of things as if that had been her concern all along. We saw how the knowledge Peter and Marie had needed and used while writing the local version of the project design (which was approved, with alterations, by the National Labor Market Authority) were of a more general nature than the specific knowledge which was activated when adapting the project to concrete situations they envisioned. We learned how subsequently the specific knowledge Marie used when she helped write the first draft for a local version of the project design was annulled by the specific knowledge she held when facing an individual man who pleaded to be exempted from her good intentions. The conception of "local knowledge" which must spring from the ethnography in this book is one in which "knowledge" is both fragmentary and contradictory in its nature; and the current problem a person is trying to solve or address is determining for the kind of knowledge invoked in that moment and thus of an entirely situational nature.

Thesis 4: planning continues throughout the implementation process

Safe to conclude now, that the relationship between the realms of project design, guidelines, and evaluation, and the realm of practical implementation is of a non-exhaustive and non-linear nature. Just as the official evaluation of *Active—Back Sooner* does not begin to exhaust the actual implementation practice or to capture the effects of *Active—Back Sooner*, such is the case in the relationship between the official guidelines for the content of the municipal follow-up and the numerous and highly heterogeneous practices that took place. It is also true of the converse; to understand the initial stages of policy design and the official life of a policy only in the light of its subsequent fate as a guide for practice would be a most reductive understanding of the work carried out at this stage and in the realm of policy-making (cf. Latour 1996; Mosse 2005). This takes me back to the idea proposed earlier—that the reductive understanding of reality which brackets off expectable interference from the socio-economic or organizational context for implementation has less to do with sloppy work than it has to do with the nature of policy-making itself.

Insights of this sort may be found in the work of both James Scott (1998) and

David Mosse (2007). Scott distinguishes between a project design's function as a plan versus its function as a scheme (Scott 1998: 228), arguing that while as a written plan a project design can be well crafted in meeting current development trends and criteria for allocation of resources, it might simultaneously fail as a scheme for the development it envisions. This gap, he argues, is due in part to planners' preference for "administrative ease" (ibid.: 242) or their conviction that "they alone knew how to organize a more satisfactory, rational, and productive life for their citizens" —what he terms the "hubris of planners" (ibid.: 247). The "gap" is theorized differently by Mosse who points out that the primary goal of a policy is not to orientate practice. Rather, before it leaves the offices of the policy-makers a policy must primarily serve the purpose of legitimizing an intervention. In this sense it is a site for both negotiating allocation of resources and for mobilizing support for the intervention, centrally and locally (Mosse 2007: 460). This purpose, he writes, defines the crafting of the policy much more than its need to orientate subsequent practice. Therefore the discrepancy between policy in its design-phase and policy as a set of realizable guidelines is not—in Mosse's view—owed to "hubris" or self-sufficiency on part of the planners but may rather be put down to the incongruence of the complexity of a social reality and the simplicity of a piece of policy crafted to meet political requirements for consensus and the theoretical "state of the art." This in turn makes translation back and forth between policy and practice both necessary and unavoidable—a condition Scott himself realizes when he faults policy-makers for their failure to acknowledge that the efficiency of any plan depends on "the response and cooperation of real human subjects" (1998: 225). We see this dependency in the contrast between *Bending the rules and agreements* and *The end of meaning* which illustrated the vulnerability of officials plans to the caseworkers' and employees' creative engagement in reformulating and reinterpreting the rules, laws and agreements—vulnerable because the informal work they carried out both sustained and distorted the initial policy.

In other words, both Scott and Mosse draw our attention to the fact that the planning phase of an intervention continues throughout its "implementation." It is, however, the latter analysis by Mosse with which my data most agree. Through the eight portraits we see how on the one hand *Active—Back Sooner*, in its official version, grew and became internally inconsistent as it took on more and more agendas (to save public budgets, to introduce an evidence-based approach to policy-making, to assist people back to work, and so on), while its multiple practical versions mutated, split, or died off as they were implemented in the municipal context and at the private employment agency ENGA. In the Municipality alone, *Active—Back Sooner* existed in the shape of three non-corresponding paper versions before it reached the first participants: first, it existed as a piece of nationally promulgated policy (presented in the portrait *The perfect plan*), next as an official local version of the same project and finally—after the first two meetings in the project group—it existed on paper in an unofficial adaptation as the local project design, the crafting of which is portrayed in *The project multiplies*. When the practical implementation of *Active—Back Sooner* began, the caseworkers' attempts to minimize the nuisance and harm generated by the project, while optimizing the conditions for working their total caseload, triggered a series of what I called "ad hoc plans." These deviations from the paper versions of *Active—Back Sooner* had sometimes very little to do with what was projected in the original national policy.

The theory of implementation that the material presented in this book must give rise to is one in which re-design and adaptation of plans and policy takes place throughout implementation and one that must embrace the non-linear nature of such an effort. What is important to note here, is that the mutation of the policy happened not only at the local level usually associated with implementation, but that it continued to mutate centrally in the Ministry too. In portrait 5 *The purpose multiplies* and later in portrait 6 *The productivity of controversy* we saw how the official, original policy evolved and adapted of its own accord and without necessarily feeding back into the realm of "implementation." In this light, we will misunderstand "implementation" if we regard it primarily as a practical executive phase subsequent to policy-making or "planning." Rather, it would be most correct to regard implementation as a second design phase in its own right, albeit a highly unstable one.

Thesis 5: policy disintegrates and the contradictory nature of bureaucracy is fed by attempts to make something sensible take place

If we take a few analytical steps back from the process of implementation with its flow of seemingly random decision-making and outcomes, a pattern becomes discernible. If project designs, purposes, and criteria for success got multiplied throughout the implementation of *Active—Back Sooner* the guiding principle under which the trial's multiple planners approached its realization was unambiguous: they all wanted *Active—Back Sooner* in its multiple guises to "make sense" in the concrete situations in which decisions had to be taken.

The scrutiny of the trial by the media and the scientific community was sparked, as we saw in portrait 6 *The productivity of controversy*, by the reporter's conviction that something did not make sense or did not add up. In the job center, every conscious diversion from the original plan was initiated by some claim that something did not make sense or was not expedient, and the resulting production of new plans and directives, as we saw in portrait 3 *The trial mutates*, was caused by decisions to move in a purposeful, meaningful, or sensible direction. When, during the midway seminar, the civil servant from the National Labor Market Authority (described in *The productivity of controversy*), lamented the changed criteria for exemption and the adjustments of the project's requirements for follow-up it was because these changes prevented the eventual measuring of whether or not the intervention they had originally envisioned "made sense." On the other hand, when the criteria and guidelines *were* changed intermittently, it was in response to external claims (from media and caseworkers) that the intervention did not make sense as it was. When Peter and Ulla had wanted the job center to be part of the intervention to begin with it was because, as we saw in portrait 1 *Making a difference*, it held the promise of being a meaningful way of working with sickness benefit cases while it simultaneously also "made sense" for them to be up-front with the development. Throughout the portraits, *The trial mutates* and *Satisfying needs*, we saw how the caseworkers tried to make sensible decisions in relation to economy, time, energy, the project design, administration of the project, or the estimated impact on the individual case.

If we zoom out further and look at the wider administrative municipal context in which the project was implemented, in portraits 5 *The purpose multiplies* and 7 *"Bending" the rules and agreements*, it becomes clear that not only were the multiple goals of *Active—Back Sooner* internally inconsistent, on a larger organizational scale this project was but one among many overlapping plans and projects all of which aimed at improving the casework. The trial's target figures, which the caseworkers and employees at ENGA had to meet, were just one of a set of many different goals and targets within their purview. Seen from this perspective, the implementation of *Active—Back Sooner* may best be described as a series of highly uncoordinated attempts to make sensible decisions, which took place on all organizational levels in parallel, and to a wide extent unrelated, ways. Before I move on to argue how these individual attempts to "make sense" not only tore *Active—Back Sooner* apart but in fact rather than producing sense contributed to the very opposite, I allow myself a brief and relevant digression.

In February 1968, journalist Patricia McBroom wrote a column in *Science News* reporting some new results from the behavioral sciences. A number of experiments conducted by professor of psychology, Dr Eliot Aronson, showed that by prohibiting children from playing with the toys they had showed a preference for they created in the children a "cognitive dissonance" between the desired and the possible. This led the children to fabricate their own justifications for the rejection of the previously desired toy—in other words they began to actively prefer a different and available toy and to actively down-rate the previously preferred. The basic method of the experiment was to create a situation in which the pressure for someone to behave contrary to their inclination would be strong enough to induce them to change their behavior but not so strong as in itself to justify the change of behavior. In Aronson's experiments, and other subsequent experiments applying the same methodology, the conclusion was that the weaker the justification (usually a punishment of sorts) provided by the "outside" (by circumstances or by a concrete person) or the milder the repercussion for not changing behavior, the more likely it was that the test subjects would make up a justification of their own. The hypothesis the methodology built on was, according to Dr Aronson that "[people] have a drive for consistency, a drive to convince themselves that their behavior is not absurd" (McBroom 1968: 193).

In Dr Aronson's hypothesis the experience of absurdity arises from the conflict between the desired and the possible and it is a condition from which people will try to escape. So too in Thomas Nagel's philosophy (1971): "In ordinary life," he writes, "a situation is absurd when it includes a conspicuous discrepancy between pretension or aspiration and reality" (Nagel 1971: 718). The discrepancy between what we wish and what we are able to do, he continues, is something from which most people will seek to distance themselves: "When a person finds himself in an absurd situation, he will usually attempt to change it, by modifying his aspirations, by trying to bring reality into better accord with them, or by removing himself from the situation entirely" (ibid.). We have seen in this book how all the different "planners" of *Active—Back Sooner* tried to overcome the internal contradictions of the intervention throughout its implementation by these exact techniques: some tried to distance themselves from the situation, as Kirsten did by requesting to be exempted from the project, while other case-workers contemplated quitting their job in the municipal job center entirely ("I am asking myself whether I wouldn't rather be unemployed"); some remodeled the plans and purposes to fit what they deemed sensible ("surely this wasn't meant to make people worse"); and some remodeled their own expectations ("there are certain things one has to accept in order to work in a place like this").

However, as Nagel argues, we are not always willing or able to extricate our-selves from positions whose absurdity has become clear to us (Nagel 1971); nor does a remodeling of our expectations or the purpose of our actions necessarily remove the contradictions we have become aware of in anything but a temporary manner (se also Rapport 1999). In Nagel's treatise on absurdity, as in Goodwin's analysis of institutional absurdity, the "decision" therefore becomes a central act. It is in the moments in which we have to make decisions—where we have to decide what to take note of and by the same token what we will ignore—that absurdity threatens to overwhelm us. In the moment of taking decisions (of putting words on paper, making a referral, formulating a purpose for referral, planning a prac-tical course of action, issuing a public document, putting together a timetable) a selection between possibly conflicting values, goals, contents, or purposes takes place and we must recognize that by pursuing one purpose or goal we might undermine our possibility of complying with another. In these moments of dis-engaged reflection we realize that our decisions and certainties "are possible only because there is a great deal we do not bother to rule out" (Nagel 1971: 723). For instance, it is only sensible to adhere strictly to a project design if one maintains the conviction that one is performing a controlled trial while blocking out every-thing that could indicate that what was, in fact, taking place was something dif-ferent. It only makes sense to base one's decisions on administrative ease if one blocks out everything that could indicate that one is, in fact, not contributing to the overall policy aims of one's field of intervention anymore.

In the material I have presented in this book, many of the caseworkers' decisions were of such a nature that any decision taken would work directly against another pressing concern: The more time the municipal caseworkers spent working thoroughly on one specific case the less time they had for the next "specific case." The faster they worked, the less arguments Peter had for getting the Central Administration to allocate extra resources to the unit. By changing the criteria for exemption and the instructions concerning the exe-cution of *Active—Back Sooner* the civil servants in the National Labor Market Authority undermined the opportunity to see if the intervention worked or not. Yet had they not done it they would deliberately and, despite knowledge to the contrary, have endorsed a course of action deemed by most parties involved to be counterproductive—i.e. not an option when working with health-related issues and when using public funds. While all the caseworkers' and civil servants' attempts to foster a sensible and purposeful "system" had an erosive effect on *Active—Back Sooner* and the policy aim it represented, these very attempts were directly contributing to producing an ever more contradictory organizational environment. Yet the more contradictory the organizational environment the caseworkers and civil servants found themselves in, the stronger the experience of the absurdity grew, and the more impetus there was to "bend and stretch" in attempts to force something meaningful, purposeful, and expedient to take place. And round and round it goes.

At ENGA the employees could put in extra time and render unpaid services to make the local labor market effort meaningful but this was at the same time the very thing that sustained the continuation of a practice they believed was fundamentally senseless; by sustaining them by working extra hours, offering unpaid services, and cutting unofficial agreements they deprived their managers of the very means they needed to argue their case with the municipal Central Administration and potentially obtain a more expedient practice regarding referrals and contracts. In the job center, when the caseworkers did their utmost to identify or even invent sensible purposes for people's referrals to the private employment agencies they created an overload of work for both themselves and their colleagues in the private sector. This overload of work directly contributed to preventing the very kind of work they all deemed to be necessary and expedient.

Here we may at last identify the central circular principle by which the contradictory nature of bureaucracy feeds. What the absurdity of bureaucracy really can teach us is that people's well-meant attempts and almost primal instinct to compensate for malfunctioning bureaucratic systems—by repairing them, short-cutting them, or surpassing them—is in fact what they feed on and what sustains their malfunctioning.

Epilogue: bureaucracy—choose your own adventure

1. Team meeting (from 19 and 26)

On a Thursday morning in November 2009 you walk down the linoleum clad staircase leading from the 3rd floor canteen back to your ground-level office. You could have opted for the old squeaky elevator but after sitting still during the weekly team meeting you feel like walking. You have recently been employed in a Danish municipality as a caseworker. Your primary task is to make assessments of the right to sickness benefit in cases where people who are ill long-term cannot tend to their current job or apply for one in any meaningful way. When you cycled to work a few hours earlier the moisture of the autumn air crept through your coat and shirt and made you cold to the bone. Although situated in a shabby building in a shabby street, the local job center, like all public buildings in Denmark, is blessed with district heating. Yet you hold your coffee mug tight between your hands to warm your fingers while trying not to spill any, hugging your notebook and a stack of papers in the nook of your arm, as you turn a corner. You balance your mug briefly on the Xerox as you collect your mail from the pigeon holes before continuing down the corridor of offices and enter your own.

Once back in your office, you sort through your post. Among some letters containing medical records submitted by your clients' GPs you find a catalogue where the private employment agencies in the municipality present their so-called "active offers." Recently, due to a revision in the sickness benefit legislation, it has been possible to refer recipients of sickness benefit to "active courses." It has been decided by the Minister of Employment that maintaining a degree of physical activity and social contact during prolonged periods of illness might further one's chances of returning to work as soon as possible. Furthermore, the legislation is meant to counter the documented tendency that people who suffer from a period of long-term illness are at high risk of becoming permanently unemployed, and thus possibly permanently reliant on public benefits.

At the meeting your team manager, Peter, complained that several of you caseworkers have too many cases. One of your colleagues, Jo, a young woman known for her efficiency and ability to close cases, asked Peter what he expects you all to do when the waiting room is stuffed with people as it was on the previous Tuesday. At the moment, Jo said, she has got more cases on her case-management sheet than any of you—130. Peter insisted that according to the number of cases per hour, divided by the number of caseworkers, nobody ought to have more than the maximum number of cases on their case-management sheets—about 90. After this, one of your colleagues, Frank who, unlike Jo, rarely participates in discussions, raised his voice:

> *Frank*: Well, we already told you that your numbers do not reflect our reality. We cannot do this by averages and say we each speak of such and such a number per hour. Some might finish only one meeting the first hour because the citizen is crying and is completely miserable. Then somebody else will have to take four that hour.

> *Jo*: We are also dealing with the new extended requirements for record keeping. Qualitatively that means that I can only do half the number of cases I could before.

> *Peter*: If we look at the numbers we reach our goals.

The discussion is yet another rendition of your unit's main problem; while you all feel that you do sloppy work and have routinized your casework beyond the acceptable, on the face of it your unit more than complies with the requirements in your performance contract. This makes it hard for Peter to argue convincingly that further resources be channeled into your unit. If you leave the discussion feeling slightly uncomfortable, knowing that you are definitely not one of the caseworkers who has more than the required number of cases on your case-management sheet, **go to option 2**. If after the morning's discussion you are tired of your colleagues' constant complaining, then **go to 13**.

2. Pulling a case (from 1)

You were quiet during the morning's discussion and didn't know exactly what to make of it. You cannot decide whether being one of the caseworkers with only the required number of cases is a good thing. It should be, since you are complying with the directives of the management but there is something about the general tone amongst your colleagues that makes you think otherwise. You sit down by your office desk and begin to arrange everything for the morning's first meeting with the new citizens—those who have just reached the 8th week of sickness absence and are therefore summoned to an obligatory meeting with the munici-pality. On the shelf beside you, you keep various letters and papers that you might need to give the citizens, and consent forms they will possibly need to fill in so that you can legally request their medical papers. When everything is ready you walk back down the corridor and past the waiting area which today is stuffed with people waiting for their obligatory meeting. You walk up to a tall coffee table by the reception desk and get behind the line of caseworkers waiting. When you get to the table you take the top cardboard file and sign your name next to the citizen's name on a list; with this gesture you have become their caseworker. You take a quick look inside the file before turning towards the waiting crowd to call out the name on the front of the file. You finish the morning's first conversation quickly and are soon back to take the next file from the pile. It is now 10:20am and the waiting room is still full of people. **Go to 7.**

3. A third case? (from 7)

You inform the woman briefly about the requirement for activity and tell her that you will get back to her after she has seen her doctor. You reason that the woman has enough on her mind already and need not deal with the demand for activity just yet. You have now spoken to the number of citizens who you are supposed to this hour. According to Peter, your team leader, if everybody does this there ought to be no case-files left on the coffee table in the waiting room. However, it is only 10:40am and you can see that the waiting room is still full of people. If you remember Peter's caution about the case-management sheets and wait until 11am before you pull your next case, then **go to 5**. If you remember your colleague Frank's point about some cases requiring more time than others and therefore decide to pull another case before taking a break, then **go to 8**.

4. Further into the case (from 7)

You decide that this is a case that might need some extra effort and care. You are concerned about the reference the woman made in passing to a number of previous periods of sickness absence. You know that she will only be entitled to a total of 52 week of sickness benefit within any one period of 18 months and you decide to open the woman's electronic journal to see how many weeks the woman has left until her right to sickness benefit runs out altogether. You see that because the woman has worked 14 months in succession there is plenty of time left but you also notice that she has had multiple periods of prolonged sickness in the past. You therefore decide to find out if there is anything in the woman's current occupational choices that might present a recurrent problem and you ask her about her education and professional area. The woman begins to weep again. "I cannot work with people anymore, I panic," she sobs. You make a mental note to look into the possibilities for re-schooling, but you do not bring it up now since you do not want to get the woman's hopes up in case she is not eligible. Instead you go on to tell her about the requirement for her to attend a course of at least ten hours weekly or return part-time to work in order to maintain her right to sickness benefit. You dread her reaction and have already made the decision to exempt her from the obligation if she resists. To your surprise she responds positively to the idea of being referred to a private employment office for relevant course work. You tell the woman about a course which might help her reach a degree of "clarification about her current problems." You quote an oft used sentence from the catalogue you received earlier. You never completely understood what hides behind this phrase but luckily the woman does not inquire about its meaning.

After the woman has left, you notice that the conversation has taken 45 minutes and the next hour of consultations has already begun. You feel bad as you hear your colleagues in the corridor talking about how busy this past hour has been. Later in the day during the lunch break you overhear the ever efficient Jo complain about the fact that "as long as some people insist on chitchatting with the citizens the rest of us will have to run all the faster." You don't say anything but wonder how your colleagues can do the job so much faster than you can. **Go to 8.**

5. You wait (from 3)

You decide to wait, and spend the time until next hour's round of conversations begins making yourself a fresh cup of coffee and typing the woman's information and your agreements into the electronic journal. A few minutes later, the efficient Jo pops in on her way down to the reception area. "Hey, do you mind giving a hand? The waiting room is still busting full" she smiles. You nod and hurry after her. The reception area is beginning to fill up with the citizens who have an appointment for the following hour and there are still quite a few people left from the first intake hour. This means they have waited at least 45 minutes by now. **Go to 8.**

6. Booking a course (from 10, 16, 17, 23, 25 and 31)

When the two hours of conversations are over you have six new cases in the pile on your shelf. You eat lunch with your colleagues and you discuss how busy these hours have been. Some of your colleagues have acquired seven new cases. They complain about the management's poor planning of your unit's work and point out the fact that despite several of your colleagues being either sick, on holiday, or attending courses, they still summon the same number of citizens every morning. You shut the complaints out and return to your office to begin filling in the records of today's cases. You start with the case of Ali and open the electronic portal through which you communicate the contracts with the private employment agencies. While the system opens you consider what to write in the box where you have to indicate the purpose of the referral. You are not entirely convinced that a referral will help Ali in any way but at a recent meeting a senior colleague of yours reminded you all that the Municipality will have a higher per-centage of their expenses reimbursed by the State if you make referrals and you reckon there is always the chance that Ali might benefit from what they can offer at the agency. If you make a referral straight away to the agency where you told Ali you would refer him then **go to 22.** If you are hesitant to make a referral due to Ali's strong objections, **go to 28.**

7. A complicated case (from 2)

The middle-aged woman whose name you call out is sitting in a chair some distance away from the rest of the waiting people. When you extend your hand to greet her she briefly meets your eye, quickly shakes your hand, then looks away.

As you walk with her towards your office you notice she is crying and you sense that she is very uncomfortable with the situation. Back in your office you begin by informing her about the law: what possibilities and what obligations receiving sickness benefit entails. You always begin the conversation by informing citizens about the law to get it over with since, in your experience, people do not listen anyway. The woman weeps while you talk. When you are done, you ask her if she has a job. She says she does not. She tells you that she has been on sick leave before because of stress and because she feels "worn out."

> *Woman*: I was on sick leave before but then I was no longer entitled to sickness benefit and I had to find myself a job. I applied for a temporary position as a nursery teacher and got it. I did not see anybody outside work during those 14 months, not my children, not my grandchildren. I just cried every day. I wanted the job so much. I just had to go through with it. But I couldn't.

The woman sobs violently now and you hand her some tissues you have standing on your table. You ask her if she has been to see a psychologist. She tells you she cannot afford it. Your office deals strictly with work retention and sickness benefit but you inform her that she can apply for financial support at the social security office. Then you ask her if she has seen a psychiatrist or takes any kind of medication. She tells you she has been trying to see a psychiatrist but that there is an 18-month waiting list. You suggest she get on the waiting list in case she might still need it in 18 months' time. Then you suggest she makes an appointment to see her doctor in order to get some medical treatment started. The woman agrees with your advice and thanks you. The conversation has lasted too long already and you have not even informed her of the new legislation that demand you refer her to course of "activity" at a private employment agency in order for her to remain entitled to sickness benefit. If you inform her about it briefly and tell her you will talk more about it on the phone after she has been to see her doctor, then **go to option 3**. If you decide to go further into her case now, then **go to 4.**

8. Record-keeping (from 3, 4, 5, 8, 15, 20 and 30)

Before the daily intake of new sickness benefit cases is over you have added five new cases to the pile of cardboard files that has been growing steadily during the past few weeks on the shelf behind your chair. You decide to spend the time until the daily "phone hour" by completing the record-keeping pertaining to cases from the previous week. You take the bottom file from the stack and search your memory for the person whose name is on the flap. No matter how hard you try you cannot recall the person or your meeting. You open the file and reread the handwritten notes you took during the meeting. The case gradually returns to you and you open the electronic journal and being typing the data and agreements into the system. You make it halfway through before the phone rings. Since it rings before 2pm when the official phone hour begins, you know it is most likely to be a colleague. If you pick up the phone, then **go to 11**. If you pull out the phone cord to get some uninterrupted work done before the phone hour begins, **go to 21.**

9. You take Ann's call (from 18)

Knowing that with the way the phones are currently wired there is no guarantee that the woman will get hold of Ann tomorrow you decide to see if you can help her. However, it turns out that the woman has tried to get hold of Ann because she has decided that she would like to be referred to an "active offer" by one of the private employment agencies or alternatively to return to work part-time. She has called to make arrangements. You had imagined that the woman perhaps just wanted to enquire about the specifics of the law so this is a bit more casework than you had imagined. You open Ann's electronic calendar and see that the next meeting between the woman and Ann is in three weeks' time. You ask the woman to wait until her meeting with Ann to submit her request. Within the next half hour you take another 11 phone calls, many of which are for Ann, while the open record entries pile up on your computer desktop. **Go to 19.**

10. You refer Ali to a different "package" (from 22)

You are not used to working with referrals to "packages." It is only since the revised sickness benefit legislation that it has been part of your job description and you know very little about the content of the different "packages." So far you have just referred people to "sickness benefit packages" since they are on sickness benefit but maybe in Ali's case a "job seeking package" would not be a bad idea. You decide to look up the agency's course description and think to yourself that as Ali is likely to move on to professional rehabilitation this course sounds like a good opportunity to work towards this goal. Alternatively, if the application is rejected he needs to find out what he wants to do instead of being a chauffeur. All the obstacles have got you thinking and you write extensively to the agency about what you intend with Ali's referral. You also remind them that Ali is sick and might have trouble showing up on a regular basis. As you send off the contract through the electronic portal your phone begins to ring. As you pick it up you hear the phones ringing out from every office in the hallway. The phone hour has begun. **Go to 18** to continue or **go back to 6** to handle the casework differently.

11. You answer the phone (from 8)

You decide to pick up the phone and it turns out to be one of the interpreters used by the Municipality in cases where recipients of sickness benefit do not speak sufficient Danish. The interpreter is calling on behalf of an Asian woman whose case has kept causing you problems. The woman has repeatedly not shown up for the meetings you have summoned her for and you are growing impatient. The interpreter informs you that there are significant social problems in the family—as one of her children has died the mother is utterly depressed. Meanwhile the other son is in constant trouble with his school, and so on. You had meant to do something about this case long ago. You had the sense something outside the normal routine was needed but at the same time this is why you have kept putting it off and then forgotten about it. Meanwhile the woman's case is now 26 weeks "old" and this means you will have to transfer it to a different team. This is an internal procedure recommended by a private consultancy company commissioned to optimize your work flow. You tell this to the interpreter. After you hang up the phone you decide to transfer the case immediately while the conversation is still fresh in your memory. You open the internal mail system and begin typing the mail. You pause for a moment and contemplate whether this would be a case in which the department of employment, of which you are part, ought to work together with the department of social services, which is involved in the Asian woman's life as well, due the problems in the family. You have the sense that this is an obvious case in which the departments ought to collaborate, but at the same time you know what the busy colleagues in the team you now must refer her case to will think about the extra work this will necessarily involve. If you decide to recommend collaboration then **go to 12**. If you decide to pass on the case and let the caseworker who will from now on be working the case make the decision, then **go to 20**.

12. You recommend collaboration (from 11)

You decide to write into the note to the team, who will from now on be working on the Asian woman's case, that you recommend collaboration with the social service office. You feel a bit naughty when you click on "send" and the case-file is officially transferred to the other team. Since you have written a recommendation into the actual file you know it will be hard for them not to follow your advice and you know how time-consuming that is going to be. You are also fully aware that if you had had more time to work your individual cases you would have realized the need for such collaboration long ago. Therefore a recommendation at this late point will reflect badly upon you.

Now that the Asian woman's case is out of your hands you turn to your cardboard files from the previous week to resume the paperwork. You finish the casework you were interrupted in and decide to proceed with the referral of the woman you spoke to this morning. You told her that you would get back to her when you had decided which course would match her requirements best. You have no real sense of what is going on in the different agencies and as you leaf through their written presentations you find that they are all rather alike. As you read carefully through the presentation material you are interrupted by a sudden symphony of ringing phones that sound from the open office doors all the way down the hallway. The phone hour has just started. **Go to 14** to continue or **go back to 8** for a chance to handle the cases differently.

13. Pulling a case (from 1)

You leave the meeting feeling sympathetic to the frustrations of your colleagues, which you share, but you are immensely tired of their constant complaining no matter what Peter and the management try to do. You are determined to maintain a positive attitude despite the fact that you have 13 case-files sitting on your desk, which you still have to find the time to type into the electronic journal. You think that there are certain things one has to accept in order to work here, like the low pay, the law, and the general busyness. "If one cannot accept them one better find somewhere else to work": you say that often. This morning you arrived an hour early to catch up with some of the paperwork from the previous days and if things go as usual you will probably be the last to leave as well. Working more than the 37 hours on your contract is a prerequisite for you to keep up with the intake of cases. The hours you accumulate on your "flexi account" as a result will enable you to take an extra-long summer vacation. You shake off the morning's discussion, pick up the large glass you prefer to drink your coffee from, and walk down to put it into the sink in the coffee area. Then you walk towards the waiting room, pass the citizens who have turned up and get in the line behind your colleagues who are all waiting for their turn to pull a case-file from the pile on the tall coffee table next to the reception desk. When it's your turn, you pick up the top cardboard folder and take a quick look inside it before turning towards the waiting crowd to call out the name on the front of the file. You quickly finish your first conversation and return to the bustling waiting room to take your second case. "Ali!"

The man who gets up to shake your hand is Middle Eastern. Like most men from the Middle East that you see here, he works with unskilled labor. You quickly establish that he has been working as a chauffeur but has been fired during his period of sickness absence. His problem is a serious case of back pain for which he takes strong pain killers. Had Ali still been employed you would have been required by law to make contact with his employer and see if he could be temporarily placed in a less physically strenuous position within the company. As this is not an option you must now see if you can otherwise make Ali return to work as soon as possible so that he will not be reliant on public benefits. You tell Ali about the requirement for activity during the period in which he receives sickness benefit. To your surprise, Ali brings up the topic of professional rehabilitation instead and he turns out to have an elite education from the military which makes him a likely candidate for re-schooling. You tell him you will transfer his case to the team that works with professional rehabilitation applications and that, in the meanwhile, you will refer him to a course. As things are, Ali does not want to be referred to "activity." He pleads with you and reminds you that he is sick; that his back hurts; that the strong medication he takes sometimes makes him too dizzy to even get out of bed. **Go to 16**.

14. Phone hour (from 12, 15, 20 and 30)

The phones are open one hour each day. This is when the citizens whose case-worker you are can call you and ask you about their case or tell you about any development that relates to their health situation and planned return to work. The first person who calls you is a woman who suffers from depression and anxiety. With the 20 new cases you have added to your case-management sheet just this previous week you have no immediate recollection of her. As she talks you quickly look her up in the electronic journal. You see that the woman's case is your colleague's, who you know is currently sick. If you take the conversation yourself then **go to 24**. If you decide to leave a message for your colleague and end the conversation here then **go to 27**.

15. You call the man (from 21)

You ask the caseworker to scan and send you the document the man has signed and decide to call him at once to get the matter out of the way. You know that a date can often be written wrong or a wrong box ticked. A few minutes later you receive the document in your email and you call the man, who answers his phone. He tells you that he did not understand the information sheet and just signed it when his employer presented him with it. He also tells you that he still has not heard from the private employment agency you said you would refer him to. He is getting nervous that he might have overlooked something or that the letter has been lost in the mail and he is worried he might lose his right to sick-ness benefit due to this. You inform the man about his mistake and tell him that you have not had time to book a course for him yet. You promise that you will do it straight away and also that you will make sure his case is opened again. You hang up and email your college in the economic section asking him to reopen the case immediately. You then type up the man's explanation for returning the form incorrectly in the electronic journal and open the electronic portal through which you must book the courses. You choose the agency you decided on earlier and begin filling in the box in which you must inform the agency's staff of the purpose of the referral. You quickly copy-and-paste a standard formulation into the box—"citizen must be clarified in respect to return to work"—and send it off. Now the man can expect to hear from the agency within the next few days. As you return to the journal to type your information and decisions into the man's now active case you are interrupted by a sudden symphony of ringing phones that sound from the open office doors all the way down the hallway. The phone hour has just started. **Go to 14** to continue or **go back to 8** for a chance to handle the case differently.

16. Referral (from 13)

You decide that Ali's back pain is not an obstacle to his participation in the course. You remind him that everybody who attends these courses is sick. You tell him that you will refer him for activity 25 hours a week and you turn to your notice board where you have a list of the different agencies hanging, specifying their target group and their address. You look up Ali's address and tell him that there is an agency just a few blocks from where he lives and asks him if he would like you to book a course there? He consents and you briefly inform him about his rights and obligations before wrapping up the conversation. By now it is 10:40am, you are done handling your second case this morning and there ought to be no more people left in the waiting room according to Peter's calculations. However, you can see that your colleagues keep bringing people in for conversations. If, in accordance with Peter's caution about you and your colleagues' case-management sheets, you wait until 11:00am before you pull your next file then **go to 17**. If you remember your colleague's point about some cases requiring more time than others and decide to take another case before taking a break, then **go to 6**.

17. You wait (from 16)

You decide to spend the time until next hour's intake writing a request to Ali's doctor for medical papers. Before you do so, you need to use the restroom and on the way back you get yourself a glass of water from the coffee area, since there is no more coffee on the pot. As you walk back down the corridor your colleague Jo passes you on her way to the reception. "Do you mind giving a hand?" she smiles, "the waiting room is still stuffed." You nod and hurry in to your office and put your glass of water on your table before you follow her. The reception area is already beginning to fill up with the citizens who have an appointment the following hour and there is a still a considerable pile of folders remaining on the coffee table. This means they have waited at least 50 minutes by now. **Go to 6**.

18. Phone hour (from 10, 23, 25 and 31)

The phones are open one hour each day. This is when the citizens whose caseworker you are can call you and ask you questions about their case or tell you about any development that relates to their health situation and planned return to work. However, due to the way in which the phones are wired, if your phone is engaged the call will be redirected and your colleagues will end up taking the calls pertaining to your cases. And while they are busy answering your calls their calls might in return be redirected to your phone. The first call you take today is from a woman who wants to speak to Ann. Ann has left early today because it is her birthday. If you ask the woman to call back tomorrow and end the conversation, **go to 29**. If you decide to see if you might help the woman and you take the conversation yourself then **go to 9**.

19. Closing time (from 9 and 29)

At 3pm, by the official end of the phone hour, you pull the cord out of your phone to make sure you can work undisturbed for the rest of the day; you walk down the corridor to use the restroom and make yourself a cup of coffee. The phone kept ringing throughout the phone hour and you had no time to record entries in between conversations. This means that you have currently eleven open entries you need to finish before you can continue to type the case-files on your shelf into the records. By 4pm you have finished the entries from the phone hour and handled the related referrals to private employment agencies. You now turn to the stack of unfiled case-files on the shelf behind you. When you leave your office as one of the last in the unit at 5pm you have completed the records in 5 out of the 6 new cases you got today. With the 13 cases you had already this makes it a total of 14 unfiled case-files, some of which date back to the beginning of last week. Are you ready to go home? If yes, then **go to 32**. If you want to try a different path and return to the team meeting then **go back to 1**.

20. Pass on decision (from 11)

You decide to refer the case without specific recommendations. You will leave it up to the caseworker who will be handling the Asian woman's case from now on to decide what she wants to do with it. You know that if you write a recommendation to collaborate with the social service office into the woman's journal it will be very hard for the next caseworker to decide not to. You have only recently become aware of the complexity of the case and you feel that recommending such a time-consuming task just when you are about to refer it is unfair to your colleague and will reflect badly on you. You write a detailed email to the team that will handle the case from now on and press "send."

Now the Asian woman's case is out of your hands and you return to your cardboard files from today to catch up on some record writing before the phone hour starts. You begin with the case of the woman you spoke to this morning and you decide you had better get her medical papers since you have got a feeling that this case might be complicated. The woman signed a consent form when you spoke to her, so you are in your rights to get it. You open the document you have to use when requesting such information and begin typing your requests into the "free text" field. You want to know several things since you have an idea that re-schooling might be an option and you know that the team that handles such professional rehabilitation applications will need this information anyway. However, you soon have to limit your requests because the "free text" field, which is the only place you can write what you want, is locked to a certain number of words. As you contemplate how to phrase your request in the briefest way possible you are interrupted by a sudden symphony of ringing phones that sound from the open office doors all the way down the hallway. The phone hour has just started. **Go to 14** to continue or **go back to 8** for a chance to handle the case differently.

21. You pull the cord (from 8)

You decide to remove the cord from the phone which will give you about an hour to catch up on writing before the phone hour begins at 2pm. You finish writing up the case you were working on when the phone rang and pick up the next in the pile. You type the personal registration number written on the cover of the cardboard folder into the electronic case management system. While you wait for the system to open the electronic record you retrieve your hand-written notes from the folder and start reading through them. This is a case you took on earlier this week and it concerns a man you decided to refer to a course in one of the private employment agencies. When you mentioned the referral at the meeting, you were not specific. You have no real sense of what is going on in the different agencies and the written material on their "packages," as they call their courses, are all rather alike. You turn to the row of shelves behind your chair and retrieve the catalogue you got with your mail this morning. Leafing through it you settle on a "package" you think sounds reasonable.

You now turn your attention to the computer. The system denies any knowledge of an active case belonging to the personal registration number you just entered. You pick up the case-file and double check. You have entered it correctly. You now open a different system which lists the history of benefit payments and here you see that the case has been shut down by the section of the Municipality that deals with finances. The reason stated is "full return to work," which makes you suspicious, since this alleged return to work is supposed to have taken place more than a week before the meeting you had with him. You plug in the phone cord and call up the office responsible for shutting the case in order to ask how this "return" has been reported? The caseworker you get hold of informs you that the man's employer has returned an information sheet where the box "returned to work" has been ticked. The man's signature is on the document. You tell the caseworker that you are fairly certain that this is a mistake and you ask them to be ready to open the case again if you turn out to be right. If you send the man a letter asking him for an explanation, **go to 30**. If you decide to call up the man instead then **go to 15**.

22. Complications (from 6)

You decide to refer Ali to the private employment agency straight away. You are convinced that it is better for him to get out and get some exercise and meet some people than merely sit at home. But as you search for the "sickness benefit package" at the agency you chose it seems there is none. You double-check the list of suppliers of "sickness benefit packages" on your wall and the agency definitely is listed. You search through the electronic portal again but the result is the same: it seems it cannot be booked. You look up their phone number and call their reception to ask if they no longer offer "sickness benefit packages" They do, but it turns out the course is fully booked and there is no available space until five weeks' time. You unpin the list of agencies from your notice board to inspect the different addresses. You had chosen that particular agency because it was situated close to Ali who complained about not being able to get around easily. Now you scan the list for addresses that are either close to Ali's apartment or have a direct bus connection. You settle on two options and call Ali to ask him which of the two he prefers instead of the one you had agreed on originally. To your satisfaction he chooses your secret favorite among all the agencies—it is situated in peaceful and beautiful surroundings and you imagine that it would be a nice place to recuperate. When you return to the electronic portal you realize that this agency's "sickness benefit package" is also fully booked. You are embarrassed at the thought of having to call Ali again and you consider exempting him from referral altogether. But then you notice there is a space available in the "job search package." If you exempt Ali from referral to a course then **go to 31**. If you refer Ali to the "job search package" instead, then **go to 10**.

23. You pick up the phone (from 28)

The daily phone hour is not due for another hour so you know it is most likely a colleague who is trying to reach you. You therefore decide to pick up the phone; it will be quicker than answering the email you will inevitably receive if they do not get hold of you. Instead it turns out to be a young woman whose case you have handled for some time. You remember her immediately because you have had several conversations with her and they all revolve around the same problem. In summary, your conversation goes like this:

> *She*: I cannot pay my rent and expenses with the sickness benefit. I have to find a job.

> *You*: If you tell me you are in fact able to work, I am going to have to shut your case. You know that.

> *She*: I know. I am still sick. I just cannot live off what I get.

After informing her that you will shut her case you hang up. Cases such as these are what you describe to yourself as catch-22 situations: You know the young woman has been suffering from anorexia for many years which has caused her to be on sickness benefit for extended periods. But the fact that she cannot live off sickness benefit forces her to look for employment in which case she is considered to have demonstrated that she is able to work and thus not eligible for sickness benefit. However, in the past she has not been able to hold on to jobs for very long because she is in fact not well. And then she ends up in the sickness benefit system again. It is your impression that things will continue like that. Therefore you have often encouraged her to go back to work if she can at all because you are concerned that she will use up her entitlement to sickness benefit (a total of 52 weeks in any one period of 18 months), leaving potentially nothing for a more serious setback. You open her journal and begin typing up the information and your decision. Then you close her case and send her a copy of your decision through the mail. You now return your attention to the case-file you were about to type into the electronic records when you were interrupted by the phone. You are almost done when the phones begin to ring out from every office in the hallway.

The phone hour has begun. **Go to 18** to continue or **go back to 6** to handle the casework differently.

24. You take the call (from 14)

You know that your colleague will not be back any time soon because she is on sick leave suffering from stress, so you decide to take the call yourself. It appears that your colleague has referred the woman to one of the private employment agencies. The woman tells you that she feels terrible at the agency and that attending the course only makes her more and more ill. You inform her that if this is the case, then you feel obliged to stop the offer and ask for her doctor's opinion on whether she can be there or not. The woman pleads with you. She does not want you to contact her GP. She is sure that her doctor will say that there is no health risk in her being there, but she herself feels differently. A hint of irritation sneaks into your voice. You repeat to her what you can see in the file, that she has been referred for just one hour a day and that this hour consists in talking to a personal mentor. You think to yourself that this is quite a luxury compared to the general offers of following classroom teaching and it is much more expensive than the offers you normally give people. She repeats to you that she suffers from anxiety and depression and that being obliged to spend one hour a day pouring her heart out to a person who is not a trained therapist or have any clinical experience does not make things better. You tell her that if that is how she sees things, you will ask for her doctor's statement and if he does not see any obstacles to her being there and she still refuses to be there, she will no longer be entitled to sickness benefit. The woman asks you to forget she called and you end the conversation. After the conversation you are slightly irritated that you now have to make file entries in a case which is not even yours and in which nothing in the end had to be done. You begin typing the content of your conversation into the woman's file. You are halfway through the entry when the phone rings again. **Go to 26.**

25. You unplug the phone (from 28)

You decide to remove the cord from the phone which will give you about an hour to catch up on record keeping before the phone hour begins at 2pm. You consider the case-file in your hand but then put it back on top of the pile of unfiled cases on the shelf. The interrupting phone has reminded you of a call you got yesterday just as you were about to go home. It concerned the case of a woman whose right to sickness benefit was about to run out. She called you yesterday to ask if you were aware that her 52-week limit was up and asked if her right to sickness benefit could be prolonged. As her caseworker you are obliged to assess whether she is entitled to have her sickness benefit prolonged but you have to do so before the 52 weeks limit is up. Otherwise her case must be shut. Since you are aware that it is entirely your fault that it has not been done (because you have been too busy) you had planned to make a so-called "technical extension" which would buy you time to make a proper assessment. But today during the team meeting you were told that this practice which you and your colleagues use in cases such as these is strictly against the law. Now you will have to close the woman's case if you do not find the time to assess her immediately. In order to do that you need her medical papers but you know how long it might take before the doctor gets around to sending them. Therefore you phone the woman and ask her if she might obtain her papers herself and hand deliver them to you the next day. That will give you the time to see if her right to sickness benefit can be extended. After you have made the arrangements you turn to the shelf to pick up the case-file from before and begin making the required journal entries. In order to save time you have a word document with a list of generic expressions that you copy-and-paste into the journal and adapt to the present case. You complete one and a half cases before the phones start ringing from out of every office in the hallway. The phone hour has begun. If you are ready to plug the cord back into your phone and continue then **go to 18** or **go back to 6** for a chance to handle the case differently.

26. End of the day (from 24 and 27)

The phone kept ringing throughout the phone hour and when the phones shut down at 3pm you had 12 unfinished journal entries opened on your computer desktop. A fair part of these are information for other colleagues whose phones were engaged, resulting in "their" citizens being forwarded to your phone. You now take cases one by one, typing into the journals new information or changed arrangements and you email requests to your colleagues to call specific citizens back. When you are done you open your email and see that you have received similar requests to call some of "your" citizens back. At 4pm you have been at work for 8 hours and you get ready to go home. The pile of unfiled cardboard files on your shelf has grown since you came in this morning. You only had time to type two of the cases into the system, which means that referrals and other plans you have arranged with the citizens this week and the week before have yet to be put into action. You think to yourself as you do so often, that you must do something wrong, since your piles of unfinished work only seem to grow. If you are ready to call it a day, then **go to 32**. If you want to return to the team meeting and try out a different approach, then **go back to 1**.

27. You write a note (from 14)

You are reluctant to interfere with any arrangements your colleague might have made. You therefore tell the woman you will leave a note for your colleague to return the call as soon as possible. The woman asks you when that might be and you repeat that you will leave a note for your colleague to call back. The woman is insistent and wants to know when she can expect to hear from her caseworker. She wants to know if she has just gone to a meeting, if she can perhaps be reached later in the day, or perhaps tomorrow. You tell her that you are not allowed to give out such information and you repeat that you will leave a note for her caseworker to call back. You end the conversation but you do not feel good about it. You know that your colleague's sickness is of a long-term nature but you are not allowed to give such personal information to the citizens. Also, you are distressed that your team leader Peter has taken no decision about what to do with your colleague's cases. You begin typing a summary of the conversation into the woman's journal and open the email to write the request for your colleague to call back. Before you are done, the phone rings again. The next two calls are for another colleague who is currently on vacation. **Go to 26.**

28. Ali's decision (from 6)

Ali's resistance to your decision to refer him to the agency has been stuck with you throughout the day. You still think it is sensible to refer him but you do not like the idea of forcing him into it. You are concerned that the fact that he feels forced to participate might hinder whatever gain he could potentially get from it. You therefore decide to send him some presentation material from three different agencies. By allowing him some time to think it through and decide which of the three options he prefers you hope to give him a sense of involvement and gain his cooperation. You have previously had some success in overcoming people's strong objections to your decisions this way. At the same time the maneuver allows you to register an extra "follow-up" in the electronic system which brings you ahead of schedule. Two birds with one stone. You put Ali's case-file aside and reach for the case from the pile behind you. You are about to open the case-file when you are interrupted by the phone. If you answer it then **go to 23**, if you pull out the plug then **go to 25**.

29. You ask her to call back (from 18)

You know Ann will be back tomorrow so you ask the woman to call back. You need to make a brief entry in the case-file documenting the woman's call in case it turns out to be of importance to her case. As you end the entry and close the window on your computer screen the phone rings again. The next caller is a man. He has been fired from his job during a period of illness and since he therefore cannot return to work part-time there is no alternative to referring him to "activity." You have asked him to read through material from three different private employment agencies and inform you which one he prefers. It seems he has done some creative thinking since you last spoke, because he calls to let you know he considers himself "fit for duty" and no longer wishes to receive sickness benefit. He has found out that since he is not required to attend work in his notice period, if he reports "fit for duty" he neither has to go to work, nor does he have to comply with the obligations in the law on sickness benefit (and therefore need not be referred to activity). At the same time he gets back at his employer for firing him since he will no longer be reimbursed economically by the municipality while they will still be obliged to pay him a full salary in his notice period. You have often wondered why so few people figure out this "trick." During the phone hour a few more of the people you have asked to decide between different agencies call you back and you make record entries in all cases and open the electronic portal to book the "sickness benefit packages" they have chosen. In between, you are interrupted by more calls. Most of them are for your colleagues. **Go to 19.**

30. You send a letter (from 21)

You decide to send a formal letter to the man to give him a chance to explain the possible mistake. You upload the standard letter for such inquiries and write the date by which he has to return the letter. Then you print the letter, put it in an envelope and place it in the tray alongside the rest of the outgoing mail. You open his inactive case and type in your decision and the information you have. You decide to wait with the referral until you are absolutely sure he is entitled to sickness benefit. You close the cardboard folder again and place it at the bottom of the pile. As you reach for the next case-file you are interrupted by a sudden symphony of ringing phones that sound from the open office doors all the way down the hallway. The phone hour has just started. **Go to 14** to continue or **go back to 8** for a chance to handle the case differently.

31. You exempt Ali from the course (from 22)

The obstructions to your attempts to refer Ali have got you wondering again about the purpose of the referral. The more you think about it the less sense it makes. If Ali's application for professional rehabilitation is approved—which you think is very likely—he will most likely be referred to one of the agencies in any case to work out the specifics of the rehabilitation. At the meeting where your senior colleague told you to remember the Municipality's higher percentage of reimbursement in cases of referrals your in-house lawyer had immediately objected and reminded you all that you are not allowed to think about the larger economic picture when you make your legal decisions. You decide this is one of those cases in which you had best make an exemption. You call Ali and give him the news, which he receives happily. You then reopen his case-file and proceed to alter the follow-up plan to accommodate your new agreement. You are only half-finished before your phone starts to ring. You ignore it for a moment while you complete the sentence you are writing. You hear the phones ringing from out of every office in the hallway. The phone hour has begun. **Go to 18** to continue or **go back to 6** to handle the casework differently.

32. The bureaucratic decision (from 19 and 26)

You cannot know what will result from your decisions but you *can* know that whatever you decide it will have consequences. And so it is, generally, in the life of human beings. Bureaucratic decisions exaggerate the fundamental nature of taking a decision in that what we with James Scott may call the "ineffably complex web of activity" (Scott 1998: 256) has over time become so finely knit that almost every movement or action has immediate intentional and unintentional consequences—not only for the subject of the decision but for a wider and largely unknown set of relations. In this experiment, now over, you have been asked to make administrative and legal decisions in a few examples from the municipal reality. The decisions are structured so that they lead either to an addition of information or to a closure of the situation. However, it is not always possible for you to choose to go further into the examination of matters since information is lacking and must be obtained. This takes time. Yet you still have to make your decision on the imperfect basis available to you. The decisions you have been allowed to make do not take place in an ideal vacuum where you can choose between all possible ways of acting conceivable to you. You can only decide what the caseworkers decided. The only extra option you get is to terminate the situations sooner than they did.

However you decided to do something, there was always another sensible way you could have gone about it. So it is, according to Thomas Nagel, in life in general, and so it seems to be in the Danish labor market system. While this might occasionally, to the people working in it, result in the overwhelming sensation that "the system" is meaningless and that their work is pointless what we know now is that "the system" in fact abounds with meaning and that this is the empirical ground for the experience of absurdity. When the caseworkers and policy-makers decide to give priority to some concerns over others; when they turn their backs on some options, some perspectives, some information, some circumstances, these do not cease to exist or assert their influence on their individual or organizational lives: the phone not answered, the concern not addressed, the file not worked, the letter not sent are not just potentially different things they could have decided to give priority to. The case not worked, the phone not answered, and the letter not sent are pressing facts of the bureaucratic and organizational life, and they become all the more influential by the very fact that they have not been addressed. Any decision produces the grounds for a parallel or subsequent production of conflicting decisions: any concern left unaddressed by a given decision-maker might in any moment be taken up by other decision-makers or even by the maker of the first decision and produce conflicting effects or become involved in an effort to reach contradictory goals or purposes.

You go to get a cup of coffee and somebody in the waiting room might not make their scheduled appointment to see their physiotherapist; you are thorough in one case and some other case gets a superficial handling due to time constraints; you run extra fast so as not to let your colleagues down and you end up not having the time to dwell on the subtleties of a case; you decide to pick up the phone and you might end up spending time taking phone messages for your colleagues rather than answering questions pertaining to your own cases; you refer a person to a private employment agency against their will and perhaps this person will regain their footing in life. But to ponder the consequences of one's decisions is a time-consuming affair and it threatens to disrupt organizational efficiency— that is, the capacity to work on the highest possible number of cases, or the capacity to make decisions as quickly as possible. However, the effect of the busyness experienced by public sector employees is not only that people gets stressed and break down or fall ill or at the very least do not have the time to finish their tasks. The most radical effect of being busy is an over production of work which will undermine itself because people are unaware of the factors that might in the next breath work against the decided course of action. The irony is that while it looks like the organizations are increasingly gearing up and becoming more effective it might very well be that what they are productive of is primarily bureaucracy.

Appendix: data, position, method

Data

This book relies heavily on ethnographic fieldnotes. Fieldnotes may be written in as many ways as there are ethnographers, but far from being a random process of data collection it is a highly structured way of dealing with the fact that one cannot know, in the moment of gathering information, what will turn out to be relevant or useful in a subsequent analysis. So one gathers as much as possible: observations of practices; descriptions of settings and interaction; conversations overheard; questions asked and answers provided; analytical reflections; observations about one's own bias or prejudice; notes on the mismatch between read theory and what one observes and overhears; new research questions to be pursued; what one does not understand; preliminary conclusions to be run past informants for discussion.

The Municipality

The main bulk of my data stems from the seven months (January–June and November 2009) I was doing fieldwork in the Municipality which agreed to let me follow their implementation of the trial. I spent most days in this period in the job center, with the exception of three weeks in February, during which I had teaching obligations to fulfill at my university department, and two weeks in April, during which I participated in conferences. My data from the Municipality primarily consist of: daily fieldnotes from meetings between caseworkers and recipients of sickness benefit; fieldnotes from the weekly team meetings; and fieldnotes on the conversations between caseworkers or between caseworkers and myself. Audio recorded data include five interviews with caseworkers who were involved in the project and one who was not; recordings of twelve project meetings pertaining to *Active—Back Sooner*; five recorded meetings between the project group and the private employment agencies involved in the execution of the project activities; and one recorded meeting between representatives from different organizational levels in the Municipality discussing the drafting of a public procurement notice. Furthermore, my data pool includes the Municipality's local project descriptions and some internal summaries and evaluative reports they made in connection with the project.

The private employment agency—ENGA

The next big portion of data comes from the private employment agency which I have called ENGA (a meaningless acronym) and where I spent four weeks during the fall of 2009. Apart from fieldnotes and audio recordings of meetings between the employees from ENGA and the municipal caseworkers, it includes a total of eighteen tape-recorded interviews with eight employees; fieldnotes from class-room sessions with the recipients of sickness benefit who had been referred there for various reasons; notes from staff meetings and meetings between employees and recipients of sickness benefit or rehabilitation benefit. Finally, it contains fieldnotes from my own conversations with the employees and with the recipients of sickness benefit.

The National Labor Market Authority

I spent a total of one month in the National Labor Market Authority in the fall of 2009. My data from this site primarily consist of fieldnotes taken during the weekly team meetings and notes recording the daily work of the twelve employees who took turns having me sit in on one day in their work life. The data I got was rich but only little of it pertained to the trial which is the subject of this book. This data is, therefore, largely unused in this book (see however Vohnsen 2013b; Vohnsen 2016a; Vohnsen forthcoming). The primary data pertaining to the National Labor Market Authority which has been included in the book are two taped interviews with people who were involved in drafting the later adjustments of the project; some memorandums I got by requesting subject access; and finally, from the two large seminars for the participating municipalities hosted by the National Labor Market Authority. These two seminars were the "experience-gathering seminar" held in January 2009 and the "midway seminar" held in April the same year.

Recipients of sickness benefit

I furthermore spoke to a number of men and women who had been drafted into the project, in other words the recipients of sickness benefit. Apart from the people I met fleetingly at the Municipality and at ENGA, I visited six recipients of sickness benefit in their homes and tape recorded their accounts of interaction with the Municipality and, in some cases, with ENGA. Three of these I had met at ENGA and therefore saw several times. This material is largely absent in the book. Since I have limited my analytical scope to focus primarily on the implementers of *Active—Back Sooner* and their decisions pertaining to the project, plus later on the revised sickness benefit legislation, the subjects of the project and of the law take up a peripheral role in the book.

Other data

I have interviewed the following persons once or twice: the Permanent Secretary from the Ministry of Employment, a civil servant from his administration; a reporter who critiqued the legal basis of the project on the radio; and a Parliament member and former Minister who gave an account of the relationship between Minister and administration as she experienced it. Apart from this I have had un-recorded conversations with scientists and researchers who have taken an interest in the scientific basis of the interventions. My research assistant, Rasmus Kolding, interviewed a total of five caseworkers and five team leaders from six other municipalities that had chosen to be part of the controlled trial *Active—Back Sooner*. I have had these interviews at my disposal as well as some British reports on parallel efforts to reduce sickness absence in the UK which he found during his research. Further documents include: a large number of Danish public research reports and the evaluation of the project; correspondence between the National Labor Market Authority, the Ministry of Employment, the Junior Counsel to the Treasury, the Employment Region and various municipalities. Finally, I have also referred to minutes from a parliamentary debate and some of the documents that were used as basis for discussion of the project in Parliament.

Position and method

As Philip Abrams (2006 [1977]) pointed out, it is notoriously difficult to study the State. It tends to slip away between one's fingers as soon as one tries to define it. When we speak of "the State," do we talk about the government as a whole or just one minister? Or do we talk about the governmental administration or a sub-unit in a municipality? When I began my employment as a PhD student in the summer of 2008, I knew practically nothing about the way the Danish state system, as Abrams defines it "the palpable nexus of practices and institutional structure centered in government" (ibid.: 112), was structured. In high school, I was a mathematics student and the subsequent travelling in Central America and six years of training as a student of anthropology had done nothing to challenge my ignorance of the political and administrative structures of the country in which I was born. The seven months I was employed as an internal consultant in a municipality after obtaining my masters degree did provide a crash course in the working of a municipality but "the State" in which I now became employed was foreign territory to me. While conducting my PhD research I was formally employed by the Ministry of Employment, seconded to the cross-ministerial innovation unit MindLab (co-funded by three ministries including the Ministry of Employment), while being supervised from and academically attached to the Department of Anthropology, Archaeology, and Linguistics at Aarhus University. The three parties co-funded my research. The requirement was that my research would somehow "be useful" and thematically fall within the area regulated by the Ministry of Employment.

Useful to whom?

For the first year and a half of my employment as a PhD student I was based in MindLab's office situated in the heart of Copenhagen next to the Danish Parliament and a few hundred meters from the Ministry of Employment and the National Labor Market Authority. Upon my employment I soon learned that in Denmark "the State" is an administrative unit comprising the ever-changing configuration of the Danish Ministries and their subsections. "The state" however is not the only public administrative configuration. There are the five geographically based regions (primarily taking care of the public health care system) and at local level 98 municipalities that each collect taxes and have their own budgets. While bound by national law produced in "the State" and approved in "the Parliament," the municipalities have relative autonomy in terms of structuring the offers they are obliged by law to offer to the inhabitants of their municipalities. The larger part of the first year and a half, I spent circulating between the National Labor Market Authority, the municipal job center, the private employment agency ENGA, and the private homes of some of the recipients of sickness benefit whom I interviewed. The final year and a half I spent alternately at Aarhus University and the University of St Andrews in Scotland, writing and teaching.

The fact that my colleagues at MindLab were working directly with policy-makers in its three owner ministries gave me access to much background information about the world of policy-making, which has not been included in this book but which shaped my interest in implementation. The requirement that my research "be useful" took me some time to come to terms with—not least because my own understanding of "usefulness" initially was rather crude. I feared I would one day be held accountable for the time and money spent on my research and that I would be expected to provide clear cut suggestions for how the Ministry of Employment could achieve its goals. This troubled me. Not only because it seemed too great a task and was one that contradicted what I continue to see as the role of research, but also because "the Ministry of Employment" is no stable thing. Political preferences change, as do Ministers and Governments. So "useful" to whom, exactly? I am grateful to my supervisor from MindLab, Head of Innovation Christian Bason, for allowing me to work out my own take on "usefulness." My answer to the question became, "useful to those who wish to know about implementation and the practical effects of policy." I found help in the pragmatic principle that also governs the theoretical framework of this book, namely that our knowledge about the world shapes our approach to it. I wanted to offer the civil servants in the Ministry a different way to look at a familiar field of intervention "the labor market area" and a different approach to thinking about the effects of their work.

Dangerous naivety—National Labor Market Authority

My previously mentioned ignorance about the political field I entered caused problems and the fact that I chose to focus my research on the implementation of the controlled trial *Active—Back Sooner* had some unfortunate methodological implications. In the spring of 2009 *Active—Back Sooner* became the focus of a legal and political controversy—something I of course had no way of knowing when I chose it as my object of study in November 2008. That it was an attempt to work evidence-based was partly what had caught my interest in the project, and being a researcher my first move was to read up on the research it built on. In this case I had difficulties finding it and it did not take many days before I was on the phone to the National Labor Market Authority asking for references. It turned out I was not the only one who was unable to find the research the controlled trial built on. Some journalists had started to look in to the matter as well and the fact that I seemed from the outset of my research to be asking the same questions as the journalists probably did contribute to placing me in the same category in the eyes of some of the civil servants from the National Labor Market Authority. This was an image I was not able to shake off during the year I did my research. Not least because I took an interest in the subsequent legal controversy and because I continued to bounce into unspoken norms about how one acts when employed in a Ministry.

For example: at one point I made a formal request for access to the documents relating to the preparatory stages of the controlled trial in order to ensure I had all the publicly accessible documents. I was continually being told that the information I was given when I spoke to the civil servants in the National Labor Market Authority was confidential and it made me nervous. I therefore felt I needed to ensure a pool of material to which I could safely refer. My request however was taken as something akin to a declaration of war since it seemed that only reporters request subject access before they want to expose the ministries in some way. It did not help me that I requested the subject access at the very same time as did the reporter who had recently exposed them several times in the media and that I did it knowingly: my reasoning had been to save the civil servants the trouble of having to find all the documents twice since I knew it was a time-consuming affair. However, it caused a scandal and the news of my request traveled all the way up to the Permanent Secretary and talk about "the PhD student who requested document access" spread to other ministries and was the subject of horrified talk. There was information I would have liked to have but which I, unfortunately, was cut off from: one civil servant from the National Labor Market Authority put it to me quite bluntly in the fall of 2009 after having told me that she had deliberately tried to cut me off from information: "You are dangerous because you are ignorant about the ways of politics. You have no idea what might be politically sensitive and you probably have not even considered that your handing in your PhD thesis will most likely coincide with the national election." She was right. Nothing was farther from my mind. The data I did get from the Ministry, however, I owe primarily to the unshakable Head of Office in an Office in the National Labor Market Authority where I was allowed to spend a month during the fall of 2009, and to those of his employees who decided to confide in me. People from the higher administrative levels, including the Permanent Secretary himself, were more at ease with my project and were forthcoming with interviews and data.

On being a researcher—the municipal job center

Initially I had planned to begin my research in much closer collaboration with the civil servants in the National Labor Market Authority. However, at the time my research was bound to begin, there was no Head of Office in the Office which would work most closely with the translation of the *Action Plan on Sickness Benefit* into concrete implementable proposals. *Active—Back Sooner* was such a translation of the Action Plan's proposal 32, but with no one in charge of the Office, there was no one to decide to take me in and no one to forward my request to. Instead I found a list of the municipalities who had applied to participate in the implementation of the project. I decided on a municipality where a friend of mine had recently begun to work in the Central Administration and through her I got hold of one of the persons responsible for the municipality's work in the employment area. This person promised to forward my request to Ulla, the Head of the job center, with whom I had a meeting a few weeks later, and the team leader, Peter, gave me permission to follow the work in the job center. After the permission arrived that I could join the project group I was invited to every meeting that concerned the implementation of *Active—Back Sooner*. Peter officially welcomed me in the group this way:

> *Peter*: Nina, you just join whatever might be interesting for you. Let this be an open invitation. We cannot promise you the highest service level because people are busy and that is the way it is meant to be. We do not have a lot of space but there is always a free office you can use. Generally put, you can be here in whatever way you like.

And this turned out to be true. I had full access to every meeting or type of work I wanted to look at and the caseworkers were all forthcoming and generous with their time and interest. As a small but significant gesture I was given my own coffee mug on the first day of my arrival; care was taken to see that I got my own email address and password to the computer systems (after having signed a declaration of confidentiality) so I could access all the files I found relevant and receive the emails that informed me when and where beers would be drunk on Fridays. There would always be several people who had noticed when I had not been around for a few days and who would be happy when I returned. The extreme openness and the degree to which these people shared their doubts and passions about their work has given me access to stacks of data that leave them quite vulnerable to critique and makes me responsible for managing the task of presenting their work and concerns in a way that respects their openness and generosity.

As opposed to the time I spent in the National Labor Market Authority, where most employees seemed to find it uncomfortable or disturbing having someone sit on a chair and take notes while they worked, in the municipal job center it was easy for me to find a "place" in their daily work life. Here the caseworkers were used to having interns from the Schools of Social Work or the recently employed caseworkers sit in on their work for extended periods of time. They were therefore accustomed to working with an observer next to them and were in the habit of articulating the grounds for their actions. My "role" on the other hand was not that of an intern or a recently employed caseworker but exactly that of a researcher. Due to my extended stay in this organization I felt it was important that the caseworkers did not forget that I was there to collect data. One way I persistently tried to establish myself as a researcher was by taking notes overtly during conversations and meetings or by asking permission to tape record meetings or private conversations.

The importance of not being "researcher X"—private employment agency, ENGA

My contact to the private employment agency ENGA came about as a result of my participation in several meetings between their employees and the caseworkers from the Municipality. ENGA was among the two private employment agencies most used in the project and they seemed concerned to improve both the communication with the Municipality and the content of their offers. When I asked their team leader Marianne after one of these meeting if I could follow their work she told me she would think about it. She needed to confer with the director of ENGA but equally important she wanted to discuss it with all the employees attached to the "sickness benefit package" to which the recipients drafted for the project were referred. This resulted in two meetings before I was given permission to follow their work with the project. The first meeting with Marianne and one of the top managers in the organization went fine but the second meeting with participation of some of the employees from the "sickness benefit package" did not go as smoothly. Some of the employees were familiar with the work of another Danish researcher, "researcher. X," who had published a book that made an institution which was in some respects similar to ENGA appear in a very bad light. Some of the employees were anxious I would pick-up on thoughtless office talk among colleagues and present casual statements out of context as representative of their attitude towards their work and the citizens they worked with. If my primary task in the National Labor Market Authority had been to convince them that I was not a reporter, to gain access to ENGA it was crucial that I convinced them that I was not a researcher like "researcher X."

I too had read her book: it was quite a horrific read and a classic example of the "system treats little man with evil" type literature, in which caseworkers are portrayed as indifferent and sometimes even mean people who care next to nothing about the fate of their clients. I knew of her as a good and thorough researcher and had no doubts about the validity of her work, but it was representative of precisely the kind of work I had wanted to distance myself from with my own research. If her observations and critiques of the people employed in the welfare system were correct, I wanted to understand the conditions these people had for carrying out their work as they wished. Thus it was not difficult for me to argue that my research would be nothing like hers; that it would not be yet another critique of the people employed in "the system" but an exploration of implementation and the employees' conditions for carrying out official policy. In any case it turned out to be a needless concern of the employees. I never heard anyone talk about any of the citizens they worked with in anything but a respectful manner. If they spoke ill of anything it was the conditions for their work which they often found counter-productive to reach the goals they were subjected to. Hence, at ENGA they were as open and forthcoming as in the municipal job center once we had established I was not there in order to "expose them." They shared my interest in describing and communicating the conditions under which large parts of the labor market effort was carried out, and with this book I hope to have lived up to their expectations.

Use of personal names and place names

In this book I refer—as a rule—to people either by a fictional name (e.g. Ida, Marianne, Henry) or by their non-specific position or profession (a caseworker, a civil servant, a lawyer, a reporter). Exceptions to this rule is The Permanent Secretary from the Ministry of Employment and other holders of clear-cut offices, such as the Minister of Employment and the Vice Director of the National Labor Market Authority, who are easily identifiable and for that reason will simply be referred to by their titles. In one instance where I quote from parliamentary minutes I use the politicians' proper names as this information is publicly accessible. Those who are most vulnerable to identification in this book are the municipal caseworkers and the civil servants whose colleagues would recognize them because they take up a prominent role in this book. To make identification more difficult I have, in consultation with some informants, decided on the strategy of sometimes scrambling caseworkers, cases, and episodes from different days.

I have done this not only to ensure anonymity but also to present a variety of work and decisions. Information pertaining to sickness benefit cases is highly person sensitive data and in the instances where I recount conversations between caseworkers and recipients of sickness benefit I have altered central information such as illness and profession where they are so obvious as to allow the specific recipient of sickness benefit to be traced. So for instance, in the first portrait of implementation where I go through a series of meetings to present the municipal unit's work, the caseworker I have chosen is Ian who will be easily recognized by his colleagues. However, the cases and episodes, on the other hand, "belong" not only to him but to other colleagues as well. I have furthermore invented extra caseworkers or civil servants to whom I have attributed the most critical or vulnerable statements. For instance the caseworkers Ena and Frank are such fictional caseworkers whose persona the real life caseworkers occupy in turn when offering harsh critique or statements that leave them especially vulnerable. The implication of these choices, of course, is that this book can by no means claim to offer portraiture of the individual life-worlds of specific people.

While the Ministry of Employment and the National Labor Market Authority are situated in Copenhagen, the Capital of Denmark, I have been purposefully vague concerning the location of both the Municipality and the private employment agency which are included in this study. Whenever I refer specifically to these organizations and the geographical location in which they are situated, I refer to them as the *Municipality*, the *job center*, the *town* or *ENGA*—the latter being a purely fictional and meaningless acronym I have given the private employment agency to distinguish it from other private employment agencies. What I call private employment agencies are themselves organizations with often highly diverse assignments—some undertake research of their own; some offer courses directed at things other than getting people back to work. However, all of them contract with the Municipality and since it is in this capacity that they are interesting to this book, I refer to them as private employment agencies to call attention to their role as private actors in the employment industry.

Since I have been present during meetings between the Municipality and the National Labor Market Authority and between ENGA and the Municipality there are people in all of these organizations who will know which municipality and which private employment agency I am dealing with. However, while they know the identity of each other and realize that people will probably guess at their true identity, they have wished to reserve the right to "deny" which anonymity will grant them. I have, therefore, omitted information that would make their organizational identity obvious. Again there are implications. The book is curiously lacking in descriptions of organizational and geographical contexts. Yet the "content" and "context" I have needed to tell the stories in this book are not the private lives of Ida or Henry, nor the organizational budgets or the architectural details of the surrounding towns and streets. Rather I have needed descriptions of work routines, of organizational links, and of the processes through which *Active—Back Sooner* was made and unmade. Neither of this has been hindered by the above constraints on the presentation of my material.

Bibliography

Abrams, Philip. 2006 [1977]. "Notes on the difficulty of studying the State." In *The anthropology of the State*, edited by Aradhana Sharma and Akhil Gupta, 112–30. Oxford and Malden: Blackwell Publishing.

Ankestyrelsen. 2009. *Ankestyrelsens praksisundersøgelser. Sygedagpengelovens § 27 og anvendelse af retssikkerhedslovens § 7a*. København: Schultz Grafisk.

Arbejdsmarkedskommissionen. 2008a. "Oplæg til pressemøde 23 April 2008: Mere velfærd kræver mere arbejde." Accessed 26 June, 2016. www.amkom.dk/skriftlige-oplaeg.aspx.

Arbejdsmarkedskommissionen. 2008b. "Oplæg til trepartsmøde 28 August 2008: Arbejdsmarkedsreformer, der både forbedrer de offentlige finanser og øger arbejdsudbud og beskæftigelse på kortere sigt." Accessed 26 June, 2016. www.amkom.dk/skriftlige-oplaeg.aspx.

Arbejdsmarkedsstyrelsen. 2008. *Viden om sygefravær*. København: Mploy.

Arbejdsmarkedsstyrelsen. 2009a. *Midtvejsjustering af forsøget "Aktive—Hurtigere Tilbage."* Memorandum, 12 March, 2009.

Arbejdsmarkedsstyrelsen. 2009b. *Aktive—Hurtigere Tilbage! Spørgsmål/svar*. Memorandum, 16 January, 2009.

Arbejdsmarkedsstyrelsen. 2009c. *Forsøgets baggrund og praksis*. Memorandum, 10 March, 2009.

Arbejdsmarkedsstyrelsen. 2009d. *Forsøgsbekendtgørelse "Aktive—Hurtigere Tilbage." Forsøgene er lovlige*. 16 March, 2009. Journal no. 2008–0002758.

Arbejdsmarkedsstyrelsen. 2009e. *EMRK og Sygedagpengeforsøget*, Memorandum, 17 March, 2009. Journal no. 2008–0002758.

Arbejdsmarkedsstyrelsen. 2009f. *Forsøget "Aktive—Hurtigere Tilbage." Hjemmel til sanktioner*. Memorandum, 31 March, 2009.

Arbejdsmarkedsstyrelsen. 2010. *Vejviser for borgere*. Accessed 12 July, 2010. www.ams.dk/Ams/Vejviser-for-borgere/Sygefravaer.aspx.

Arbejdsmarkedsudvalget. 2009. *Arbejdsmarkedsudvalget 2008–09. AMU alm. del Bilag 185*. Council question Z, 1 April, 2009.

Bason, Christian. 2010. *Leading public sector innovation: co-creating for a better society*. Bristol and Portland: The Policy Press.

Bauman, Zygmunt. 1992. *Mortality, immortality and other life strategies*. Cambridge and Oxford: Polity Press & Blackwell Publishers.

Becker, Howard S. 1997 [1963]. *Outsiders: studies in the sociology of deviance*. New York: The Free Press.

Behn, R. D. 1995. "Creating an innovative organization: ten hints for involving frontline workers." *State and Local Government Review* 27 (3): 221–34.

Beskæftigelsesministeriet. 2002. *Aftale om flere i arbejde.* København: Beskæftigelsesministeriet.

Beskæftigelsesministeriet. 2008a. *Konklusionspapir om handlingsplan om sygefravær.* Accessed 26 June, 2016. www.ac.dk/media/31379/aftaletekst-sygefravaer.pdf.

Beskæftigelsesministeriet. 2008b. *Analyse af sygefraværet.* København: Beskæftigelsesministeriet.

Bjerge, Bagga. 2008. "Mellem vision og praksis: strukturreformen, rusmiddelbureaukrati og new public management." PhD diss., Copenhagen University.

Boden, Rebecca and Debbie Epstein. 2006. "Managing the research imagination? Globalisation and research in higher education." *Globalisation, societies and education* 4 (2): 223–36.

Boll, Karen. 2011. "Taxing assemblages: laborious and meticulous achievements of tax compliance." PhD diss., ITU and MindLab.

Boorstein, Daniel J. 1969. *The sociology of the absurd: or the application of Professor X.* New York: Simon & Schuster.

Brehm, John and Scott Gates. 1999. *Working, shirking, and sabotage: bureaucratic response to a democratic public. Michigan studies in political analysis.* Ann Arbor: The University of Michigan Press.

Broadhead, Robert S. 1974. "Notes on the sociology of the absurd: an undersocialized conception of man." *The Pacific Sociological Review* 17 (1): 35–45.

Bræmer, Michael. 2008. "Offentligt ansatte drukner i papir." *UgebrevetA4*, 28 January. Accessed 26 June, 2016. www.ugebreveta4.dk/offentligt-ansatte-drukner-i-papir_18265.aspx.

Bubandt, Nils. 2014. *The empty seashell: witchcraft and doubt on an Indonesian island.* Ithaca and London: Cornell University Press.

Casey, Michael A. 2002. *Meaninglessness: the solutions of Nietzsche, Freud, and Rorty.* Lanham, Boulder, New York and Oxford: Lexington Books.

Das, Veena. 2004. "The signature of the State: the paradox of illegibility." In *Anthropology in the margins of the State*, edited by Veena Das and Deborah Poole, 225–52. Santa Fee: School of America Research Press.

deLeon, Peter and Linda deLeon. 2002. "Whatever happened to policy implementation? An alternative approach." *Journal of Public Administration Research & Theory* 12 (4): 467–92.

Dilley, Roy. 1999. *The problem of context.* New York and Oxford: Berghahn Books.

Drost, Ulla, Lisbeth L. Espersen, and Anne Thuen. 2006. *Sygedagpengeloven. 4. udgave.* København: Karnov Group A/S.

Durose, Catherine. 2009. "Front-line workers and 'local knowledge': neighbourhood stories in contemporary UK local governance." *Public Administration* 87 (1): 35–49.

Durose, Catherine. 2011. "Revisiting Lipsky: front-line work in UK local governance." *Political Studies* 59: 978–95.

Eggers, William. D. and Shalabh K. Singh. 2009. *The public innovator's playbook.* Winnipeg: Deloitte Research and Harvard Ash Center for Democratic Governance and Innovation.

Engelke, Matthew and Matt Tomlinson. 2007. *The limits of meaning: case studies in the anthropology of Christianity.* New York and Oxford: Berghahn Books.

Eisenstein, Sergei. M. 1994. *Towards a theory of montage v. 2: Selected works*, edited by Richard Taylor and Michael Glenny. London: British Film Institute.

Espeland, Wendy N. 2001. "Value-matters." *Economic and Political Weekly* 36 (21): 1839–45.

Ferguson, James. 1994. *The anti-politics machine: "development," depolitization, and bureaucratic power in Lesotho.* Minneapolis and London: University of Minnesota Press.

Ferguson, James. 2005. "The anti-politics machine." In *The anthropology of the State: a reader,* edited by Aradhana Sharma and Akhil Gupta, 270–86. Oxford and Malden: Blackwell Publishing.

Foucault, Michel. 1991. "Governmentality." In *The Foucault effect,* edited by Graham Burchel, Colin Gordon, and Peter Miller, 87–114. Chicago: The University of Chicago Press.

Finansministeriet. 2008. *Aftale om Finansloven for 2009,* Schultz Distribution.

Finansministeriet. 2011. www.fm.dk/Arbejdsomraader/Offentlig%20modernisering/Afbu reaukratisering.aspx. [no longer available]

Garfinkel, Harold. 1967. *Studies in ethnomethodology.* Cambridge, Oxford and Malden: Polity Press and Blackwell Publishers Ltd.

Gjørup, Jes, Henrik Hjortdal, Tommy Jensen, Leon Lerborg, Claus Nielsen, Niels Refslund, Jakob Suppli, and Jasper S. Winkel. 2007. "Kronik: Tilgiv os—vi vidste ikke, hvad vi gjorde." *Politiken.* 29 March, Debate Section p. 7.

Goffman, Erving. 1959. *The presentation of self in everyday life.* New York: Anchor Books.

Goggin, Malcom L., Ann Bowman, James Lester, and Laurence O'Toole. 1990. *Implementation theory and practice: towards a third generation.* Glenwood, Ill.: Scott Foresman/Little, Brown.

Goodwin, Glenn. 1971. "On transcending the absurd: an inquiry in the sociology of meaning." *The American Journal of Sociology* 76 (5): 831–46.

Graeber, David. 2015. *The utopia of rules: on technology, stupidity, and the secret joys of bureaucracy.* Brooklyn and London: Melville House.

Gupta, Akhil. 2012. *Red tape: bureaucracy, structural violence, and poverty in India.* Durham and London: Duke University Press.

Hacking, Ian. 1991. "How should we do a history of statistics?" In *The Foucault effect,* edited by Graham Burchell, Colin Gordon, and Peter Miller, 181–96. Chicago: The University of Chicago Press.

Harman, Graham. 2010. *Graham Harman on the history of OOO and SR.* Talk given 1 December, 2010 at UCLA. Accessed 26 June, 2016. www.ustream.tv/recorded/11193628.

Harman, Graham. 2011. "Response to Shaviro." In *The speculative turn: continental materialism and realism,* edited by Levi Bryant, Nick Srnicek, and Graham Harman, 291–303. Melbourne: Re.press.

Hill, Heather C. 2003. "Understanding implementation: street-level bureaucrats' resources for reform." *Journal of Public Administration Research and Theory* 13 (3): 265–82.

Hjern, Benny and David O. Porter. 1981. "Implementation structures: a new unit of administrative analysis." *Organization Studies* 2 (3): 211–27.

Hyatt, Susan B. 1997. "Poverty in a 'post-welfare' landscape: tenant management policies, self-governance and the democratization of knowledge in Great Britain." In *Anthropology of policy: critical perspectives on governance and power,* edited by Cris Shore and Susan Wright, 217–38. London and New York: Routledge.

Indenrigs- og Sundhedsministeriet. 2005. *Kommunalreformen—kort fortalt.* København: Indenrigs- og sundhedsministeriet.

James, William. 1955 [1943]. *Pragmatism and four essays from "The meaning of truth."* New York: Meridian Books: The Noonday Press.

Joas, Hans and Richard Sennett. 2006. "Creativity, pragmatism and the social sciences." *Distinktion* 13: 5–31.

Jorgensen, Dan. 1980. "What's in a name: the meaning of meaninglessness in Telefolmin." *Ethos* 8 (4): 349–66.

Kammeradvokaten. 2009. *Hjemmel til sanktionering af sygedagpengemodtagere under forsøgsordning*, Memorandum, 12 March, 2009.

Katz, Demian. 2011. Accessed 26 June, 2016. www.gamebooks.org/show_faqs.php.

Kettl, Donald F. 1993. "Searching for clues about public management: slicing the onion different ways." In *Public management: the state of the art*, edited by Barry Bozeman. San Francisco: Jossey-Bass.

Kobré, Kenneth. 2008. *Photojournalism: the professional's approach. 6th ed.* St Louis: Focal Press.

Krause-Jensen, Jakob. 2011. "Ideology at work: ambiguity and irony of value-based management in Bang & Olufsen." *Ethnography* 12 (2): 266–89.

Labor Market Commission. 2010. Accessed 26 June, 2016. www.amkom.dk/in-english.aspx.

Latour, Bruno. 1996. *Aramis or the love of technology.* Cambridge and London: Harvard University Press.

Latour, Bruno. 1999. *Pandora's hope: essays on the reality of science studies.* Cambridge and London: Harvard University Press.

Latour, Bruno. 2010. *The Making of law: an ethnography of the Conseil d'Etat.* Cambridge and Malden: Polity Press.

Lea, Tess. 2008. *Bureaucrats and bleeding hearts: indigenous health in northern Australia.* Sydney: The University of New South Wales Press.

Lewis, David and David Mosse. 2006. *Development brokers and translators: the ethnography of aid and agencies.* Bloomfield: Kumarian Press, Inc.

Li, Tania M. 2005. "Beyond 'the State' and failed schemes." *American Anthropologist* 107 (3): 383–94.

Li, Tania. M. 2007. *The will to improve: governmentality, development, and the practice of politics.* Durham and London: Duke University Press.

Lin, Ann C. 2002. *Reform in the making: the implementation of social policy in prison.* Princeton and Oxford: Princeton University Press.

Lipsky, Michael. 1980. *Street-level bureaucracy: dilemmas of the individual in public services.* New York: Russell Sage foundation.

Luper-Foy, Steven. 1992. "The absurdity of life." *Philosophy and phenomenological research* 52 (1): 85–101.

Lyman, Stanford M. and Marvin S. Scott. 1970. *A sociology of the absurd.* New York: Appleton-Century-Crofts, Inc.

Lyman, Stanford M. and Marvin B. Scott. 1989. *A sociology of the absurd. 2nd ed.* New York: General Hall, Inc.

Matza, David. 1969. *Becoming deviant.* Englewood Cliffs, NJ: Prentice Hall.

Marcus, George. 1995. "Ethnography in/of the worlds system: the emergence of multi-sited ethnography." *Annual Review of Anthropology* 24: 95–117.

Maynard-Moody, Steven and Michael Musheno. 2000. "State agent or citizen agent: two narratives of discretion." *Journal of Public Administration Research and Theory* 10 (2): 329–58.

McBroom, Patricia. 1968. "The utility of absurdity." *Science News* 93 (8): 193–4.

Miller, Peter. 2001. "Governing by numbers: why calculative practices matter." *Social Research* 68 (2): 379–96.

Miller, Peter and Nikolas Rose. 2008. "Governing economic life." In *Governing the present: administering economic, social and personal life*, 26–52. Cambridge and Malden: Polity Press.

Mosse, David. 2005. *Cultivating development: an ethnography of aid policy and practice*. London and New York: Pluto Press.

Mosse, David. 2007. "Is good policy unimplementable? Reflections on the ethnography of aid policy and practice." In *The Anthropology of organizations*, edited by Alberto C. Jimenez, 451–83. Surrey and Burlington: Ashgate.

Mulgan, Geoff. 2009. *The Art of public strategy. Mobilizing power and knowledge for the common good*. New York: Oxford University Press.

Nagel, Thomas. 1971. "The absurd." *The Journal of Philosophy* 68 (20): 716–27.

Nygaard-Christensen, Maj (2011). Building from scratch: aesthetics of post-disaster reconstruction. *Anthropology Today*. 27 (6): 8–10.

Ong, Aiwa. 1988. "The production of possession: spirits and the multinational corporation in Malaysia." *American Ethnologist* 15: 28–42.

Osborne, David and Ted Gaebler. 1992. *Reinventing government: how the entrepreneurial spirit is transforming the public sector*. New York: Plume.

O'Toole, Laurence. 2000. "Research on policy implementation: assessment and prospects." *Journal of Public Administration Research & Theory* 10 (2): 263–88.

Patterson, Fiona, Maura Kerrin, Geraldine Gatto-Roissard, and Phillipa Coan. 2009. *Everyday innovation: how to enhance innovative working in employees and organizations*. Accessed 9 September, 2014. www.nesta.org.uk/publications/everyday-innovation.

Peirce, Charles S. 1955 [1940]. *Philosophical writing of Peirce*, edited by Justus Buchler. New York: Dover Publications, Inc.

Porter, Theodor. M. 1995. *Trust in numbers*. Princeton: Princeton University Press.

Pressman, Jeffrey L. and Aaron Wildavsky. 1984 [1973]. *Implementation: how great expectations in Washington are dashed in Oakland [...]. 3rd ed., expanded*. Berkeley, Los Angeles and London: University of California Press.

Rambøll. 2010. *Evaluering: Aktive—Hurtigere Tilbage*. København: Rambøll.

Rapport, Nigel. 1992. "Connexions with and within a text: from Forster's 'Howards End' to the anthropology of comparison." *Bulletin of John Rylands University Library of Manchester* 73 (3): 161–80.

Rapport, Nigel. 1994. "Busted for hash: common catchwords and individual identities in a Canadian city." In *Urban lives: fragmentation and resistance*, edited by Vered Amit-Talai and Henri Lustiger-Thaler, 129–57. Toronto: McClelland and Stewart:

Rapport, Nigel. 1997. *Transcendent individual: towards a literary and liberal anthropology*. London and New York: Routledge Press.

Rapport, Nigel. 1999. "Problem solving and contradiction: playing darts and becoming human." *Self, Agency & Society* 2 (1): 81–101.

Regeringen. 2002a. *Flere i arbejde*. København. Beskæftigelsesministeriet.

Regeringen. 2002b. *Flere i arbejde—et debatoplæg*. Accessed 26 June, 2016. http: //bm.dk/da/Aktuelt/Publikationer/Arkiv/2002/Flere%20i%20arbejde%20-%20et%20debato plaeg.aspx.

Regeringen. 2008. *Sygefravær—en fælles udfordring: regeringens handlingsplan for at nedbringe sygefraværet*. København: Beskæftigelsesministeriet.

Retsinformation. 2008. *Lov om ændring af lov om sygedagpenge (udvidelse af arbejdsgiverperioden)*. LAW no 389 of 7 May, 2008, Historical.

Robbins, Joel. 2007. "Afterword: on limits, ruptures, meaning, and meaninglessness." In *The limits of meaning: case studies in the anthropology of Christianity*, edited by Matthew Engelke and Matt Tomlinson, 221–4. New York and Oxford: Berghahn Books.

Rose, Nikolas. 2006. "Governing 'advanced' liberal democracies." In *The anthropology of the State: a reader*, edited by Aradhana Sharma and Akhil Gupta. Oxford and Malden: Blackwell Publishing.

Scott, James C. 1998. *Seeing like a State: how certain schemes to improve the human condition have failed*. New Haven and London: Yale University Press.

Seidman, Steven. 1983. "Modernity, meaning, and cultural pessimism in Max Weber." *Sociological Analysis* 44 (4): 267–78.

Shore, Cris and Susan Wright. 1997. *Anthropology of policy: critical perspectives on governance and power*. Routledge: London and New York.

Shore, Cris, Susan Wright and Davide Però. 2011. *Policy worlds: anthropology and the analysis of contemporary power*. New York and Oxford: Berghahn Books.

Staal, Fritz. 1979. "The meaninglessness of ritual." *Numen* 26 (1): 2–22.

Stengers, Isabelle. 2009. "Thinking with Deleuze and Whitehead: a double test." In *Deleuze, Whitehead, Bergson. Rhizomatic connections*, edited by Keith Robinson, 28–44. Hampshire and New York: Palgrave Macmillan.

Strathern, Marilyn. 2004 [1991]. *Partial connections*. Walnut Creek and Oxford: AltaMira Press.

Sundhedsstyrelsen. 2007. *Evidens i forebyggelsen*. København: Sundhedsstyrelsen.

Taussig, Michael. 1992. *The nervous system*. New York and London: Routledge.

Tomlinson Matt. 2007. "The limits of meaning in Fijian methodist sermons." In *The limits of meaning: case studies in the anthropology of Christianity*, edited by Matthew Engelke and Matt Tomlinson, 129–46. New York and Oxford: Berghahn Books.

Torpy, Janet. 2010. "Randomized controlled trials." *The Journal of the American Medical Association* 303 (12): 1216.

Tsing, Anna L. 2005. *Friction: an ethnography of global connection*. Princeton and Oxford: Princeton University Press.

Tynell, Jesper. 2009. *Metoderapport*. Accessed 26 June, 2016. www.dr.dk/NR/rdonlyres/DFF07532–8C5C–4AEC–8679–0F74273E2E35/1580813/Ministerens_mindre_demo kratiske_metoder.pdf.

VK Regeringen III. 2007. *Mulighedernes samfund: regeringsgrundlag*. København: Statsministeriet Publikationer.

Vohnsen, Nina H. 2013a. "Labor days: a non-linear narrative of development." In *Transcultural montage*, edited by Christian Suhr and Rane Willerslew, 131–44. New York and Oxford: Berghahn Books.

Vohnsen, Nina H. 2013b. "Evidence-based policy: some pitfalls in the meeting of scientific research and politics." *Anthropology Today* 29 (5): 3–5.

Vohnsen. Nina H. 2015. "Street-level planning; the shifty nature of 'local knowledge and practice.'" *Journal of Organizational Ethnography* 4 (2): 147–61.

Vohnsen, Nina H. 2016a. "Evidensbaseret politikudvikling—brudfalder mellem forskning og bureaukrati." *Tidsskriftet Antropologi*, 72: 39–60.

Vohnsen, Nina H. forthcoming. "A blind man's problem: distortion and non-responsiveness—the construction of non-futures in Danish bureaucracy." In *optimal distortion*, edited by Morten Nielsen and Nigel Rapport. London and New York: Routledge.

Vonnegut, Kurt. 1973. *Breakfast of champions*. New York: Dell Publishing

Whitehead, Alfred North. 1929. *Process and reality: an essay in cosmology*. New York: The Macmillan Company and Cambridge: Cambridge University Press.

Winter, Søren, Peter Dinesen, and Peter J. May. 2008. "Implementation regimes and street-level bureaucrats: employment service delivery in Denmark." Working paper 12. The Danish National Center for Social Research, Copenhagen.

Wright, Susan. 2008. "Measurements and distortions: a review of the British system of research assessment." Working Paper 9, *Working papers on university reform*, Danish School of Education, University of Aarhus, Aarhus.

Wright, Susan and Sue Reinhold. 2011. "'Studying through': a strategy for studying political transformation. Or sex, lies, and British politics." In *Policy worlds: anthropology and the analysis of contemporary power*, edited by Cris Shore, Susan Wright, and Davide Però, 86–104. New York and Oxford: Berghahn Books.

Index

EU authorised representative for GPSR:
Easy Access System Europe, Mustamäe tee 50,
10621 Tallinn, Estonia
gpsr.requests@easproject.com

www.ingramcontent.com/pod-product-compliance
Lightning Source LLC
Chambersburg PA
CBHW070247290326
41929CB00047B/2807